Where Are They Today?

GREAT SPORTS STARS OF YESTERYEAR

Where Are They Today?

GREAT SPORTS STARS OF YESTERYEAR

by JOHN DEVANEY

CROWN PUBLISHERS, INC.
NEW YORK

For Barbara
and all those kisses

Published by Crown Publishers, Inc., One Park Avenue,
New York, New York 10016
and simultaneously in Canada by
General Publishing Company Limited

Manufactured in the United States of America
CROWN is a trademark of Crown Publishers, Inc.

Library of Congress Cataloging in Publication Data

Devaney, John.
Where are they today?

1. Athletes—United States—Biography—Addresses,
essays, lectures. I. Title.
GV697.AID455   1985   796'.096'2 [B]   84-17475
ISBN 0-517-55344-9
ISBN 0-517-55345-7 (pbk.)

10 9 8 7 6 5 4 3 2 1
First Edition

Contents

Acknowledgments

At a party a few years ago, someone said to me, "There isn't a guy in this room who wouldn't like to do what you do."

He may have been right. Since 1956, I have traveled around the country talking to the stars of American sport. A number of magazine and book editors let me do that job, and to them I am thankful: Morris Weeks, Jr., and Jess Gorkin at *Parade*; Al Silverman, Dick Schaap, and Berry Stainback at *Sport*; Bob Hood at *Boys' Life*, and, in the book business, editors like Jim Bryans and Evan Heyman.

Two people shared with me in the creation of this book—Barbara Lowenstein, my agent, and Brandt Aymar, Crown's special projects editor—and I thank both for their assistance and advice. Nat Andriani of Wide World went beyond the call of duty in finding hard-to-locate photos. And for his helpfulness when I despaired this book would ever be done, my special thanks to the well-known author, and my good friend, George Sullivan.

Photo Credits: ABC-TV, 86, 176
AP/Wide World, 14, 25, 33, 47, 95, 103, 112, 141, 158, 196, 205, 210
Franko Khoury, 17, 78   Miller Beer, 21, 166
United Press International, 6, 18, 22, 30, 43, 46, 59, 66, 69, 70, 79, 83, 87, 91, 99, 107, 108, 111, 154, 159, 162, 163, 177, 185, 188, 209, 214, 217
Photographs for which no credits are given are courtesy of the author.

Introduction

Without heroes, we are all plain people and don't know how far we can go.
          —Bernard Malamud, *The Natural*

In March of 1956 I went to St. Petersburg, Florida, to interview a St. Louis Cardinal pitcher, Wilmer (Vinegar Bend) Mizell, for a magazine article, the first one I wrote on a person in sports. Since then I have written more than a hundred magazine articles and books about the sports stars of the 1920s to the 1970s. In this book of portraits, I have tried to sketch 52 of them: their lives before and after I met them, but mostly the way they were at that once-and-only time for each of them when they were our heroes.

Felipe Alou as an Atlanta Brave in 1966.

Felipe Alou

ON A SPRING DAY AT FORT LAUDER-dale, Florida, in 1967, I was chatting with Bobby Richardson, the former Yankee second baseman who was then a coach with the team. I told him I would be driving to West Palm Beach the next morning to interview the Atlanta Braves' first baseman, Felipe Alou, Atlanta's Most Valuable Player in 1966.

"Oh, you'll enjoy that," the ebullient

Bobby told me. "You'll enjoy talking to Felipe. He is a very interesting person."

I was not surprised that Bobby spoke with such a glow in his voice about Felipe. Both were born-again Christians who professed, as they put it, "to speak out for Christ." During the next two days, however, as I shuttled the 60-odd miles between Fort Lauderdale, where I was staying, and West Palm, where the Braves trained, I told myself more than once that I found nothing enjoyable about talking to Felipe.

I was wrong—and Bobby was right. Alou

turned out not only to be uniquely interesting, he gave me my first insight into the problems of being a Latin ballplayer in the North American big leagues. Our relationship began bumpily because he kept putting me off when I tried to talk to him. I told him I wanted to write an article about his remarkable 1966 season. He had played every position for the Braves except pitcher and catcher, hit .327, which was second best in the league, and whacked 31 home runs. On a team with Joe Torre and Henry Aaron, he had been voted MVP.

"I will talk to you tomorrow," he told me during my first visit to West Palm. I explained I had to return to Lauderdale, then drive back the next morning. He shrugged and said, "Tomorrow." I came back the next morning and he told me, "Tomorrow." On the morning of the third day, I was polite but I let my annoyance unfurl a little. I suggested that if we didn't do our interview today, we might not do it at all. His face was as impassive as charcoal, but he agreed to meet me after practice at his hotel room in downtown Palm Beach.

The room was on a high floor of the hotel. Through the window we could see the Florida sunlight shatter on the blue waters of Lake Worth. Felipe sat on the side of a bed, his large coffee-brown face solemn. But during the next three hours, as we talked, he became more animated, his hands sweeping the air; there was anger in his voice when we discussed the subject of the Latin player and his reputation for being a showboat, a "hot dog" in the parlance of the dugout.

He wore slacks and a short-sleeved polo shirt, the muscles of his upper arms bulging from the silky fabric. I was not surprised to learn, during our two days of conversation in West Palm, that he had been a champion thrower of the discus and javelin as a teenager. His longest javelin throw was still a Dominican Republic record some twenty years later.

"They say we are all hot dogs," he told me when I mentioned the flamboyance of some Latin players. He spoke English with a soft-voiced fluency, the words accented with the carioca rhythms of the Caribbean. "They say we make the easy play look hard. They say we are showboats. People here in the United States, they don't understand us. We are not German or Irish or Italian. We are a mixture of Spanish and African. Most of us grew up in poor families. Many of us didn't get a good education. All this affects our play.

"Like up here in the big leagues, I'll see a Latin player get knocked down by a pitcher. He jumps up and starts talking back to the pitcher. That's what we do back home." His large, hard face relaxed for a moment into a you-know-how-it-is smile. "But you're not supposed to do that here. So we learn not to say anything, and hit the next pitch good. You come up to the big leagues and you see how a Musial or a Mays does things. You imitate the way they behave, their approach to the game. When we go home, we show the younger players how they play up here, and you don't hear so much talk about hot dogs."

Latin players were underpaid, he told me with more resignation than anger in his voice. At a time when young U.S. high-school players were receiving bonuses of up to $100,000 to sign contracts, Alou signed with the Giants in 1956 for $200. "At the time," he told me, "my family owed the grocer $400. My bonus was so small, it didn't even pay the grocery bill." He did not smile.

Latin American players were still getting low bonuses, he said. "I know what the scouts tell them," he told me. "The scouts say, 'Where are you going to make any money in your country? Cutting sugar cane in the fields?'

"The Giants told me that—after I was a big leaguer and their best hitter. I have that letter back home in the Dominican Republic. It is a letter I will always keep. I got it in 1963.

In 1962 the Giants won the pennant. I led the Giants in hitting last year. At the time I was an $18,000 ballplayer.

"That winter I knew they would start out with a low offer. They'd offer a $10,000 player maybe a $1,000 raise. But you don't offer a guy who hit .316 for you a $2,000 raise. That was what they offered me for being their best hitter on a team that won the pennant.

"Finally I made them give me close to what I wanted. But I had to go through a lot of bad letters. They wrote things like, 'Do you think you will make this kind of money in the Dominican Republic?'

"No one likes people to say bad things about your country. And I'll tell you something. There are two million Dominicans working in the sugar fields, and they have nothing to be ashamed of. They are supporting their families."

Felipe's pride showed that afternoon when we discussed his MVP 1966 season with Atlanta. Most of the season he had played first base, even though he preferred to play where he had played for the Giants —the outfield. "I have lots of speed," he said, "and first base is like being locked in a jail. But if you are a ballplayer, you play where you are needed."

The pride also showed when he told me about a game that had given him what he called "my greatest thrill." It was the final game of the 1962 playoff for the pennant between Felipe's Giants and the Los Angeles Dodgers.

"I remember in the eighth inning of that last game, they were ahead, three to two. Maury Wills stole third and [catcher] Ed Bailey's throw got away into the outfield. Wills ran for home and Leo Durocher [then the Dodger third-base coach], he ran all the way down the line with Wills and slid as Maury slid home safe.

"Durocher got up laughing. Right then he thought he had the game won. But we got four runs in the top of the ninth [Felipe scoring the winning run] to beat them.

"I had wanted bad to win that game. But I wanted real bad to beat them after what Durocher did. Sliding." Felipe spat out the word. "Like it was a show."

It was only later that I realized why Felipe had been so angry when Durocher slid home. I put it this way in the article, titled "The Gentle Howitzer," that I wrote about Felipe in *Sport:* "It was such a hot-dog thing to do."

Felipe was born in the Dominican Republic on May 12, 1935. He grew up in Haina, a fishing village a few miles from Santo Domingo. His father owned a blacksmith shop, and Felipe grew tall and strong as he helped his father hammer hot metal. "I loved sports," he told me. "In high school I ran on the track team and threw the discus and javelin. I was the fastest in my school in the four hundred meters."

At sixteen he labored in a cement factory to help his father support a growing family that would send three sons to the U.S. big leagues. "There was this machine in the factory. We called it Korea. What you did was pick up these big rocks and throw them into Korea. And as fast as you could pick up those rocks and throw them in, the machine broke them up. For eight hours you do that, always bent over, and at six in the morning, when our shift was over, you weren't good for anything." The pay was $9 a week.

When he could, he fished. "What I liked to do was go out fishing by myself or with my brother Jesus. It's peaceful out there. And you're not hurting anyone."

In 1954 he had saved enough money to go to college to study to be a doctor. He pitched for the college baseball team. A Giant scout saw the muscled, six-foot, two-hundred-pounder hurl baseballs and signed him. In 1956 he was playing for a Giant farm team in Cocoa, Florida. He couldn't speak English and was lonely, missing his brothers. He realized that homesickness would drive him back to Santo Domingo if he didn't soon make friends. He enrolled in a correspondence course to learn English and carried a pocket English-Spanish dictionary to study on road trips.

He joined the San Francisco Giants in 1958 as a platoon player; a right-handed hitter, he batted against lefty pitching, hitting .275 and ten homers in 1959.

As we sat in the hotel room overlooking Lake Worth, he stared at the floor and said, "I used to think that if I made it to the big leagues, my problems would be over. I thought, I will have a new house, a car, and I will see my name in the newspapers all the time. I will play baseball on the same field with men like Willie Mays, big guys like that. Then, I thought, I will know real happiness.

"I got to the big leagues . . . but I found my problems were not over. I still had the problems—worry about money, worry about pain, worry about all the sorrows that mankind has.

"A friend of mine in the Dominican Republic had given me a Bible. I used to go to church. But I didn't even know there was a book like the Bible. The book told me I could find no happiness in the big leagues. The book told me of Jesus Christ and how all men need repentance.

"Now that I have accepted Jesus Christ, I have peace in my life. I'm not perfect. I'm still a sinner. Money problems still worry me. I have a lot of relatives. I know I have to argue for money for my family because God isn't going to argue for me. But now I feel happiness. I feel I am alive and before I was dead."

In 1961 he became the Giants' full-time left fielder. Two years later there were three Alous on the team, younger brothers Jesus and Matty having made the same jump from their island in the sun to the San Francisco bay. The Giants may have decided that three Alous were too many, especially after

Felipe complained to manager Al Dark that Jesus was not playing as much as he should. Felipe went to the Braves in 1964. He never had another wonderful year like 1966, his best a .317 season for the Braves in 1968. Later he played for Oakland, the Yankees, Montreal, and Milwaukee before retiring in 1974. His lifetime average was .286.

Felipe stayed in baseball, joining the Montreal Expos as a minor-league coach and instructor. In 1984 he was named Montreal's first-base coach, and in 1985 he became manager of Montreal's top farm team, The Indianapolis Indians. Each winter, though, he goes back to the Dominican Republic, where the fishing is good and the life is peaceful.

Felipe Alou as a Montreal coach in 1984.

Rick had the grim-faced look as a high scorer at Miami in 1964.

Rick Barry

I HAVE NEVER FORGOTTEN A CONVERsation I once had with Rick Barry as we stood in the corridor of the New Orleans airport on a night in November of 1969. At the time he was playing for the Oakland Oaks in the American Basketball Association, one of a long line of teams whose uniform Rick wore during fourteen seasons as a pro. He was averaging 30 points a game, tops in the league. I asked him if he was bothered by the pressure of trying to maintain that lofty average in game after game. His answer, given in a tone that questioned how I could ask such a stupid question, made me understand for the first time what it was like to be the cocky athlete who swaggers into a game certain that he will perform anywhere from good to great.

Tall (six-foot-eight) and with polelike arms and legs on a two-hundred-ten-pound frame that moved as though the pieces were hinged, Barry stopped and stared down at me. He was a tense man; a grim look usually hung on his beach-boy handsome face. Now he radiated annoyance. "Pressure to score points?" The high-pitched voice was almost a screech. "Of course not! Look, when I go out onto a court for a game, I know—I *know*—that unless I get hurt, I am going to score at least twenty points."

"How can you be so sure?"

"First of all, if I play only twenty to twenty-five minutes, I got to score six to eight points just by hanging around the basket and putting in garbage [easy two points made by tap-ins or when a ball glances off the board into a player's hands]. Then I am going to be fouled at least four or five times, so there is another six to seven points. Even if I'm off on my shooting from outside, I am going to put in at least one-third of my shots [his average was around 50 percent]. If I take fifteen shots during twenty-five minutes and I make only five, there's another ten points. Add that up and what have you got—at least twenty-two points, which is only eight below my average. And that's on a bad night. On a good night I'll play thirty to thirty-five minutes, I'll shoot above my average, and I have to make thirty-five to forty points."

Two of his Oakland teammates were Doug Moe, later an NBA coach with Denver, and Larry Brown, later both a pro and college coach, most recently at the University of Kansas. They had given Rick a nickname: Linus. Linus was the character in the comic strip "Peanuts" who was so insecure he walked around clutching a security blanket. In calling Barry a name like Linus, Moe and Brown were, of course, jesting. Rick Barry,

then twenty-four years old, was as insecure as another comic-strip character, Popeye, after quaffing a can of spinach.

Failure had been a stranger in his life. He was born in Elizabeth, New Jersey, on March 28, 1944, attended high school in Roselle Park, a bedroom suburb of New York City, then went to the University of Miami. On that campus in the sun, he fitted in perfectly, the fair-haired, handsome surfing type. He married Pam Hale, the pretty daughter of Bruce Hale, his college coach. In the 1964–65 season he averaged 37 points a game to rank among the nation's high scorers, and he made just about everybody's All-America. Still he seemed too skinny to be a high scorer amid the flailing elbows of the National Basketball Association. I can recall predicting that he would be one of those All-Americas who disappear swiftly beneath the turbulent waters of the NBA.

The San Francisco Warriors chose him in the first round of the 1965 draft. Almost from his first game, he showed us skeptics a quickness in dodging those flailing elbows and he soared over those aiming to mug him. He leaped, twisted, bent, and swooped with a body control unlike that of few, if any, white players before him. Barry has been called (somewhat to his annoyance because I think he considers the comparison racist) the first white player to play black. "I don't believe in that nonsense," he once told me. "Sure, I believe there are different styles. But I don't like the idea of having to say white or black. If a man, whether he be white, black, blue, or green, has an abundance of God-given talent and if he grows up in an atmosphere that is conducive to playing basketball a majority of the time, he will develop a certain style. If he comes from a black ghetto, he will play with a style that people call black style. If you had the same number of white children growing up in the same ghetto environment, you would have far more white players playing the same

7

way. And then people would call it white style."

Barry was chosen the NBA's Rookie of the Year in the 1965–66 season. The next year he led the league in scoring. He was a white face in a sport that was filling with the faces of black stars, and so was sought after as a drawing magnet by the teams of a new league, the American Basketball Association. In 1967 when one of the ABA owners, singer Pat Boone, signed Bruce Hale to be the coach of his ABA Oakland team, no one was too surprised when Rick also signed, apparently not only for a good father-in-law relationship. Rick's salary was said to be $75,000 a year for each of three years, a whopping sum at a time when few NBA stars were earning over $50,000 a year.

The Warriors screamed loudly in courtrooms, asking for an injunction against Barry's jump to the ABA. He had to sit out the 1967–68 season and the Oakland team played so ineffectively that Hale was replaced by a veteran NBA coach, Alex Hannum, for the 1968–69 season, Rick's first in the new league. ABA owners hoped that Rick would pull people into ABA games.

Late in November of 1968 I joined the Oaks on a road trip from New Orleans to Miami to Louisville for a story that *Sport* titled "Rick Barry's Save-a-League Crusade."

I met Rick in a New Orleans hotel room. The floor was strewn with clothing, a typical scene in the room of athletes always on the move. As we talked, Rick stuffed sneakers, uniforms, and wrinkled shirts and slacks into bags.

Did he feel nervous about being the one who was supposed to draw people into games and save a league? As usual, the face was grim, his manner cocky. "Naw," he said, "I don't let it bother the way I play, if that's what you mean."

That night the Oaks played the New Orleans Bucs. The crowd was announced at 3,225, well above the average for Buc games when Rick wasn't here, but a disap-

pointment to the Bucs, who had expected 4,000 in an arena that held 6,000.

The Oaks won easily, 121-108, Rick the high scorer with 35 points. After the game a group of us—Rick, Hannum, Larry Brown, Doug Moe, and Oakland writer Paul Murphy—squeezed into a rented car and drove to the airport for the flight to Miami. Murphy said that he had read recently a comment from a columnist: that Rick Barry playing in the American Basketball Association was like Van Cliburn playing piano for an out-of-tune singer like Tiny Tim.

I laughed, but no one else did. Rick gave me his grim scowl. "That columnist is trying to make our league sound like a minor league. You take away seven or eight of the NBA's top stars and the two leagues are not that far apart."

He turned toward Hannum as our car, driven by Larry Brown, sped through the dark streets, the time near midnight. "In the NBA I didn't have to work to score against your club, did I, Alex?" Hannum nodded. "I didn't have to work against Boston— Satch Sanders wasn't always that tough. Or Detroit. Or Baltimore. I did have to work against Dick Van Arsdale in New York."

"And against Tom Hawkins in Los Angeles," Murphy said.

"Some nights, yes, but that was about it, all around the league."

He hadn't convinced me that the ABA was even close to the quality of the NBA in talent, but I said nothing. I sensed early that in a debate Rick Barry did not concede easily or happily.

On the plane to Miami I talked to Doug Moe, a hulking forward who grinned, eyes twinkling, as he told me this story about Linus. He and Rick liked to play I.Q., an electronic game then popular in airports. Questions flashed on a screen. The faster you answered the question by pressing one of five buttons, the higher your score. One day, as Moe played and Barry watched, this question jumped onto the screen:

WHICH FAMOUS BASKETBALL PLAYER
IS BRUCE HALE'S SON-IN-LAW?

Moe's jaw dropped, that son-in-law standing next to him. Five names showed on the screen—Chamberlain, Barry, Baylor, West, Robertson—but Moe was too rigid with shock to find the right button in time.

Barry had been embarrassed. Moe would not let him forget. In the airplane he shouted loudly enough for Barry to hear: "Which *famous* player is Bruce Hale's son-in-law?"

Barry's face reddened, but he shot back down the aisle: "And you, you dummy, you blew the answer!"

Even with Rick Barry, Oakland could not draw enough people to make the franchise lucrative. It moved to Washington and then to Virginia, Rick still the league leader in scoring. He went to the ABA's New York Nets in 1970 and helped the Nets win the ABA title in 1972. He jumped back to the NBA and the Warriors, now based in Oakland, as the two leagues closed toward a merger. He was the high scorer of a Warrior team that surprised many people by winning the NBA title in the 1974–75 season. He played for the Houston Rockets in the 1978–79 season, then retired to be a CBS sports commentator.

He talked candidly on TV about the lack of teamwork in NBA games. "We have great shooters, great jumpers," he told me in 1979. "If they could play the entire game, like moving without the ball as well as they move with the ball . . . oh, it's just incredible what this game could be like. It's a great game now, but what a game this could be— if only . . ."

He left CBS in 1981 but returned to sports broadcasting in 1984, teaming with Bill Russell on WTBS cable telecasts of NBA games. Still as grim looking as ever, he played in an NBA old-timers game in 1984, leading everyone in scoring. Living in Mercer Island, Washington, he tried to play golf but "that's too relaxing a game," he told an interviewer. He and his wife, Pam, took up tennis

and became one of the country's best amateur mixed-doubles players; they won a husband-wife regional tournament in Eugene, Oregon, in 1983. Now answer this quickly, Doug Moe: "What famous basketball player, now retired, won a tennis championship with his wife?"

Rick still looks grim playing in an old-timers game in 1983.

Nick Buoniconti as a Dolphin in the 1970s.

Nick Buoniconti

IN HIS PRO FOOTBALL CAREER NICK Buoniconti straddled both sides of the tracks. He had come into pro football when it was not a rich man's game and, as his wife once told me, "It was really something to be a hard-nosed guy making $10,000 a year." By the time his career was at its peak, Nick had crossed over to the other side of the tracks. He saw a time coming when defensive players like himself would be earning anywhere from $100,000 to a quarter of a million dollars a year. As we sat by the side of his pool near Miami on a fall day in 1972, he talked enthu-

siastically about a game that was making its quarterbacks overnight millionaires. But there was a touch of longing in his voice for a time when he was a rookie—a time only a decade earlier when he had played for the Boston Patriots and the players, allowing for inflation, were not appreciably higher paid than the players of the first days of pro football in the 1920s.

He talked, with the broad a's of his native Massachusetts in his voice, of the evenings, after Patriot practice sessions, when the team gathered at a tavern. His brown eyes, set above a curving Roman nose on a broad and swarthy face, gleamed as he said, "I still miss how we used to get together every

10

day after practice at the Red Boot in Taunton, and we had a hell of a time over beers and sandwiches. Tuesday was always the married guys night out, and there'd be twenty of us on the defensive unit who'd get together at the Bolo Lounge near Fenway Park for a night of bull throwing and beer drinking.

"Pro football's not like that anymore. Today's players are more selfish. We go to practice, then go out on our own as businessmen. The players today look out for themselves. Hell, look at me, I'm one of the worst offenders. I got a law practice, a radio show, a half-dozen other things. Our selfishness is warranted. A player is foolish if he doesn't take advantage of the opportunities. Today you get $500 to speak. Then, in the old days, $50 was a big deal. Still. . . ." There was a long pause as he stared at the turquoise water of the pool that sat at the edge of his large ranch-type home. "Still," he said, obviously thinking back to those days at the Red Boot and the Bolo Lounge, "I miss how we used to get together."

The thick-necked, five-foot-eleven, two-hundred-twenty-pound Nick seemed small and squat when I saw him standing with his fellow linebackers on a practice field. But Nick was the heart and brain of a bunch of relatively unknown players who became famous as the Miami Dolphins' No-Name Defense of the early 1970s. That defense, and the offense steered by quarterback Bob Griese, achieved that rarest of pro football records, going without a defeat through the 1972 National Football League season, the Dolphins becoming the only team to go undefeated since the Chicago Bears of 1942. The Dolphins won Super Bowl championships in 1973 and 1974, joining the Green Bay Packers as the only team up to then to win two in a row.

Nick was the last of the lightweight linebackers, most of whom, in his time and since, weighed at least two-hundred-forty pounds. "At two-hundred-twenty pounds,"

he told me one afternoon as we sat on stools in the Miami training room, Nick peeling off his practice uniform, "I am going up against linemen who are two-hundred-fifty pounds and bigger. The key for me is quickness and agility—not bigness and speed. In a 40-yard dash I wouldn't be in the top twenty fastest on this team. But I have the quickness to start before those fast running backs can start. And I've got the agility to avoid those big linemen so they'll get no more than a hand on me."

I talked to his coach, the square-faced Don Shula, who said of Nick: "When Nick sees something, it doesn't take him long for what he sees to go from his mind to his feet."

Nick was the only athlete I have ever written about who was also a practicing lawyer. (*Sport* titled my article, "A Brief for Buoniconti.") In 1962, shortly after he came out of Notre Dame to join the Patriots of the American Football League, he was chatting with a friend who was a lawyer in the friend's office on Boston's Commonwealth Avenue. Nick mentioned in an off-handed way that he had often thought about studying to be a lawyer.

The lawyer stared for several moments at Nick, then laughed. He said he just couldn't imagine a burly linebacker as a lawyer. A football player arguing before a jury—the image caused the lawyer to laugh out loud.

"Nick came home steaming," his wife, Terry, told me. "That was all Nick needed—someone to tell him that he wasn't able to do something."

Nick promptly went off to night school, studied for four years during his evenings away from football and off-season jobs, and passed the Massachusetts bar examination. For a while he was a state prosecutor working in a Boston office. When he was traded to Miami, he took and passed the bar exam for the state of Florida.

That lawyer friend was not the first to intimate to Nick that he might not be able to do something. Nick's college coach once told him that he would never be a pro football player.

His pathway to the NFL began in Springfield, Massachusetts, where he was born on December 15, 1940. He attended Cathedral High School where he won the annual award for being the outstanding high school football player in the area during his senior year. He went to Notre Dame on a football scholarship, playing for Joe Kuharich, who had once coached the Philadelphia Eagles of the NFL. In his senior year Nick was named to several All-America teams. He talked to Kuharich about his future as a pro. "I'm sorry, Nick," Kuharich told him. "You certainly played good football for us. But I don't think you're big enough to play pro football and because I don't, I won't recommend you. It wouldn't be right."

At the time Nick claimed he was five-foot-eleven and weighed two-hundred-fifteen pounds, but I have always believed that Nick, in claiming to be five-foot-eleven, attached an inch or two. In any case, he told me that day as we sat by the side of the pool, "I was really down, really crushed. I had always thought that I could make a pro team that needed linebackers. All I wanted was the chance to prove myself—and now I knew I wouldn't even get a fair shot."

No NFL team, perhaps heeding Kuharich's concern about his size, drafted Nick. The time was 1962. The two-year-old American Football League was grasping for any talent it could find, even has-beens and never-weres who had been let go by NFL teams. But no AFL team was interested in Nick until the Boston Patriots, on the thirteenth and near final round of the AFL draft, picked him with no particular enthusiasm.

A grateful Nick signed to play for the Patriots for a $1000 bonus. When Nick heard the news in South Bend, where he was living off campus in a tiny cottage with his new bride, Terry, a former nurse in Springfield, he ordered $1000 worth of beer. A row of

trucks dumped a large hill of beer cans onto his front lawn and the party went on for two days (cops came by at least eight times to try to shush the celebrants). "One thousand dollars," Terry told me. "It was a tremendous amount for us to spend in those days. And we threw it away."

That kind of free-spiritedness made Nick one of the ringleaders of the happy-go-lucky Patriots during guys nights out. It also made him a far-ranging, blitzing linebacker who seemed to bump into ballcarriers with almost magical regularity. "He is so good at guessing where you are going," the best running back of his time, O.J. Simpson, once told me. "Do you know what I do when we're playing against Buoniconti? I go to a hole where I am not supposed to go. We improvise a lot against him. But the way he reads what hole you are going to, it amazes me. He knows where you are going before you start to go there."

Nick was an All Pro linebacker for six of his seven years in Boston. In early 1970 he was traded to Miami where Don Shula and his defensive coach, Bill Arnsparger, fit Nick into the middle of a defense they were building. "In Boston," Nick told me one afternoon as he drove me from the Dolphin training base at a local college to his home, "I freelanced all over the place. Here I became one man, a cog if you will, in an eleven-man piece of machinery in which every section of the machine feels part of a whole."

"Nick was always prepared to do the physical part," Shula told me. "Now he is giving a lot more thought to the mental part."

In 1969 the Dolphins had been among the league's busted suitcases, finishing at the bottom of the AFL's Eastern Division with a record of 3 wins, 10 losses, and 1 tie. In 1970, Nick's first with the team, the Dolphins rose to second in their division with a 10–4 mark. In 1971 they were first with a 10–3–1 record. They beat Shula's old team, the Baltimore

Colts, for the championship of the American Football Conference and were matched against the Dallas Cowboys in Super Bowl VI. The Cowboys broke through the middle of the No-Name Defense as though it were a door with broken hinges, gaining 252 yards rushing, which was at the time a Super Bowl record. The Cowboys breezed to a 24–3 victory. After the game Nick was among the first to say that a good share of the fault for all those yards was his.

As we sat by the side of the pool almost a year later, there was a rueful look on Nick's face. "Dallas took advantage of my quickness," he told me. "One of their backs, usually Duane Thomas, would take off toward the right, and I'd sense he was going to the right and flow toward the right. Then one of the Dallas linemen would nudge me even more to the right. Thomas would cut back toward the middle, going against the flow, and he'd gain five or six yards before I'd get back to help cut him off. This year I'm working hard on cutbacks, staying behind the ball a little more than I've done in the past."

Indeed, Nick and the No-Name Defense did many things right during that 1972 season, winning all 14 games of their season. The No-Name Defense was made up of relative unknowns like Vern Den Herder, Don Reese, Bob Mathewson, Mike Kolen, Manny Fernandez, and deep backs Jake Scott and Dick Anderson. That defense excelled in the Dolphins's second-straight Super Bowl, shutting out the Washington Redskins for the entire game. (The Redskins did score once in a 14–7 Miami victory when Washington blocked a field goal; Miami kicker Garo Yepremian picked up the bounding ball and threw a pass, right into the hands of a Washington player, who ran into the end zone for the touchdown.) The Dolphins went to a third straight Super Bowl the following season, 1973, beating Minnesota, 24–7, the only touchdown given up by Nick and the No-Name Defense in eight quarters against the best of the National Football Conference.

In 1975 Nick was injured and out of action for the entire season, and in 1976, after playing off and on, he retired at the end of the season. Today he has his own law firm in Miami and also serves as a corporate lawyer for the U.S. Tobacco Company, splitting his time between the U.S. Tobacco headquarters in Connecticut and his office and home in Miami. What he is especially proud of is a campaign that reduced his weight from the two-hundred-eighteen pounds of 1972 to the one-hundred-eighty-eight pounds of 1984. In 1985 Don Shula still had not forgotten all the things that Nick could do at two hundred and eighteen pounds. Shula was talking about his sensational quarterback Dan Marino. "It doesn't take long for a message to go from Dan's eyes to his feet," Shula said. "Nick was like that."

Nick is a corporate lawyer in Florida and Connecticut.

Lew (*left*) poses in 1960 with Warren Spahn and Gene Conley, fellow Braves pitchers.

Lew Burdette

I WATCHED LEW BURDETTE PITCH THE seventh game of the 1958 World Series, a Series I recall with relish for two reasons. First, the Yankees were losing in the Series, 3 games to 1, when I bet a friend $20, getting 4–1 odds, that the Yankees would win. "I don't know if the Yankees can win the next three games in a row or not," I told myself,

"but when will I ever get the chance to bet on the Yankees and get odds of 4–1?" My second reason for remembering that Series, and in particular that seventh game, was this: I predicted correctly for the only time in my life the imminent downfall of a pitcher.

Burdette retired the first two Yankees in that inning. But I had seen something that told me he was weakening. "Burdette's fastball is coming in too high," I told someone who was watching the game with me on

14

television. "He's not bending his back, as the coaches say, because he's tiring. He can't keep throwing those high fastballs to a power-hitting team like the Yankees and get away with it."

The Yankees had won 2 games in a row to tie the Series at 3 games apiece. In this climactic game, the score was tied 2–2 in the top of the eighth inning. And after their first two batters were retired, the Yankees struck. They scored one run off Burdette and two Yankees were on base. Bill Skowron stood at bat. Burdette threw another high fastball that Skowron took. "If he does that again," I said, "Skowron will hit it out." Burdette threw two low pitches, then came in with another high pitch, either a slider or a fastball. Skowron "got all of it," as the hitters say, and slammed the ball into the left-field stands of a suddenly quiet County Stadium in Milwaukee. The Yankees led, 6–2, and a few minutes later they were world champions and I was $80 richer.

I met Burdette for the first time some five years later. During spring training in 1963, I interviewed him for an article about the struggle of an aging pitcher—Burdette was then thirty-six—trying to hang on to a big-league job. When I arrived at the Braves' clubhouse in West Palm Beach, the long and narrow room was empty. An attendant told me that all the ballplayers were out on the field. Through the open windows I could hear the distant cracks and shouts of baseball. I walked to Burdette's dressing stall and saw his uniform hanging there. As I turned, he was striding toward me, head down, apparently late for practice hurrying to change from his street clothes and go out onto the field.

I introduced myself. He nodded, ground out a cigarette, and yawned. Despite a crew cut, he looked older than thirty-six, his leathery face deeply lined. As he pulled off his short-sleeved polo shirt, he asked softly, "What kind of an article are you doing?" His eyes had been appraising me and I guessed

he was wondering why I would be interested in a thirty-six-year-old pitcher whose days as a headliner were behind him.

"I want to do an article about how a veteran pitcher like yourself has to fight in spring training to hold a job, and how a younger pitcher, like Denny Lemaster or Bob Hendley on your club, has to fight to win one."

"Hah!" It was a hard, dry, mirthless laugh. His square-cut face worked angrily for several moments as he tried to bring out the words he wanted to say. "Why didn't you tell me that before?"

He stared for a while at the floor as he pulled on his baseball stockings. "Look," he said finally, some of the anger apparently ebbing. "This is a ticklish situation. Sure, it's a true situation that you're talking about, but it's ticklish. Anything I say might make me sound bitter."

A little later, his uniform on, his cap slapped slightly askew on his head, he stood in a tunnel that led under the stands to the field. "Oh, I'll talk to you," he said. "I'll talk to you." He paused. "But if you crucify me, then I'll find a way someday to crucify you."

The next day we sat together on stools in the clubhouse, which was again empty, the other players out on the field. Burdette, who had been running in the outfield, had come into the clubhouse to change his wet shirt. As he smoked a cigarette, he talked about what baseball had meant to him. "This is a wonderful goofy business. It's been my life. I don't really have anything else except my family and a couple of little businesses in Sarasota [where he lived during the off-seasons]. But they're nothing to write about. When I'm finished, what I would really like would be some kind of coaching job in base-ball.

"I try to help the kids now. Like with Hendley. I'll holler at him from the dugout to keep the ball low. If he asks me how to pitch, or how I throw a pitch, I'll show him. All this talk about not giving away secrets, that's so much shellac. As long as I can pitch, I will have a job. When I can't, then someone else will take over. That's all there is to it."

But, of course, there was more to it—the agony, both mental and physical, as a player of that time tried to force a thirty-six-year-old body to do all the flowing things it did so easily at twenty-six. And the worry: What will happen to him and his family when he must leave this world of high pay and enter that bigger world which may demand skills he might not have? The manager of the Braves at the time, Bobby Bragan, gave me, in his brisk no-nonsense fashion, a look at the death rattles of a terminal case.

"You can tell it with the older guys, when they don't have it anymore. They stand out there on the mound, the poor suckers, throwing the ball so hard the sweat stands out in beads and runs down their faces, but the ball doesn't move like it should and you know they're through."

Burdette's big-league career began with the team that was both his victim and his conqueror in two successive World Series— the New York Yankees. He was born on November 22, 1926, in Nitro, West Virginia, the son of a factory worker and a semipro baseball player, Selva Lewis Burdette, who gave his son his full name. (Lew sometimes spelled his name Lou when he signed autographs, but historians have continued to spell his name as his father spelled it.) "He could throw rocks farther than any boy in town," his mother once said. As a teenager he played for one of the industrial teams in Nitro as his father did before him. He went into the army during the last two years of World War II; when he came out of service in 1946, he enrolled at the University of Richmond, and played on the baseball team, a strapping right-hander who startled batters with the velocity of his fastball.

His coach knew a Yankee scout, who signed Lew. By 1950 Lew was wearing pin

stripes in the Bronx but late that season the Yankees sent him to Boston in exchange for Johnny Sain. In 1953 the Braves moved to Milwaukee, and Burdette teamed with a rawboned left-hander, Warren Spahn, and a sinewy slugger, Hank Aaron, to help win two successive pennants in 1957 and 1958. Burdette was the hero of the 1957 Series victory over the Yankees, winning three games.

He and Spahn had become buddies, a love of laughter their bond. In clubhouse skits both spun their hats and crossed their eyes to play loony drunks. One of their favorite practical jokes was frightening the new driver of a bus taking the Braves from a hotel to the ball park.

"Back it up a little more, bussy," Spahn shouted as the driver twisted the bus through a crowded parking lot. "A little more . . . a little more . . ." Then both Spahn and Burdette whacked their palms against the sides of the bus, the sudden sound of a collision that lifted the driver off his seat while the Braves shook with laughter.

Burdette's best years were from 1956 to 1961. In those six years he won at least 17 games each season, winning 20 in 1958 and 21 in 1959, and his earned-run average of 2.70 led the league in 1956. He pitched a no-hitter against the Phils on August 18, 1960. In 1962 he struggled through a 10–9 season, was consigned to the bullpen for much of the time, and began to feel forgotten.

Now, at the start of the 1963 spring-training season, I had come to him to talk about an article that would be titled, "An Old Pitcher Against the Challenge of Youth." Lew's good buddy, Warren Spahn, seemed more annoyed than Lew when he heard why I was there. One day I was interviewing young Denny Lemaster when Spahn crept up behind me, poked his Ichabod Crane face over my shoulder, and peeked at what I was scribbling. When I turned he smiled innocently and said, "Don't let *me* interrupt you." He put on one of his goofy cross-eyed grins. Lemaster laughed.

"Maybe you can help, Warren," I said. "I was going to ask Denny whether it's tougher for an established pitcher, like Burdette, to hold a job, or for a younger pitcher, like Denny, to win a job."

The grin drained from Spahn's face. He stepped back, doing a mock stagger. "Oh, no," he said loudly. "Oh, no. That's a personal story. I've got nothing to say to you. Nothing!" He stopped, wagged his finger in front of his banana nose, and said, "No, sir, that's a personal story." He stepped into the tunnel and vanished.

The next day I passed him as he sat on the bench in the dugout. He was alone, staring at the green outfield. "You've got a good story there," he said. "You can't miss—the old guy and the young guy." His voice dripped with sarcasm.

I said nothing. But later I wondered if Spahn, sitting there on the bench and staring at the outfield, wasn't seeing a future spring when he would feel youth's hungry breathing on his shoulder, challenging him for a job.

As in most conflicts in sport between youth and age, youth was the victor in Burdette's struggle to stay with the Braves. He was traded to the Cardinals early in that 1963 season. Later he pitched for the Cubs, Phils, and California Angels before retiring in 1967 with a career record of 203 victories and 144 losses. He lives now in Sarasota. I talked to him briefly in the fall of 1979 when he came to New York to be honored by *Sport Magazine* as one of the twenty-five previous World Series Most Valuable Players. I told him what I sincerely meant: that he looked no older than he had when I'd first met him some sixteen years earlier. He had looked older than thirty-six in 1963, but then, of course, he had been looking over his shoulder at something that was catching up to him.

Lew gets ready for a 1984 old-timers game.

Don Carter

I HAVE NEVER SEEN A BOWLER ROLL A perfect game of 300—that is, twelve straight strikes. Few people have; a perfect game is rare. On a spring day in 1960, watching Don Carter bowl at a lane in Toledo, Ohio, I came literally within a fraction of an inch of seeing that perfect game, thrown by a bowler who was unquestionably the best of his time and perhaps the best ever.

I had been traveling through the Midwest with Carter for much of a week. We had been in Detroit for most of the day. Carter had dashed from one department store to another in downtown Detroit, signing autographs and otherwise promoting his line of Don Carter bowling shirts and Don Carter bowling gloves. Suddenly he glanced at his wristwatch and realized he would probably be late for an appearance in Toledo more than a hundred miles away.

We jumped into a rented car. With us were a photographer and a business associate of Carter's. We talked about stopping to eat since none of us had eaten since breakfast, but decided there was not enough time. Carter had been up since before six that morning, jogging for several miles, and since then he had been almost continually on the go. Normally an amiable and often witty man who resembled a younger Bing Crosby, Carter was quiet for most of the trip, and near the end he seemed irritable. We arrived at the bowling center in Toledo at about five in the evening, about an hour late. A crowd of perhaps 500 was seated and milling around in the center as we came through the entrance. People let out a low murmur of recognition when they saw Carter's thick-shouldered, six-foot figure, familiar to them because of his many appearances on televised bowling shows.

Don Carter gets set to roll in 1959.

The owner of the lanes scurried up to him, looking upset. Carter apologized for being late. He said that he had missed lunch and asked if he could have a cup of coffee and a sandwich before he bowled against a local professional.

"I'm sorry, that's impossible," snapped the owner. "These people have been waiting for you for an hour or more. They want you to bowl right away."

Carter shrugged. He walked down the steps to the bowling lanes, a stage smile masking his tiredness. The crowd applauded politely but only moderately; a few stopped him to ask for autographs. Carter shook hands with his opponent. He had time for only a couple of practice rolls, and then the match began.

Carter rolled a strike. He rolled a second. He rolled a third. When he rolled the fourth, the roaring filled the place. I was standing, my tiredness from the trip vanished, wondering if I was going to see a perfect game.

Carter came up to the line to roll his fifth frame, the ball gripped at his side. He let it fly. It skidded down the lane, then began its roll. It smashed into the head pins, curving slightly, and the crowd broke the hush with another roar, believing he had knocked down all the pins for another strike. But one pin—I believe it was the ten pin—was still upright, teetering from side to side. It held. Carter knocked it down on his next roll for a spare. Then he rolled strikes the sixth, seventh, eighth, ninth and tenth frames for a score of 280.

He bowled two more games against the pro, winning all three. "I feel good," he told me between games. "Once you start playing, all the energy comes back."

His bowling style made other pros wince and say that Carter did nothing right except win. He approached the line by taking four slow, choppy steps, seeming to be more hesitant than most pros, who glide to the line. Carter reminded me of someone doing the rhumba for the first time and being very self-conscious about the way he looked. Instead of swinging the ball in a graceful arc behind him, Carter kept the ball close to his body, his elbow bent at an awkward angle, resembling a father carefully tossing a ball to his four-year-old son. Yet Carter released a ball that flew with astonishing speed and accuracy to curl into the pins with flattening force.

That kind of bowling had made him the National Bowling Champion five times and the Bowler of the Year five times (nobody else had ever held either title more than twice). When I met him for the first time, in Akron where he was beginning his tour of the Midwest to sell his shirts, slacks, and gloves, he had seemed too listless to be a champion. We had dinner in an Akron restaurant with Eddie Elias, a young man who had helped Carter and other bowlers organize the Professional Bowlers Association. The PBA, directed by Elias and Carter, was trying to give to pro bowling the prestige and prize money that the Professional Golfers Association (PGA) had given to the pro golfing tour. As Carter and Elias talked to me about the goals of the PBA, I could see that I was wrong about Carter being listless. He had been tired after a day of personal appearances in Toledo but as we sat he drummed his fingers on the table and when he wasn't chewing gum he was smoking a cigarette. "I could never sit around the house doing nothing," he told me at one point during our travels together. "I'd go clear out of my head."

He rarely sat around for long at his house in St. Louis, where he lived with his wife, LaVerne, who was also a pro bowler, and their two children. In fact, he told me, he was on the road for five days of most every week of the year. "I'm making money that's going to make a lot of difference for my youngsters," he told me one day as we drove from Akron to Detroit. "I am making a lot of money— more money than I thought there was just a

few years ago. That money is going to help my children have all the things I dreamed about when I was a kid."

His childhood had made him long for the good things of life. He was born in St. Louis on July 29, 1930. "We lived in St. Louis and my mother got a job in a factory," he told me during that drive from Detroit to Toledo. "I can't say we were ever starving, but the Carter family, let me tell you, knew what hunger was. I was a scrawny kid until I went into the navy. Then I filled out. I played some baseball and developed into a fair pitcher. I signed a contract with the St. Louis Browns organization after I got out of the navy, and I pitched a year of minor-league ball at $150 a month. I could see that I was never going to make it to the majors, so I quit.

"I'd always been a fair bowler, and I worked on it while I bounced around in several jobs. In 1949 I got a job teaching in a Chicago lane, and I began to compete in professional bowling."

Only two years later he was the national champion. He was not a rich one. "There was no big money in bowling tournaments until about 1955," he told me. "The Brunswick Corporation signed me up to make personal appearances, but I was lucky to make one a week. And at that time there were none of the television shows that came later offering big prize money."

In the mid-1950s new bowling centers, as they were called, began to sprout in shopping malls. Shiny and luxurious, their golden-yellow lanes gleaming, they were equipped with new automatic pin-setters that replaced the old-time pin boys who had squatted in the smoky "bowling alleys" of the 1940s. Lanes were open twenty-four hours a day and armies of bowlers, formed into leagues, filed into the centers in long and seemingly endless lines. There were leagues for married couples, day workers, night workers, high-school students; most

ml:antm
every office and factory had its own leagues.

Brunswick, which made automatic pin-setting equipment and therefore wanted to see the mushrooming of more bowling centers, sent Carter around the country to show bowlers how to boost their averages. "I was appearing in new lanes across the country as often as seven times a week," he told me. "And then came the television shows."

There was "Jackpot Bowling" and then "Make That Spare," the top pros competing on TV for as much as $10,000 a night. "A lot of the pros," Carter told me, "were making more money in one night on a TV show than they had been making in a year."

He and the other pros hopped from one PBA tournament to another on spring tours that were telecast, each Saturday afternoon, on ABC-TV. (They still are telecast and ABC claims the PBA spring tour are the longest-running sports show in TV history.) By 1964 prize money on the PBA tour had more than quadrupled to $1,200,000. Bothered by leg and knee aches, Carter began to appear less often on the tour and by the late 1960s the bowling craze had begun to subside.

I once asked Carter what advice he would give to a woman bowler who wanted to average 200 like her husband. "Practice making spares," he told women in an article he and I wrote. "Aim from the left to pick up pins on the right side, from the right to hit pins on the left. Your husband may score more strikes, but by converting spares, you can beat him."

He also suggested "making the ball, not your arm, supply the power." Using photos of his wife, Laverne, to illustrate his tips in the article, he pointed out that "on her second step—on the right foot—she pushes the ball straight out at arm's length. The weight of the ball, not her arm, swings it down."

In 1970 Carter was elected to the American Bowling Congress's Hall of Fame and in 1975 to the PBA's Hall of Fame. In 1970 a

group of bowling writers named him the greatest bowler in history. Divorced from Laverne, he married another pro bowler, Paula Sperber. They live in Miami where Carter owns a number of bowling centers. He also keeps busy appearing with other former athletes in TV commercials for Miller beer.

Don Carter gets ready for a Miller beer commercial in 1984.

Wilt shows his grasp of basketball in 1959.

Wilt Chamberlain

WILT CHAMBERLAIN ROSE FROM THE stool on which he had been seated in the Madison Square Garden dressing room. As he rose, my head tilted back to follow the progress of his scowl. He and the scowl climbed majestically. The scowl stopped inches below the ceiling of this narrow, steamy room, filled with shouting reporters and sweaty half-dressed or nude basketball players. The scowl, now some seven feet high, flashed sparks of annoyance, and the words boomed down as though from a

Moses speaking on a mountaintop: "I don't want to be hard, my friend, but I don't need any stories written about me."

I hid my disappointment by forcing a smile. I had come here in the winter of 1965 to try to wheedle an interview from Wilt the Stilt, the highest scorer in basketball history. He was being paid $125,000 a year by the Philadelphia 76ers at a time when few people in sport made more than $50,000. He owned a $17,000 Bentley motorcar, a Harlem nightclub, and real estate on both coasts, including a palatial home in southern California. Indeed, I thought, Wilt Chamberlain needs no interviews, no magazine articles, no songs written about him.

But I persisted because I had been told there was one way to get by Wilt's guard and talk to him close up. The guard dropped, I had been told, when Wilt was asked about a favorite subject of his: the possibility that he might be the world's greatest athlete. "It would make a great magazine article—is Wilt the world's greatest athlete?" Haskell Cohen, the bespectacled publicity director for the National Basketball Association, had suggested to me a few days earlier. Haskell had known Wilt when the gawky kid from Philadelphia worked during the summers as a bellhop for Kutscher's, one of the Catskill Mountain resorts in upstate New York that is part of the Borscht Belt.

"Wilt would love to talk about his being the world's greatest," Haskell told me. "He believes he can beat anyone in anything. He'll play you cards, pitch pennies, dominoes, and be convinced he can accomplish just about anything."

Now, looking up at the scowl, I told Wilt I wanted to write an article that would try to resolve the question: Is Wilt Chamberlain the world's greatest athlete?

He nodded. (Did he smile? I wasn't sure.) He said he would give me an interview in Philadelphia before the next 76ers home game a week hence. "Just fifteen minutes, my man," the voice boomed.

"Fifteen minutes will be fine," I lied, willing to settle for half a loaf and hoping I could slice more when we met in the 76ers' dressing room. A week later Wilt spied me entering the dressing room, which was filled with his teammates dressing or undressing. I noticed that many wore silk underwear, a symbol of their rapidly improving economic status. Wilt perched himself, cross-legged, on a large table in the corner. I sat on a chair, looking up at his giant Buddha-like figure, and was quickly reminded by Wilt that he could give me only fifteen minutes. I asked him to tick off the sports apart from basketball in which he thought he would do

well enough to be titled the world's greatest athlete.

"I would love to play football," he roared, the voice so loud it could be heard across the noisy room. He told me that Hank Stram, then the coach of the Kansas City Chiefs, had told him that no pass defender could stop him from catching passes. Indeed, I thought, Wilt might catch any ball thrown reasonably close to his long arms and huge hands. I could see Wilt standing under a goalpost, reaching up to catch an arching pass, while Lilliputian defenders swatted helplessly somewhere below his belt buckle. "I hope something can be worked out so I could play pro football until December," he told me, "and then turn to basketball. Football . . . *that's* my sport."

We talked about other sports. A Baltimore Oriole scout had seen him pick up a basketball the way you or I would grip a softball, and told him he would be an overpowering baseball pitcher. He hit golf balls 250 yards and bowled around 200. I knew that Cus D'Amato, who had trained Floyd Patterson, wanted him to fight the current heavyweight champion, Cassius Clay, a.k.a. Muhammad Ali. "With Wilt's long reach," D'Amato had told reporters, "he would open holes in Clay's skull."

Traditionally, I pointed out to Wilt, the accolade of world's greatest athlete is granted to the winner of the Olympic decathlon. Wilt said he was confident he could win or place high in most of the decathlon's ten events. He had the endurance for the long runs. Didn't he run a couple of miles each night, often at full speed, during a basketball game? As for the shorter runs, he had competed in both the 60-yard dash and the quarter-mile run in college and been clocked near Olympic times. "I'm the fastest man on this team," he told me, and while I had no way of checking that, I knew he had once raced a quick guard, Hal Greer, in a foot race and won.

As for the decathlon's strength events, I

knew he had thrown the discus and shotput in college and come close to matching the distances of Olympian Bill Neider. On a dare, the 260-pound Wilt had once picked up the rear of a Volkswagen—with one hand, or so I had been told. Certainly, standing close to him, seeing the weightlifter's curving muscles on those treelike arms and legs, I had no reason to doubt he might have picked up the rear of a Ford truck.

Wilt suddenly looked at me and said, "My man, your fifteen minutes are up."

"One last question then. Do you think you are the world's greatest athlete?"

He laughed loudly and threw down a sly look. "I don't take myself lightly, my man," he said, roaring now, turning to pull on a 76ers shirt.

Wilt was born in Philadelphia on August 20, 1936, the son of a maintenance worker. Both his father and mother were of normal height. At sixteen he stood six-foot-nine as he wheeled, spun, and hooked at Overbrook High with the grace and quickness of a five-foot-nine guard. At the University of Kansas he scored 40 and 50 points a game and got a nickname he hated—Wilt the Stilt. "It sounds," he once rumbled, "like some jungle bird." He glowered when people said he was a high scorer only because he stood seven-foot-one. He had all the quick and graceful moves of smaller men, he snapped. When he heard himself referred to as a "goon," he growled, "Nobody roots for Goliath."

He left Kansas after his junior year to sign with the Harlem Globetrotters. He toured the world and later boasted of his ability to pick up quickly a number of languages, including French, German, and Spanish.

In 1959 he joined the NBA, playing with the Philadelphia Warriors. In one game he scored 100 points, still a record 25 years later. During the 1961–62 season he averaged 50.4 points a game, a season's mark that no one has since come within 20 points

of matching. "Scoring fifty points a night was just an average night's work for Wilt," his coach, Frank McGuire, has said. "Afterwards he'd stroll off the court, drink a half gallon of milk, and take a cab back to his hotel. Then he'd have a T-bone steak, french fries, and about a half dozen bottles of soda while he watched TV. I don't think there will ever be anyone quite like him again."

An insomniac, he watched late movies on TV and prided himself on his knowledge of old-movie trivia. A Philadelphia teammate, Larry Costello, once told me that "Wilt is so good he can tell you the number of teeth in the mouth of Buck Jones's horse."

Critics said he didn't win the big games—and a championship. He blew that charge out of the water as his Philadelphia team won the 1966 NBA title. A year later he was traded to the Los Angeles Lakers where he teamed with Jerry West and Elgin Baylor to win another championship in 1972. He retired after the 1973 season, at thirty-seven still a high scorer and terrifying shot blocker. During the 1973–74 season he coached a San Diego team in the American Basketball Association. Then he said his adieu to pro basketball—but in 1981 he coyly listened to offers to come back to play in the NBA before saying no.

He retired as basketball's highest scorer. There is no telling how many points he would have scored if he had been able to sink free throws—he made only a high-school percentage of 51. As he was, he scored 31,419 points, more than any player before him. That record was broken in 1984 by Kareem Abdul-Jabbar, but Wilt still held a slew of records, including the highest average points per game (30). Of the record broken by Kareem, Wilt said, "Well, it's only one of about ninety I held."

After leaving basketball, Wilt became president of the International Volleyball Association. He was also one of the league's best players, soaring high above nets to "spike" balls that few opponents could return. He has lived in houses and apartments in New York, Philadelphia, and Los Angeles, his Los Angeles home a king-size mansion. In 1983 he appeared at an old-timers game at Kutscher's, where he had once been a bellboy. When he slam-dunked a basketball, the crowd roared, wrote one reporter, "as if Wilt the Stilt had never missed a season." Wilt, I thought, must have groaned when he read that, aware he is still the Stilt to a new generation of writers. In 1984 he showed off his muscles as a costar with weightlifter Arnold Schwarzenegger in a barbarian history movie, *Conan the Destroyer*. I wasn't surprised to learn that Wilt, once, arguably, the world's best athlete, was trying to be the world's best barbarian-movie actor. Of the spiked club he carried in the movie, he said proudly: "I designed it myself."

Wilt shows his strength posing for a cover of *Women's Sports* in 1983.

Larry Costello demonstrates his two-hand prowess in the 1960s.

Larry Costello

I WROTE ABOUT LARRY COSTELLO DURing two climactic periods in his life. The first: when he was ending his career not only as a player in the National Basketball Association, but as the last of the two-handed set shooters. The second: when he was coaching the Milwaukee Bucks to the team's first NBA championship.

I met him for the first time in 1967 because of a remark I had made to an editor during a cocktail party. I said to the editor: "Do you realize that of all the famous two-handed set shooters, going back to Nat Holman in the 1920s, Bobby Wanzer and Bob Davies in the 40s, Dolph Schayes and Bob Cousy in the 50s and 60s, only one is left—Larry Costello?"

We agreed there was an article on Costello—"The Last of the Two-Handed Set

Shooters," as the piece about him was titled. We also agreed that the article should look back at the history of the two-handed set shot and the reasons for its becoming extinct.

I knew well the two-handed set, having tossed more than my fair share of them as a boy playing in the schoolyards of the South Bronx in the 1940s. "It was," I wrote in *Sport*, "a beautiful shot. You dribbled to a spot behind the key, suddenly stopped. You held the ball lightly with both thumbs and the other fingers, the ball at chest level. You flicked the ball toward the hoop, the arms and fingers giving the ball a touch of backspin. If you needed extra distance you rose slightly off the toes, both feet square to the basket. The arms rose high, forming a frame as you viewed the ball as it arched, backspinning, toward the hoop (coaches told you to aim at the front rim). The arms came across, hands almost touching, as the ball made that deliciously sweet swishing sound as it whipped through the nets . . ."

In the late 1940s the shot got its first serious challenge. Jumping Joe Fulks, who came out of the South, showed the pros his turn-around jumper. He took the ball with his back to the basket, whirled and corkscrewed into the air to face the basket, his opponent still rooted to the floor. Then, with one hand (sometimes two), Jumping Joe flicked the ball into the hoop, unopposed, his man rising too late to stop the shot. Jumping Joe led the NBA in scoring his first season. Immediately high-school kids across the country were trying to do the turnaround jumper. By the early 1950s one of those kids, Paul Arizin, out of Villanova, was jumping to shoot while facing the basket. In 1955 Arizin finished second in NBA scoring, playing for Philadelphia, and he converted many of the two-handed set shooters, like Cousy and Schayes, to the one-handed jumper.

Two NBA rules hastened the demise of the two-handed set. One was the rule requiring teams to shoot within 24 seconds. Most two-handed set shooters needed to pop from behind a screen of teammates so the shot wouldn't be blocked. Now there wasn't enough time to set up those screens. Second, new foul rules allowed bonus shots after a certain number of fouls. These bonus rules made the jump shot, which was more likely to draw a foul, more attractive to coaches than the two-handed set.

"All of a sudden," Larry Costello told me one cold and gray afternoon in the winter of 1967 as we sat in the living room of his home in Bala-Cynwyd, a Philadelphia suburb, "I looked around and I was the only one left. They're all gone now."

Basketball, I soon discovered, was the most important thing in Costello's life apart from his wife, Barbara, and their children. He talked about playing the game with a missionary's fervor, animation in his voice, his eyes gleaming, his hands moving as he showed the routes of players, and if need arose he'd whip out paper and pencil and draw you the X's and O's of a play.

Before coming to Bala-Cynwyd, I had talked to coaches about Costello. I had asked the veteran LIU coach, Clair Bee, why he thought that Costello had survived as a two-handed shooter. "Costello needs no screen to shoot from behind," Bee told me. "Of all the set shooters I have seen in fifty years, none got off the shot faster than Costy."

"That's right," Costello told me, perched on the edge of a couch as he spoke. "It's my strong wrists that give me that quickness. I can hit from the top of the key, say thirty feet away, with my feet flat on the floor, using only my wrists."

At thirty-five he was the oldest player in the league. Costy, as the players called him, stood an even six foot, weighed a chesty one hundred eighty-five pounds, and his sharply planed face and wide nose gave him a pugilistic look. The 76ers' "old man" had been playing only ten to fifteen minutes a game, yet was averaging 10 points a game. I asked him how he was scoring at such an impressive rate.

He leaned forward on the couch. "First of all, there's my two-handed set shot. If you give me enough time, I can stand out there and throw in seven, eight, even nine out of ten from as far as twenty-five to thirty feet away."

"But you are a small man in this league," I said. "Why don't they play you close and block those two-handed sets?"

"It's true, no question about it, the two-handed set is easier to block than the jumper. But I have very strong legs"—he patted massive thighs—"and so I am always a threat to drive around a man who plays me too close. I give my man a good fake with my right leg—like this . . ."

He jumped off the couch and thrust his right leg forward. "My man has to fall back when I make that move. If he doesn't, I'll drive around him. When he does fall back, then I have the time for my two-hander."

He was also picking up points from the foul line, putting in nine of ten free throws. "It's a sin to miss from the line," he told me. "If I have the time I can hit a high percentage from anywhere on the floor. At the line you have all the time in the world."

He walked back to the couch. "Frankly, though, it's not my nature to enjoy scoring. I enjoy working up something. Like when I have a rookie guarding me, I'll yell to [fellow guard Hal] Greer, 'Let's weave it, Hal.' The rookie immediately looks for me to cut toward Hal to start the weave. Instead I break to the basket before the rookie knows what happened. I get a pass and I score. I used to get a basket a game that way."

He laughed. "But there are no smarts in basketball anymore. The jump shot took away the smarts. How many teams will take twenty seconds to set up a play when they can get the same two points in five seconds with a jump shot?"

Costello was born near Minoa, in upstate New York, on April 15, 1932. When he was eight he nailed an apple basket to the side of his grandfather's barn and began to throw in those long two-handed set shots that would later make his wrists so strong.

He attended Niagara University where he played on the basketball team with Hubie Brown, another guard who later became the coach of the New York Knicks. He came into the NBA in 1955, joining the Syracuse Nats. In 1963 the team moved to Philadelphia and became the 76ers. In the 1964–65 season the 76ers came close to winning an NBA championship, but lost in the finals for the Eastern title, 110–109, beaten by the Celtics. Costello announced his retirement after that season, although at thirty-three he was still considered one of the league's best guards both offensively and defensively. He went back to Minoa to teach at a local high school and coach the basketball team. But when Philadelphia's new coach, Alex Hannum, asked him to come back for the 1966–67 season, Larry returned. "I wanted a championship," he told me in Bala-Cynwyd. "That's something I'd never had after ten years in this league. I figured I could help this team go all the way."

He and the 76ers went all they way that 1966–67 season to win the NBA championship. He retired as a player to become the assistant to 76er coach Alex Hannum. In twelve NBA seasons he averaged 12.2 points a game. He led the NBA in free-throw shooting in 1963 and in 1965. In 1968 he became the head coach of a new NBA franchise, the Milwaukee Bucks.

At the start of the 1970 season he seemed to have the makings of a championship team, having obtained the seven-foot-three Lew Alcindor (later Kareem Abdul-Jabbar) from UCLA and the six-foot-five Oscar (The Big O) Robertson from the Cincinnati Royals. The Bucks had what many thought were the best big man and the best little man in the game. I decided to write a book about the Bucks, planning to follow them through most of the 1970–71 season and watch, I hoped, how a team comes together to win a championship.

I flew to Milwaukee where I met Larry in the team's offices. Looking at his chesty frame, I said, "You look like you could still throw in those long two-handed sets."

He laughed, but didn't disagree—and with reason. Later that season I watched him toss in ten straight two-handed sets from the foul line during a Buck practice session.

He was as didactic about coaching basketball as he had been as a player. "Basketball is a simple game, really," he told me later that day. "It is a game of one on one, two on two, or—at the most—three on three. Our offense is designed to keep the odd fourth or fifth man out of the play.

If you see Oscar and Lew working a pick and roll against two opponents, you don't run over to their side with your man so that he can help on the defense, do you? Common sense, that's all it is."

The Bucks won the NBA championship that 1970–71 season. I watched them play as often as I could from their first game to their last, when they swept by Baltimore, four games to none, for the title. What I remember best about Costy—all during the season and even in the closing minutes of a game the Bucks had clearly won—was the intense look on his face during team huddles as he scrawled X's and O's on yellow legal-size sheets clipped to a board.

His Bucks won division titles the next three seasons, but never another NBA title. Oscar retired and Kareem demanded to be traded after the 1975 season. In 1976, without Kareem, he coached the Bucks to another division title, but the team lost quickly in the first round of the playoffs. Early in the 1976–77 season he was fired. He coached the Chicago Bulls briefly and then was a scout for Houston. When he left the NBA as a coach, he had the best won-lost record (430 wins, 300 losses) of any active NBA coach. In 1979

he coached the Milwaukee Does of the short-lived Women's Professional Basketball League, then went back to upstate New York to live near Utica and coach the game he still loves dearly at Utica College. Every once in awhile, he'll stand back 20 or 25 feet from a hoop and show his Utica players what it was like when the two-handed set shot was such a thing of beauty.

Larry is a Utica College basketball coach today.

Bob was the MVP winner at the 1957 NBA All-Star Game.

Bob Cousy

I MET BOB COUSY FOR THE FIRST TIME ON an Arctic, snowy night in Boston during the winter of 1957. I and a photographer, Ben Ross, had come to Boston where the annual NBA All-Star game was being played that year. We wanted to take closeup color photos of five of the NBA's top stars for a cover of *Parade* magazine. We found an empty, unheated room in the concrete bowels of Boston Garden. Ross set up his cameras and electronic strobe lights. I went to the dressing rooms of the East and West teams and,

one by one, led Dolph Schayes, Bob Pettit, George Yardley, and Neil Johnston to the room. Ross took photos that showed each star in an action pose—Johnston, for example, tossing a hook shot.

Cousy was the last man on our list. I walked into the East's dressing room and saw the black-haired Cousy curled up alone in a corner, wearing, as I recall, only his basketball shorts and socks. He seemed nonchalant, even dreamy, ignoring the loud talk and laughter of the other East players in the room for this prestigious game. From above the room we could hear the sounds of the crowd. I knew this Boston crowd would expect a bravura performance against the best of the league's West by this Celtic hero, famous for his behind-the-back dribble, fancy passes, and ball-handling magic.

Cousy seemed too dreamy and faraway to be aware of the crowd and its expectations. Hesitantly, I broke into his reverie to ask him if he would come to the small room for a posed photo of him dribbling a ball. He nodded, still seeming remote, and promised he would be there in a few minutes.

He didn't arrive until a few minutes before the teams were scheduled to take the floor for practice. The room was icy cold. He stripped off his warmup suit. In his basketball shorts and shirt, he bounced a basketball, face impassive. Ross pressed a button. The strobe lights, apparently short-circuited by the cold, did not flash. Ross checked his connections, shook wires, jabbed at his gadgets. No lights flashed.

Cousy stood silent, expressionless, but I could see the goosebumps on his bare legs and arms. I was shivering in an overcoat. And from above us I heard the expectant roar as the East and West teams began to assemble to come onto the floor.

"We can't keep you any longer, Bob," I said apologetically. "You had better go."

He nodded and pulled on his warmup pants and jacket. As Cousy zipped the last zipper, Ross pressed something and the lights flashed. "I got them working!" Ross said, eager to get this picture we badly needed for the cover. "Never mind, Bob," I said. "You had better leave or you'll miss a chance to warm up."

He said nothing. He stooped down, pulled up a zipper on his pants leg, and began to peel off the warmup suit. He picked up the basketball and said softly, "Okay, if you're ready."

We took the picture. We thanked Cousy, who nodded and left the room, a man seeming to be staring at something far away. That night his East team won and he was selected the game's Most Valuable Player.

Some twenty years later I learned why he had seemed so distant before this important game. He and I wrote a book together, *The Killer Instinct*, and in the book he told why he went into a trancelike state before a big game—and what he was thinking about in that state. "I'd lock myself in a room and I thought about the guy who would be guarding me that night. I think that if that guy had walked into the room, I might just have leaped at his throat and tried to strangle him."

That killer instinct, he told me, was a necessary evil in competitive sport. "You need talent to succeed," he said in *The Killer Instinct*, "but as you rise to higher levels you are going to be competing against people who are equally talented. Then you need intensity, a killer instinct that impels you to succeed when other people have to stop or slow down."

Cousy's killer instinct flared even during the most trivial of competitions. One evening, while I was with him in Worcester, Massachusetts, where he still lives, he played a neighbor a game of tennis. The match was close, but Cousy was the loser. For the rest of the evening he mumbled his unhappiness with himself for having lost a match he believed he should have won.

"You'd be playing against Cousy in a little pickup game of basketball at his summer camp in New Hampshire," another friend, Andy Laska, once said. "You'd steal the ball away from him during the game. He'd knock you into the woods to get it back."

"I believe that if I had never had this killer instinct, this inner drive to keep going when others slowed down," he wrote in *The Killer Instinct*, "I would have been just another one of those six-foot guards who wander briefly into the National Basketball Association and disappear without a trace."

The son of French immigrants, Cousy was born in New York City on August 9, 1928. He grew up in Queens, not far from present-day Kennedy Airport. Small and skinny as a teenager, he got little attention from the basketball coach at Andrew Jackson High School until his senior year. That year, 1945, he played often enough and well enough to be picked on an All-City team.

I once asked him if he had had any boyhood heroes and he said no, not in the sense that his friends had idolized Joe DiMaggio and the other stars of the day. "My heroes," he told me, "and they weren't really heroes, were much closer at hand. There was Frank Higgins, for example. During my last year in high school, he was the best player in our neighborhood. Frank became my idol in the sense that I wanted to be as good as he was. And as the months went by, playing with him in high school and on the playground, I could see I was edging closer to him in ability."

In 1946 Higgins went to Boston College, Cousy to nearby Holy Cross. "During the next four years," Cousy told me, "I played against Frank four times. He developed into a fine player—but never once did he and his Boston College teammates beat Holy Cross." (Years later I was playing basketball at a YMCA in Manhattan and a player I knew only as Frank made several spectacular shots and passes. After the game I said in a jocular tone, "You were like a Cousy out there today, Frank." Frank smiled and said nothing. Later, talking to a friend of Frank, I learned I had been playing against a now-fortyish Frank Higgins.)

An All-American during his last two seasons at Holy Cross, Cousy became the idol of millions of high-school kids as he dribbled behind his back or dished the ball to a fast-breaking teammate on his left while looking to a teammate on his right. Cousy's sleight-of-hand tricks with a basketball won him the nickname the Houdini of the Hardwood.

Pro scouts looked at the scrawny six-foot, one-hundred-seventy-pound Houdini and shook their heads: "too small for the rough-and-tumble ways of pro basketball" was a near-universal opinion. "The first time he tries to make a pro look bad with that fancy dribbling of his," one scout said, "he'll get elbowed into the upper balcony."

Boston Celtic coach Red Auerbach showed little interest in Cousy. Cousy was chosen in the 1950 draft by a team that went out of business before he'd played a game. At a special draft held in a Manhattan hotel room, three teams—Boston, Philadelphia, and New York—had to choose among two veteran guards, Andy Phillip and Max Zaslofsky, or the rookie Cousy. All three teams wanted the two veterans, none wanted the rookie. Finally, after much haggling, the three names were put into a hat. Celtic owner Walter Brown picked first and, to his chagrin, drew Cousy.

Almost immediately Cousy was the league's most talked-about ball handler. His passes seemed to fly magically out of his hands and land in the open palms of teammates. And he could dribble a ball for as long as a minute during the last stages of a close game, "freezing" the ball when the Celtics had a narrow lead and opponents tried desperately, and usually unsuccessfully, to get it away from him and score. Freezing the ball to protect a lead, however, made for boring basketball in the last min-

ute of a game, when it was supposed to be the most exciting. The NBA came up with the rule requiring each team to shoot within 24 seconds.

No league could legislate against his passes to teammates, and he led the league in assists from 1952, his second season in the league, to 1956. During those years, however, he often didn't have the ball as often as the Celtics would have liked. They lacked the skyscraping center to pull down rebounds and feed the ball to the fast-breaking Cousy. In 1956 they got that center by signing a six-foot-nine leaper from the University of San Francisco, Bill Russell. During the next seven seasons, from 1956 until Cousy's retirement in 1963, the Celtics won six world championships.

He left pro basketball holding the record for the most assists in a career (he was later surpassed by Oscar Robertson and Lenny Wilkens). What is often unpraised is his scoring. In one playoff game in 1953, he poured in 50 points, a record at the time. He averaged 18.5 points a game, and what basketball aficionados liked about Cousy's scoring was the timing of his baskets. In the first half he fed the ball to teammates, "passing around the sugar," as he called it. But late in the game, when a shot could win a game or lose it, it was Cousy who called for the ball and took the shot. Unlike some high scorers, Cousy did not vanish when the win-or-lose shot had to be taken.

He retired as a player, but never left basketball. Living in Worcester with his wife, Marie, and their two daughters, he accepted a head coaching job at Boston College, only an hour from home. He turned around a so-so basketball program at BC, and in 1966 the Eagles came within one game of going to the National Collegiate Athletic Association's Final Four—the World Series of college basketball. In 1969 the team lost in the finals for the National Invitational Tournament.

By then, however, Cousy had become dis-

Bob poses with old Celtic pals Red Auerbach and Tom Heinsohn at the Basketball Hall of Fame in 1983. Note the photo of victorious Celtics—and a somber Bob—on the wall.

heartened by having to kowtow to good high-school players—"blue chippers" in coaching parlance—to lure them to Boston College. And he had become aware that to be a winner in college basketball, a coach had to enter what he called "gray areas"— places where a coach, at best, was creeping around the recruiting rules, and at worst was breaking at least a few of them. In 1969 he decided to leave college coaching. Winning was important to Cousy, "the only thing," he once said, paraphrasing the late Vince Lombardi, but he was unwilling to cheat to win.

He accepted an offer of $100,000 a year, probably the highest salary of any NBA coach at that time, to coach the NBA's Cincinnati Royals. The Royals had two outstanding players, Oscar Robertson and Jerry Lucas, but lacked the towering center that every NBA team since Russell's Celtics have needed for a championship. The team lost about as often as it won, both in Cincinnati and later in Kansas City. By 1973 a string of losing seasons had worn down Cousy, a proud man accustomed to being with winners. At the start of the 1973–74 season, edging closer to physical and emotional collapse, he suddenly quit and went back to Worcester.

Today he is a television commentator for New England college and Boston Celtic games. In 1983 he played in an old-timers game at Monticello, New York, to raise funds for needy players. Newsweek reported he "handled the ball with magical dexterity." A Houdini, it seems, is always a Houdini.

Dave DeBusschere

DAVE AND I WERE CRUISING IN HIS three-year-old Ford along a street in downtown Detroit on a brisk, sunny afternoon in December of 1966. I remarked that most athletes I had known would not have been caught within twenty feet of a three-year-old car, most preferring shiny new ones right out of the showroom. He nodded. "Cars," he said, "have never seemed very important things to me; I don't know why." At that moment a wave of pedestrians suddenly materialized in front of the windshield, a light apparently having changed quickly in their favor, and Dave had to jab hard at the brake, the car lurching as it skidded to a stop.

"Sorry about that," he said nonchalantly, and then he went back to crooning, in a nasal tone, a then-popular tune that a singer was wailing on the car's radio, "What's newewwww, pussycat, what's newwwww. . . ."

I waited for the song to end and the light to change. When we were rolling again, I asked the question I had thought about for the two days I had been with DeBusschere. What was it like, I asked the only player-coach in the National Basketball Association—and the youngest man to boss a big-league team in more than fifty years—to be the young leader of hardened veterans and highly skilled but sensitive rookies?

He started to answer. He stopped in mid-sentence and stared silently for several seconds before he began again. "I'll tell you," he said, "all of us like to take the easy way out. It's my job to make sure they don't take the easy way out."

"Right there, from this boyish-looking young coach," I later wrote, "I heard wisdom that I have not heard from the distin-

Dave shows his shooting form as a Detroit Piston in the 1960s.

guished and graying in sport. For, indeed, doesn't that sum up what being a boss, in sport or in anything else, is really all about—keeping the people under you, and you yourself, from taking the easy way out?"

What struck me about DeBusschere, during the week I traveled with him when he coached the Detroit Pistons, was the way that older people, people with power, sought him out. He was only a month past his twenty-fourth birthday in November of 1964 when an older man, Fred Zollner, an NBA pioneer owner, picked him as his head coach. Not since Roger Peckinpaugh, at twenty-three the manager of the Yankees some fifty years earlier, had anyone so young been named the boss of a big-league team.

When I arrived in Detroit, I sought out a friend of Dave's, Piston publicist George Maksin, and I asked him why Zollner had picked Dave. "Dave has always been a ferocious winner," Maksin said. That ferociousness, hidden behind a casual and sometimes lethargic exterior, would be the reason other men with power would seek out DeBusschere and at thirty-five he would be the commissioner of a major basketball league and at forty-one the front-office boss of a major-league franchise.

Indeed, as Maksin had said, Dave had always been a winner since his schoolboy days in Detroit, where he was born on October 16, 1940. He grew up on a tree-lined street in the working-class east side where his family owned a small tavern. An A student at Austin Catholic High, he pitched the baseball team to the city's Catholic championship and led the basketball team to the state championship.

At the University of Detroit he averaged almost 25 points a game. In Dave's three years on the varsity, the team went to two NIT championships and one NCAA tournament. To Detroit headline writers he was "Big D."

When Dave graduated in 1962, the Chicago White Sox gave him a $70,000 bonus and that summer he was pitching in Comiskey Park. He appeared in 12 games, neither winning nor losing a game. That fall he shucked his baseball uniform, slipped on the uniform of the Pistons, and was immediately a starter. He averaged 12 points a game and the Pistons made the playoffs. "One of the big reasons," said coach Dick McGuire, "was Dave."

During the next three seasons—1963, 1964, and 1965—he pitched for the White Sox and their top farm team, Indianapolis. He won 25 and lost only 9 over a two-season span with Indianapolis and in 1965 was second in strikeouts among all Triple A pitchers.

But by 1964 Piston owner Fred Zollner had seen that he owned more than a six-foot-six, two-hundred-thirty-five-pound forward who was among the league's reliable scorers (16 points a game) and best rebounders. He talked Dave into saying goodbye to baseball and pouring all of his physical and mental ferociousness into being the player-coach of the Pistons.

Two years later, at the start of the 1966–67 season, the Pistons had added a rookie, Dave Bing, who was averaging 20 points a game, and with DeBusschere scoring 18 and leading the team in rebounding, the Pistons seemed to be a playoff contender. I watched them play the Boston Celtics as part of a doubleheader at Madison Square Garden. The Pistons were losing, 34–25, when DeBusschere brought in a slim guard, Eddie Miles. Jackknifing over the Celtics, Miles rained in nine of thirteen jumpers and at the half the Celtic lead was shaved to 2, 60–58.

DeBusschere did not start Miles at the start of the second half. The Celtics crept ahead. When Miles did come back, his hand had turned cold. He made only three of thirteen shots, and the Celtics won, 130–111.

When I entered the dressing room, I saw Dave staring angrily at a wall. I asked why he hadn't started Miles in the second half.

Considering the state of things, his manner and tone were pleasant. "I was hoping Ed would come in late in the third period, when the score was close, and give us three or four quick baskets to break the game wide open," he said.

He was still staring at the wall. "But maybe I made a mistake. Maybe I should have kept him in there while he was hot. But sometimes, when you do that, they stop hitting." He laughed, the grimness suddenly gone from his long-jawed face. "It's a funny game."

An hour later he and I were seated in a jet rushing at six hundred miles an hour toward Detroit. He had a bourbon and water in one hand, a crossword puzzle on his lap. "I like doing crosswords," he told me. He had been reading a paperback, *If Morning Ever Comes.* The cover blurb said the book was "for the millions who loved *To Kill a Mockingbird.*" "That's why I bought it," he said. "I thought *To Kill a Mockingbird* was the best book I ever read."

While we were talking, he suddenly raised one hand. "Wait a minute," he said. "I want to hear this." He had slipped on earphones, listening to the jet's stereo system as we talked. Playing now was "The Impossible Dream."

"I think that's a great song," he told me a little later. "I love the words about dreaming impossible dreams and fighting unbeatable foes."

In Detroit the next afternoon, George Maksin told me about the social side of being a young player-coach. "On the road it's hard for him. As a player Dave could sit around and have beers with the boys and talk about the game. He can't anymore. Oh, he can go out with Donnie Butcher (the assistant coach) or myself, but if we are off somewhere, he's alone. We went out in Philly the other day and he said to me, 'This is the first beer I've had in four days.'"

He loved his beer, as I would discover during a conversation I had several years later with Alex (Fats) Delvecchio, Dave's good friend and the center for the Detroit Red Wings' hockey team. Dave and Alex, along with two friends, played a round of golf one hot summer's day in Detroit. Before starting out, the foursome loaded a case of beer onto the cart. That was quickly gone and they ordered another. Some four cases of beer later, the foursome weaved onto the eighteenth hole. "Who won?" I asked Fats.

"Who knows?" he said, laughing. "I don't even remember playing the eighteenth hole."

"I don't either," DeBusschere told me. We were riding on a Long Island Rail Road train toward Manhattan on a wintry evening in 1971. Four years had passed since I had last talked to him in Detroit. He had been unable to turn the Pistons into winners, was replaced as coach, and then late in 1968 was traded to the Knicks. He and his wife, Gerri, were living on Long Island.

"It was the luckiest thing that ever happened to me," DeBusschere said of the trade as he and I walked down Eighth Avenue toward Madison Square Garden and a game that night against the Chicago Bulls. It may also have been the luckiest thing that ever happened to the Knicks, who hadn't won an NBA championship since the league began in 1946. With Willis Reed at center, DeBusschere and Bill Bradley as the forwards, and Walt Frazier and Dick Barnett the guards, the Knicks won the 1969–70 NBA title.

Before the game against the Bulls I talked to Knick coach Red Holzman. "DeBusschere is the complete player," he told me. "Sometimes he'll score only four or six points in thirty-five minutes. People say to me, 'How come you play him so long?' I tell them that he does a hell of a rebounding job for us, a hell of a job on defense for us. If he can get the rebounds and play good defense, we got the other guys on this team who can score."

I saw what Holzman meant during the game that night. Dave was guarding Chet Walker. Someone bumped Dave in a melee under the basket. For a moment Walker was alone near the foul line. He had the ball. As Walker went up for the jumper, Dave leaped at him, belly to belly, hand high to block Walker's view. The shot hit the front rim. The Bullets' Bob Love grabbed the rebound. Dave dropped off Walker and harried Love, who missed the short shot. Dave grabbed the rebound. He dribbled upcourt like a ball-handling guard, evaded one man with a quick move, then passed the ball to the towering Willis Reed, all alone underneath. Reed jammed the ball through the hoop— the basketball-wise Garden crowd erupting with applause. Indeed, I thought, Dave is the complete and ferocious winner.

I can never go to the Garden without seeing, in my memory, the ceaseless crisscrossing of Bradley and DeBusschere under the basket. Perhaps no two forwards ever knew how to "move without the ball," as the coaches say, better than Bradley and DeBusschere. Running, running, and running some more, from left to right and right to left under the hoop, they passed each other elbow to elbow. Then, suddenly, when a defender bumped against another defender and was picked off by his own man, Bradley or DeBusschere was open for a split second. In came a pass, a short jumper—and a basket. Though DeBusschere was not a good outside shooter, nor was he quick enough to drive to the basket like most power forwards, he dropped in enough of those short jumpers from around the basket to be a consistent scorer of 15 points a game for the Knicks. He averaged 16.3, second highest on the team, as he and the Knicks won their second NBA championship in 1973.

"Dave is the most efficient ballplayer I have ever seen," Knick sixth man Mike Riordan once told me. "He is one hundred percent efficient in that what he puts in, his work input, is roughly equivalent to what he gets out, his work output. There is nothing wasted."

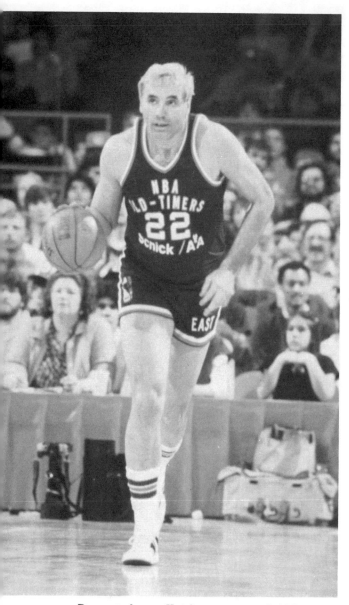

Dave, today a Knick executive, dribbles in a 1983 old-timers game.

DeBusschere nodded when I repeated that to him one day. "When you're younger," he said, "you waste a lot of energy with moves that won't get you anywhere. As you get older, you see some small things and you say to yourself, 'Ah, if they do that again, then I can do so and so.'"

All of the Knicks told me about the savage battles underneath the boards between DeBusschere and Baltimore's Gus Johnson. "When Dave and Gus go up against each other," trainer Danny Whelan told me, "it's like Ali against Joe Frazier." I got some idea of the ferocity of those battles when Chicago's walloping six-foot-seven, two-hundred-forty-pound Paul Silas told me, "Dave keeps coming back at you. You hit him hard once to block him out, but he bangs right back in there again. He never gives up."

He finally did give up, retiring as a player after the 1974 season in which he was the team's number-one rebounder and number-two scorer with 18 points a game. The American Basketball Association, trying to compete with the NBA, hired him as its commissioner. He was ABA commissioner from 1975 to 1976. After the better ABA teams merged with the NBA, DeBusschere joined the Knicks as front-office boss. He is heard and seen frequently on New York radio and television stations, shouting, "This is Dave DeBusschere!" and then telling people why they would be smart to take their automobiles to a sponsor's repair shops. Whenever I hear those commercials, I think: Someone else with power and money has chosen a ferocious winner.

Alex Delvecchio

FATS AND I WERE SEATED IN THE SPAcious living room of his ranch-type house in a suburb of Detroit. Like millions of other suburban American males on this wintry afternoon in 1971, a cold wind blowing drifts of snow across his backyard, Fats was watching a college football game on the color TV. He sipped from a steaming cup of coffee as the colored images flickered on the screen. He was wearing slippers, iron-gray slacks, and a green turtleneck that hugged his boxy body.

His wife came into the room and asked, "Dad, when would you like to have dinner?" In about an hour, Fats said. He ran a hand through his graying hair, yawned. After the game and dinner, he said, he just might take a nap.

That evening, awakening from his nap and putting on a hip-length black fur coat and a white Tyrolean hat, Fats walked down the icy walkway of the house to his Cadillac. He scraped the snow and ice off the windshield, then drove to his job at the Olympic Arena in downtown Detroit. In a large dressing room he shed his suburban coat and slacks and loafers and began to make the transformation from Fats the suburban sports fan to Fats the Hall of Fame hockey player.

In 1971 Alex (Fats) Delvecchio was only the eighth man in the history of the National Hockey League to have played twenty seasons. In that time he had scored more than

Alex as a Detroit Red Wing in 1961.

400 goals, exceeding anyone except four legends: Gordie Howe, Maurice (Rocket) Richard, Bobby Hull, and Jean Beliveau. With deft passes of the puck to teammates, he had assisted in the scoring of more than 700 other goals for the Red Wings. In a career that so far had spanned 1,134 games in the uniform of the Red Wings, he had accounted for more assists than any hockey player ever with the exception of Howe, and more scoring points (one point for each goal and one point for each assist) than anyone except Howe and Beliveau.

Fats did all that? Even as I scanned those statistics in the press box at the Olympic Arena that night, waiting for Delvecchio to play his 1,135th game, I had trouble matching that incredible record with the face and figure of the quiet-spoken, forty-year-old Fats with whom I had whiled away most of a quiet afternoon.

I was not alone in underestimating Fats. Later I talked to his teammate, Gordie Howe, up to then the Babe Ruth of scoring, owner of most of the scoring records of his time. Alex had passed the puck to Howe for many of Howe's goals. "Alex is the most underrated player in the game today," Howe told me with a regretful smile on his long, crooked face. "He is an All-Star without a title."

Before I flew to Detroit to interview Delvecchio, I talked to some of the Boston Bruins about him. I had just finished an article on Phil Esposito, the high-scoring center for the Bruins, and I told Phil I was planning to write articles on all the Italian centers in the league. Phil laughed, but his face turned somber when I mentioned that Delvecchio had played more than twenty seasons. Phil had played only a half dozen. He shook his head and said, "I can't imagine anyone playing in this league for twenty seasons— I'd be a wreck." Of Delvecchio he spoke with the admiration of a fellow center—"a good playmaker, underrated by everyone but the players."

The willowy Bobby Orr came by as we talked. Bobby had been two years old when Fats played his first NHL game. "You got to be sure to take his body when you check him," Orr said in that close-lipped way he has of speaking. "You can't play the puck against him. He's so quick and smart with the puck, he'll go right around you."

I spoke to goalkeeper Ed Johnston. "Maybe the most deceptive shooter in the league," Ed told me. "He doesn't take a big windup. Just sort of slaps at it, but he gets an awful lot on it."

A few days later I sat down with Fats in his living room. The Red Wings called him Fats because of his round face and soft underbelly of a chin, but I saw little softness on his stocky five-foot-ten, one-hundred-ninety-five-pound body. He settled into an old-fashioned Morris chair in that careful middle-aged way of Archie Bunker hunkering down for a night of watching the TV. It would take a trip that night to a hockey arena to convince me that I had been talking to a flesh-and-bone hockey player.

He lit a long cigar, one of the dozen or so Antonio and Cleopatras that he smoked daily, and as he puffed leisurely, I asked him how he had been spared from the sticks that so often slash the faces of hockey players. His softly rounded face, I had read earlier, had required only twenty to twenty-five stitches during his entire career, the number that some players need in half a season. He had rarely been hurt seriously; in fact, he once played in 630 consecutive games, and during another span for 548 straight, two Iron Man records that are among the longest in hockey. "You don't get hurt in this game," he told me, "if you keep your head up and watch what's going on around you."

He had a reputation for being a clean hockey player, three times the winner of the Lady Byng Trophy for gentlemanly play. He smiled slightly as he puffed on the cigar. "I'll trip a man or hold him if he's about to break away," he said. "There's a fifty-fifty chance the referee will miss it. But I don't believe you win games by collecting foolish penalties. I know because I used to be that kind of player."

He was born in Fort William, Ontario, on December 4, 1931. The son of an Italian immigrant, he was skating when he was four and playing this Canadian game of ice hockey when he was six or seven. Alex was one of a half dozen Fort William kids who were signed by NHL scouts in 1947. As a seventeen-year-old center for Oshua in the Ontario Hockey Association, he was the slashing and tripping kind who went frequently to the penalty box. One day his coach, Larry Aurie, a former Red Wing, sat down with him and said, "You're doing neither yourself nor us any good with that chippy stuff. Stay away from those foolish penalties."

He joined the Red Wings at the start of the 1951–52 season, replacing the retired Sid Abel on the Detroit Production Line that had Ted Lindsay and Gordie Howe as the wingers. During the next nineteen seasons, as Fats fed Howe the puck and Howe lashed it into cages, the Red Wings won three Stanley Cups (1952, 1954, and 1955), and went into the Cup finals five other times. But the Canadiens won most of the big ones, including five straight Cups from 1956 to 1960. "You could argue all night about the best team of the 1950s, us or the Canadiens," Alex told me as we sat in his living room. "But I think we might have been better defensively."

I asked him if he had resented Howe's publicity while he got relatively little. He puffed several times on the cigar before replying, again with the serene smile. "Not at all. Just getting on the ice with the big fellow even after twenty years, it can still electrify you. He does so many things with a puck that are unbelievable. I look up to him because he is the one who had to put it in the net. That's the toughest job. I wouldn't have done half of what I have done without him."

Today Alex is the chief executive officer of his own firm in Detroit.

He drew once more on the long cigar. "And I guess," he said, "he wouldn't have done half of what he has done without me. So it is one hand feeding the other."

Later, at the Olympia Arena, I was told that Howe would not play that night against Buffalo because of an injury, so I did not get the chance to observe the one hand feeding the other. Early in the first period Alex collected the puck near the Buffalo cage. He saw, as he had hoped, that a Buffalo defenseman was coming out to challenge him, vacating the area in front of the cage. The Red Wings' Frank Mahovlich swooped into the open area. Fats snapped the puck to Mahovlich, who smacked it into the cage for a goal and Fats' 709th career assist.

A little later he crossed behind the Buffalo cage, then whirled and anchored himself no more than 6 feet from the goalkeeper's right elbow. He was unnoticed as skaters blurred around him. "I didn't holler for the puck," he told me later, laughing. "You hope nobody notices you when you are that close. They whack you in the ankles and jab you in the ribs with their sticks, trying to move you out of there."

"There" was the place called "the slot" by hockey scorers, a favorite location for launching pucks at the goalkeepers. When Delvecchio told me what the painful penalties were for being caught in the slot, I could understand why Phil Esposito, who loved dearly to sneak into the slot, would say he could not imagine paying those penalties for twenty seasons.

Fats didn't pay the penalty this time—he was not noticed by the Buffalo defense. A teammate slid the puck to Alex and, with a backhand swipe, he drove the puck into the cage for his 408th goal.

He went home that night in his big Cadillac and again was the relaxed, fatherly suburbanite who played in the violent and often bloody world of hockey during the seasons and relaxed in the summers with his golfing and beer-drinking buddies. At the start of the 1973–74 season, now forty-two years old, Fats retired as a player to become the Red Wings' coach. In 1974 he was awarded one of hockey's most coveted trophies, the Lester Patrick Trophy, for distinguished service to hockey. Later he was both coach and front-office general manager of the Red Wings. In 1977 he left the Wings; today, still easy-mannered, he is a successful Detroit businessman, the chief executive officer of Alex Delvecchio Enterprises.

Phil Esposito (*right*), and a Black Hawk teammate, share the bubbly enthusiasm after a 1965 playoff victory.

Phil Esposito

I WALKED INTO THE BOSTON BRUIN dressing room minutes after a game in the winter of 1972. Phil Esposito, pulling off thick hockey stockings, was chatting with teammate Derek Sanderson. I stopped to ask Espy, as the Bruins called their high scorer, a question for a magazine article I was writing about him. He didn't answer the question; instead he threw one at me: "Hey, is the magazine putting me on the cover?"

"No, I'm afraid not."

"See," he said, turning to Sanderson, "I've never been on a magazine cover. Not one. Even my little brother gets on a cover."

"The magazines put Bobby Orr on their covers," I said.

"Ah," Esposito said slowly and meaningfully, raising one hand and looking at Sanderson. "You hear, Turk, you hear?"

"You're chopped liver, like me," Sanderson said. Chopped liver was then one of Sanderson's favorite descriptions of something to be ignored.

Esposito saw the fair-faced, gangling Orr walking down the aisle of the dressing room toward the shower, a towel wrapped around his waist. "Hey, cover boy!" Esposito shouted. Orr turned, startled, then saw who it was: the eternal needler, Espy. "Aw, shaddup, Espy," Orr shouted over his shoulder as he turned again for the showers. The

Bruins were big that year in yelling "shad-dup!" at each other. The six-foot, broad-backed Esposito stood up, grinning, and winked at Sanderson.

Orr and Esposito. Esposito and Orr. They were the one-two punch of a Bruin team of the early 1970s that won itself a name: the Great Boston Scoring Machine. In the 1970–71 season, Esposito led the National Hockey League in scoring with 152 points (goals plus assists), more points in one season than anyone before him in the history of pro hockey. Right behind him, the league's number-two scorer of points, was the blond Bobby Orr. He scored more goals (37) than any defenseman before him, and he collected more assists with his passes than anybody ever. The two set a string of scoring records. Among them:

• Most goals in a season by a center—Esposito (76).

• Most points in one season by a defenseman—Orr (139).

• Most points in one season by a center—Esposito (152).

In the Stanley Cup playoffs of 1969–70, Esposito set another scoring record—the most goals and assists ever scored up to then in the playoffs. The Bruins won the cup. But it was Orr, not Esposito, who was picked as the league's Most Valuable Player. And it was Orr, the brilliant and flashy skater, who excited the fans and who was on his way to becoming hockey's first highly paid player. At the time Esposito was making about $30,000 a year. I wondered if Esposito was beginning to be envious of all the attention and money being poured on Orr.

Happily for me, the subject came up without my having to introduce it to Orr or Esposito. I was in Boston during the 1971–72 season writing an article about Esposito and a book about the Bruins. Esposito invited me to a postgame party at the Boston apartment of Orr, who was a bachelor. Orr had invited about a dozen of the players, their wives and girlfriends, and when I got there Bobby was happily carrying highballs and cocktails on a tray to the guests milling around in a large living room.

Sipping a drink, I was chatting with a girlfriend of Orr's as we stood near a large picture window, looking down at the wintry darkness of Boston some fourteen stories below. Orr came up behind us and said to me, "Hey, are you trying to steal my girl?"

I turned to face a grinning Orr and a laughing Espy, who had overheard. Phil was twenty-eight at the time, tall and broad-shouldered. He reminded me of a younger Dean Martin. A gold wristband gleamed from one wrist, and his cufflinks flashed in the light of a nearby lamp. His dark hair was wavy and long, his sideburns halfway down the sides of his face. For a moment I expected him to burst out singing "That's Amore."

"Hey, Bobby," Esposito said, "how come you never invited me and my wife to your apartment until now? What's the matter, you don't like us?"

Orr turned to me and said, "That's what some of the writers try to make out—that we don't get along, that we're jealous of each other." Both men laughed. In the days that followed, as I traveled with the Bruins, I saw the respect that existed between the two. Like all hockey players, Esposito was in awe of Orr's skating and stick-handling brilliance. Like all the Bruins, Orr watched with a younger brother's respect and excitement as Esposito put a record number of pucks into nets.

During a plane ride to Chicago a few days later, Orr told me that Esposito liked to station himself in what is called "the slot," a spot ten or fifteen feet to the left or right of the cage. Big for a hockey player at six-foot-one and two hundred ten pounds, Esposito stood like a skyscraper, smaller defensemen bouncing off him, as he waited for a pass from Orr or one of his wingmen.

"He's got such long arms," Orr said, "he can reach out with his stick and get a pass ten or fifteen feet away from him. With that reach he can stay out maybe twenty or twenty-five feet from the cage, and defensemen can't come out that far to check him or they leave themselves open in the rear. When the puck comes within ten or twelve feet of the cage, Phil can reach it while most centers aren't able to."

In Chicago I talked to Black Hawk goalkeeper Gerry Desjardins, who told me what Espy looked like when he had the puck on his stick. "He is all arms and legs and looks like he's twelve-foot wide. He doesn't get excited or rush the shot. He'll make two or three moves with his stick. He gets you down on the ice, and then the game is over. I wouldn't say he has a hard shot. It's only average speed, but he is very accurate at picking the corners."

Espy did more than score goals; he passed the puck to either of his open wingers. In 1968–69 the line he centered—Esposito, Ken Hodge, and Ron Murphy—scored the most points up to then by a single line, and Esposito set a record for the most assists by a center. "You've seen kids play shinny hockey?" then-Bruin coach Tom Johnson asked me one day as we talked about Esposito. I said I hadn't. He explained, "That's the game where one kid tries to keep the puck as long as he can until someone takes it away from him. Phil would keep the puck all day."

Phil first played shinny hockey in Sault Ste. Marie, Ontario ("The Soo" to its natives). He was born there on February 20, 1942, the son of a factory worker. He and his brother, Tony, only a year younger, played hockey for a neighborhood team. Phil was the scorer, Tony the goalkeeper. In one game Tony let two long shots skid by him and the team lost, 2–1. Phil lambasted Tony, calling him "a blind jerk." A few weeks later Phil had to apologize; Tony had been examined by an eye doctor, who prescribed glasses.

In 1963, after a steady climb up the Black Hawk farm system, Phil joined Chicago as the center on a line with Bobby Hull. "Before I met Bobby," Phil once told me, "I was a bit of a rebel. I'd dropped out of school in the twelfth grade. The hell with the world, I thought. I just didn't care all that much about the feelings of other people. I think I've changed. I'll sign autographs now more than I did then. I'll stop to talk to people who come up to say hello. I saw the way Bobby Hull treated people, how nice he could be to people, and that took some of the rough edges off me."

In the 1965–66 season Esposito fed the puck to Hull so well that the Golden Jet scored more goals and more points than anyone before him. But the burly Esposito wasn't nimble enough for the Black Hawks. In 1967 they traded him to Boston for quicker skaters. Hull was openly unhappy. "I lost my right arm," he growled, *"my right arm."*

(The Black Hawks kept another Esposito, a goalkeeper named Tony, whose vision had become so good that he would soon become one of the best, if not the best, NHL goaltenders.)

Esposito joined a Bruin team that had failed to make the Stanley Cup playoffs in eight years. At a team meeting the loud Esposito told them emphatically that they could be winners. He became the team's scoring leader and three years later, in 1970, the Bruins won the Stanley Cup.

"Boston thought Bobby Orr was going to lead them out of the wilderness," Bobby Hull once told me. "But Orr couldn't do it alone. Orr and Esposito, they complement one another."

Phil brought more than a Stanley Cup to the Bruins. He gave the team a *joie de vivre.* "The Bruins," I once wrote, "have been likened to the old Yankees because of the depth of their talent, and to the old Cardinal Gas House Gang for the laughing way they go to work. Esposito keeps them laughing, and around him the others cluster, shouting

'Espy, Espy,' after he made them believe they could be champions."

When I traveled with the Bruins, I watched Esposito kidding the Bruins and kidding himself. I saw Orr look at him one day, as Esposito crooned "Oh, mama mia" in the aisle of an airplane, and Orr said, admiringly, "Look at him, he keeps everyone relaxed and loose. He brought all of us together and made us believe we could win."

In Boston Phil knew who the stars were: Carl Yastrzemski in baseball, John Havlicek in basketball, Bobby Orr in hockey. "I'm not a Bobby Hull, a Gordie Howe, or a Bobby Orr," he once told me. "Have you ever seen me on the cover of a magazine? No. Why? It's simple. I wouldn't sell copies. I've never made people rise to their feet with spectacular plays. I just do my job. To tell you the truth, I wouldn't walk across the street to see myself play."

But that night at Bobby Orr's apartment, as he sipped a beer, he told me, eyes gleaming, "All I want to prove is that I am one of the best. I am never going to prove I am the greatest, but maybe I can prove I am one of the greatest."

Esposito did prove himself one of the greatest as he led the NHL in scoring for five of six years from 1969 to 1974. In 1975 he was traded to the Rangers in New York, a place he had always said he detested. In Manhattan he became the hockey star and the popular personality he had never been in Boston, seen often in the swinging East Side places. TV sports network bosses recognized both his engaging personality and his ability to explain hockey; for several years, when the Rangers were out of the playoffs, he was a color commentator during Stanley Cup finals, so candid in his comments that he once scolded brother Tony on television for missing a shot.

In 1981, his knees aching, he retired after eighteen seasons in the NHL, leaving hockey as its second highest scorer behind Gordie Howe. He lives in Manhattan with his wife and keeps active as a TV commentator and interviewer. He is the director of the Phil Esposito Foundation, which stages Master of Hockey games around the country. Participants in the games are former stars like himself, Orr, Hull, and Howe. The games raise funds for the foundation, which gives career help and financial and medical assistance to former NHL players. "What we try to do," Phil told me in 1983, "is prepare hockey players for life after hockey." In 1984 he was elected to Hockey's Hall of Fame.

Phil is still the laughing man in 1985 as head of the Phil Esposito Foundation.

Chuck is congratulated by his family after hitting the record two pinch hit homers in 1959 Series.

Chuck Essegian

LOOK AT THE RECORD BOOK AND IT WILL tell you that Chuck Essegian was the first baseball player to hit two pinch-hit home runs in a World Series, a feat he accomplished as a Los Angeles Dodger in the 1959 Series against the White Sox. Some twenty-five years later, he was still the only player to own that distinction. The record book will also tell you that Charles Abraham Essegian played in the big leagues from 1958 to 1963, and was a member of a half-dozen teams: the Phils, Cardinals, Dodgers, Orioles, A's, and Indians. Unlike most of the other people in this book, he was never a star, but I will always remember writing

about Chuck Essegian because his career told me more about what it was like to be a professional baseball player in the 1950s than does the career of any star. Like thousands of others before and after him—quick but not quick enough, strong but not strong enough, skilled but not skilled enough—Chuck Essegian gambled that he was good enough to be a big league player—and lost.

"It comes down to this," he told me one day in the spring of 1962 as we sat in the lobby of the Hotel Biltmore in Manhattan, waiting for a bus that would take him and the other Cleveland Indians to Yankee Stadium for a game that night. "I'm gambling I can put together a few good years in baseball. Then I'll have some dollars to help out when I start another career, something outside baseball. The money I make in baseball is important—nobody wants to knock his head against a wall for nothing. But, truthfully, the money isn't the big reason why I'm sticking. The big reason is to prove something to a lot of people in baseball."

He was proving something during the first few months of this 1962 season. On this hot June day, as the Indians' chartered bus rocked along First Avenue toward the Bronx, Chuck Essegian was batting .347, second best in the American League. He was trying to prove that a lot of labels stuck on him during the past five seasons were wrong and that at the age of thirty-one he belonged in the big leagues as a starting leftfielder.

A number of managers to whom I had talked during the spring were doubtful that he belonged. "He is a real power hitter," an American League manager had told me after asking that our conversation be off the record. "Make a mistake and he'll hit the blank-blankety out of here. But when he's not hitting, he strikes out too much. He takes his eyes off the ball. He stops following it."

"I would not have the Chuck Essegian kind of ballplayer on my team," Cardinal manager Johnny Keane told me in an empty clubhouse in St. Petersburg that same spring. "There's something—you can't put your finger on it—that stops him from being the complete ballplayer. He's the kind who stopped here"—Keane waved his arm at chest level—"and never went any further."

Those World Series pinch-hit home runs had given him a reputation. "In baseball they put tags on you," Met outfielder Richie Ashburn, who had played with Essegian on the 1958 Phils, told me. "Chuck's got the utilityman tag—a good righty pinch hitter. Sometimes a man has to fight for all of his career to get rid of a tag like that."

At thirty-one, Chuck was hoping that he had finally shed that tag; he was the regular leftfielder for an Indian team that was locked in a tie with the Yankees for first place. When he came out onto the field on that evening in 1962 at the Stadium with the other Indian regulars to begin batting practice, he was surrounded by a small gang of reporters. They asked him how he could explain his .347 batting average; playing off and on in 60 games for the Indians the previous season, he had batted .289.

"Well, I don't know if I can keep on doing it," he said. "I haven't been going so good for the past week." In his last 23 at bats, he had collected only four hits.

"You used to have trouble hitting the inside pitch at the knees, didn't you?" a reporter asked.

I thought to myself: another tag—can't hit the inside pitch at the knees.

Chuck frowned; he may have been having the same thoughts. "I'm hitting good because I'm getting to play every day," he said quickly. "That's all there is to it. Baseball isn't a test of a few days. You have to get the chance to show what you can do over a season, even over a couple of seasons."

The reporters drifted away. He stood at the batting cage, a quiet man. When he smiled, which was not all that often, he seemed to do so with difficulty, like someone with a headache forcing a grin. Although articulate, he spoke in a flat, expressionless tone. As he stood somberly at the cage in the evening light, he seemed to me to be the archetypical ballplayer: tall, heavy-shouldered and thick-chested, narrow-waisted, slim-hipped, and long-legged. He had a handsome face, his skin burnished golden by both California sun and the bequests of his Armenian ancestry. His hair was coal-black. He resembled the actor who portrayed Dr. Ben Casey on a popular television show of the time. Dark and handsome, he had played small roles in Hollywood-made television westerns.

Hollywood, in fact, had been close by during his teenage years. He was born in Boston on August 9, 1931; his family moved to California when he was in grade school. He attended Fairfax High School in Los Angeles. "I made All-City in both baseball and football," he told me later that night as an airliner carried the Indians to Boston for their next series (they had lost to the Yankees at the Stadium, dropping out of first, and Chuck had only one hit in four at-bats). "I got to college on a football scholarship."

He carried the ball for a Stanford team that won 9, lost 1 and went to the 1952 Rose Bowl. After graduating, he signed a contract to play baseball for Sacramento, an independent team that had no connection with a big league club. "Nobody was interested in teaching you anything," he told me, his voice cutting through the airplane's drone. "You weren't being groomed by an organization." He was sent to lower minor league teams like Little Rock and Tulsa. "All they wanted, those independent clubs, was a .350 hitter to pep up the box office, and if you didn't hit .350, goodbye."

He stared out the window into the darkness. "Sometimes I wish I had tried pro football. There, at least, you find out right away if you are going to make it or not. There's no bouncing around the minor leagues, no gambling with time.

"That's what I'm doing—gambling with time. At Stanford I took pre-med courses which you must take if you want to go to dentistry school. I like dentistry. You study a problem, like a lawyer studies a problem, but the dentist gets to solve the problem himself—with his own pair of hands. I like working with my hands.

"When you're young, things like baseball seem important. When you get older, you look ahead ten years—you wonder where you are going—and baseball doesn't seem so important. All of us, I guess, look back and think: Maybe I should have done that. Or that.

"Sure, I have regrets. It eats at me inside sometimes. But you can't keep second-guessing your life. It can drive you crazy."

In 1956 he worked himself loose from the Sacramento team and signed with the Phillies' organization. "I went to spring training camp with the Phils in 1958. But (manager) Mayo Smith had a pack of outfielders. When you got a chance to hit, you went up pressing—to stay in the lineup. That's what kills an in-and-out ballplayer. You try too hard and they get you out. Then you sit on a bench for a week and you go cold. I stuck with the Phils only part of that 1958 season."

The Phils sent him to the Cardinals, who sent him to the Dodgers, who sent him to Spokane, their top minor league team. By now, he felt, he had been assayed by baseball's scouting system and weighed as being not quite good enough. "Three years ago, a scout saw you. You couldn't hit a curve. You get the label: Can't Hit Curve. But after three years you've learned to hit curves. It makes no difference. You have the reputation for not hitting curves, so the reputation sticks."

Late in 1959, the Dodgers brought him up and threw him into a dogfight with the Giants for the pennant. In 24 games he batted .304. "Playing on that team," he told me as the plane cruised toward a landing in Boston, "it was my most gratifying experience in baseball. Everyone pulled for everyone else. Having guys like Gil (Hodges) and Duke (Snider)—men you had read about for years—pulling for you to get a hit, it was a real thrill. We won the pennant and then I hit those two homers in the Series. But the Dodgers didn't play me much in 1960, and I asked (general manager) Buzzie Bavasi to trade me."

The Dodgers sent him to Baltimore, who sent him to Kansas City, who sent him to Cleveland—three teams in the first three months of the 1961 season. "They didn't think much of my ability. But that was their opinion, not fact. Baseball is based on opinion.

I'm up here to have good years and put away some money. But I'm also up here to show these guys, all the people who said detrimental things about me, that they were wrong."

The next evening, as we strolled to Fenway Park from our hotel, he talked about his life away from baseball. "I like to be with musicians when they're working. When I'm in New York, friends take me to recording sessions when someone like Ellington or Basie is cutting. Back home in Los Angeles, my father and I have a built-in hi-fi set for our house; we can pipe music into most every room."

A bachelor ("the way I've been bouncing around, what kind of life would that be for my wife or family?"), he spent much of his spare time, he said, listening to music or fishing with friends. "In the off-season some friends and I, we go up maybe 10,000 feet in the Sierras, fishing for golden trout, which are indigenous to the area. You hit a stream and just wade along; it's real peaceful. Sometimes I don't even try to catch anything. I'll stop fishing and take some pictures, or we'll kick a football around, or just talk. We talk politics, books, inventions that would be successful. Anything except baseball. To tell you the truth, I don't really enjoy talking baseball."

At Fenway that night, however, he had to talk baseball to reporters wanting to know about his dipping batting average. A few days later he was benched, and never again was he a big-league regular, although he finished the season for the Indians with a respectable .274 batting average. The next season, 1963, he was back at Kansas City, where he hit only .225 in 101 games before being let go. His career batting average was .255.

Chuck Essegian, having lost his gamble with baseball, would win a third gamble, but only after losing a second. He went back to Los Angeles and took a job as a production assistant at 20th Century-Fox. He stayed there five years on the gamble that a friend would rise in the organization and he would rise with him. But the friend decided to leave, and Chuck had to go, too. Now near forty, he decided to try an entirely new field—law. He attended a small Los Angeles law school at night, graduated, passed his bar exam in 1974, and became a Los Angeles County prosecutor. Today he has his own successful law firm in Encino, where he lives with his wife, Gayle, and their three children. He looks back on that lost gamble with baseball and laughs. "Gayle," he says, "tells me it's a good thing I hit those two homers in the Series, because I wouldn't be remembered for anything else."

Today Chuck is a successful lawyer in Encino, California.

Clyde as a Knick in the early 1970s.

Walt Frazier

THE YEARS FROM 1970 TO 1973 WERE THE sweet years for the fans of the New York Knicks. They were the years of Willis Reed, Dave DeBusschere, Bill Bradley, Dick Barnett, Earl Monroe, and perhaps the most popular but certainly the most spectacular of them all—Walt Frazier, known to both teammates and fans as Clyde.

I talked with Clyde off and on for much of a week during the middle of the 1971–72 season. He was living in the penthouse of an apartment building on Manhattan's East 53rd Street between Second and Third Avenues. The apartment was bare-walled and empty of furniture except for a long couch sitting on the rugless floor; the place had a warehouse look to it. Frazier told me he had just moved in. "The furniture will be here in a few days," he said, obviously pleased by the size of the place and its panoramic view northward. He strode to the picture window and looked out, a taller man than I had expected. On the basketball floor he had seemed dwarfish next to six-foot-ten teammates. But he was close to six-foot-five. I had to look up at him as we talked.

Famous for his expensive, fashionable, and sometimes flashy clothes, he was dressed in dark, sleekly fitting slacks and an egg-white shirt, open at the collar, and obviously also expensive. His face was decorated with a full beard—later that season he trimmed it back to mutton-chop sideburns—and the beard made him look older than his twenty-six years.

Smiling, chatting about the view, he walked back from the picture window, seeming to bounce as he came toward me. I sensed a man in command of more than this new apartment. He was idolized by millions in the city spread below him, knew it, appreciated it, and was obviously relishing the chest-filling joy of it all.

I remarked that he seemed much more ebullient than the poker-faced Knick guard I had seen play the night before, one who had seldom showed emotion when things were going bad or when they were going well.

"Learned that from Elgin Baylor," he said quickly, eyes flashing delight. "In one game I put this fierce look on my face when I was guarding him. I got up on him. I applied pressure. I went into this tough stance."

He spread his arms and feet wide, then glared at me, teeth clenched.

"Elgin looked at me like he was saying, 'Hey, kid, whatcha think you're doing?' Then he went through his moves like I wasn't there. Wow! He blew my mind. It was the worst feeling I ever had. I thought I was a strong player and he destroyed my ego.

"But I learned I could do that, what he had done—that I could psych out an opponent. The way I do it, their pressuring may be bothering me, but if I have the same look on my face all the time, my opponent can't see it's bothering me. But I can see on their faces that our pressuring is bothering *them*."

Up until this 1971–72 season he had been the ball-handling guard who brought the ball across the midcourt line, then the passer who fed the ball to the open man. And on defense he had been the long-armed, quick-handed pressure guard who stole the ball to start a Knick fast break. "Our offense," Dave DeBusschere once told me, "comes out of our defense." This 1971–72 season, however, the Knicks' towering center, Willis Reed, was injured, and Frazier had taken over as the team's number-one scorer.

"I see more aggressive defenses now," he told me as he settled into the long couch. "They work to keep me from the ball. That's all right. I run without the ball. I go backdoor without the ball, get a pass, and get my points that way. I never let my man relax. And when the other team keys on me, that opens up shots for other people."

"But you have always been at your best and in command of the Knicks when you have the ball," I said. "You have been the one who passes the ball to Bradley, DeBusschere, or whomever's open or has the hot hand. How can you be in command of the Knick offense when you don't have the ball?"

"Being in command isn't that important until the last five minutes of the game. Down the stretch I know my man will be tired after working hard to keep me from the ball all during the game. Then, with my man tired, I go get the ball. I learned that this year: When the team needs me, that's when I am really in command."

He showed me what he meant a few days

later during a game at the Garden against the Milwaukee Bucks, then the defending NBA champions. He was guarded for much of the game by Oscar Robertson, who had limited Clyde to only 6 points in the first half. In the second half he began to run Oscar into picks set by Jerry Lucas and Dave De-Busschere; alone for an instant, he was popping in his best shot, 12- to 15-foot jumpers. The Bucks had led most of the way but after five straight one handers by Clyde, the lead had shrunk to 2 points, 99–97. Then, as the capacity crowd stood and roared, he tossed in a sixth and the score was tied, 99–99.

There was less than a minute left as the Bucks brought up the ball. A Milwaukee pass was deflected, the ball hopping along near the foul circle, pursued by two Knicks and a Buck. One of the Knicks was Frazier, who dived and hugged the ball to his chest. Coach Red Holzman was on his feet, shouting for a time out. Frazier's hands formed a **T**.

Holzman told the Knicks to wait until the last few seconds to take the final shot of the game. Frazier took the pass from out of bounds. Glancing at the clock, he dribbled the ball outside the foul circle, Oscar Robertson watching him warily. As the electronic clock blinked off the final five seconds, Clyde suddenly swerved to his right. Oscar slipped—and Clyde shot by him. He raced to the foul line, saw the giant seven-foot Kareem Abdul-Jabbar come out, hands poked high and ramrod stiff to block a shot or pass. Clyde skied upward, then flipped the ball over the straining fingers of Jabbar. The ball cut through the basket and the Knicks ran off the court 101–99 winners.

"Guys have always looked for me to lead," he told me later. "In high school I was the quarterback in football, a catcher on the baseball team, and in basketball I was always the guard who was in command." He was born in Atlanta on March 29, 1945, and grew up playing basketball on a dirt playground. Even then he was adept at passing the ball to the free man underneath while tossing in looping, flashy one-handers. He went to a small school as basketball powers go, Southern Illinois, and although the team did not play a big-time schedule, Frazier was picked on at least one All-America second team. In 1967 he was the Knicks' first-round pick. In Frazier's rookie season, 1967–68, Red Holzman became the Knick coach. He began to assemble the team that would win two world championships in four seasons, the first in the 1969–70 season. They won with an interlocking all-for-one-and-one-for-all defense that intercepted passes and stole the ball from dribblers, the chocolate arms of Walt Frazier as busy as a pickpocket's. And they won with an offense that began with Frazier bringing up the ball. "When you come up," he once said, "there are basically three things you can do. You can pass off to the left, you can pass off to the right, or you can take it in yourself. Before you decide, you must consider a couple of things. One, who has the hot hand, or who has the weak defender against him? If Reed has made three jumpers in a row, or Barnett has the range from his corner, you want to work the ball so that he ends up with it and takes the shot. Two, you want to mix things up so that everybody gets involved, everybody gets his shot."

Commenting once on how Clyde decided who got the ball and when, Reed once said, "On the Knicks, the ball belongs to Frazier. He just lets the rest of us play with it once in a while."

In his early days as a Knick, Walt wore wide-brimmed hats, wide ties, and wide-lapeled jackets. It was a 1920s look that got him the nickname Clyde, a nickname borrowed by the Knicks from the then-popular movie of two 1920s gangsters, *Bonnie and Clyde*. By the time I met him in the 1972 season, he had shucked those clothes for more modern stylings that were nonetheless spectacular. He was once described this way by a fashion-conscious writer, Edwin Kiester, Jr., as Clyde left a Knick practice: "The

Knicks' star guard, basketball's most elegantly dressed player, was rigged out in a camel-hair topcoat with matching flat cap. His suit was a blue-gray whipcord, with riverboat-gambler lapeled vest, and beneath it a pale blue shirt, with a fashionably wide white tie showing in the V of the lapels. He wore two-tone box-toed shoes, charcoal gray and mauve . . . a bracelet studded with diamonds, spelling 'Clyde,' his nickname, flashed from his right wrist." I once asked Clyde how many suits he owned; he "guessed" the number was more than fifty.

Clyde and his Knicks won another championship in 1973, their second in four seasons, with Frazier the team's high scorer with 21 points a game. Reed was the first to retire, and then DeBusschere, then Bradley and Barnett. Frazier stayed with the Knicks through the 1977 season, then went to Cleveland, where he played two more seasons before retiring in 1979. In 1984 he was still the Knicks' all-time leader in every major statistical category except rebounds, including games played (759), assists (4,791), and points (14,617). His number 10 jersey was retired in 1979 and in 1984 he was inducted into Madison Square Garden's Hall of Fame. Still a bachelor ("nobody wants me"), he lives now in Atlanta, where he is president of Walt Frazier Enterprises, a sports management company, negotiating contracts for athletes. Of his years as a Knick, he told me in the summer of 1984, "they were so good, everyone in the big city knowing who I was. They were real heady years, enough to make your head spin, but then I went to Cleveland, where I was just another ballplayer, and that brought me down to earth. It was a good thing that happened, because now I'm just an ordinary person making a living, and I am rid of any illusions that all my life I should be an idol."

Clyde is interviewed after entering Madison Square Garden Hall of Fame in 1984.

Rod as a Ranger in 1968.

Rod Gilbert

THE TWO OF US WERE SEATED ON
stools at the bar in Il Vagabondo, a dimly lit
Manhattan restaurant of Italian persuasion
that was much in favor among the Giants,
Jets, and Rangers of the early 1970s. As rain

beat hard on the windows during a dark stormy winter afternoon, the Rangers' Rod Gilbert (pronounced Jill-Bear) was telling me and Dave Zoni, the owner of the restaurant, a story.

"I remember when I was younger," Gilbert said with only a trace of French, his only language until he was sixteen, in his voice. "And I had the big head, you know? I met this girl in Florida and I told her I was with the Rangers. 'Oh,' she said, 'does that mean you work in the forest?'"

Gilbert laughed, pinpricks of amusement in his coal-black eyes. This was the Rod Gilbert I had come expecting to see on this December day in 1972: the rich, carefree, laughing playboy bachelor who was the high-scoring star of a big-league hockey team. But later that afternoon and during the next week I saw the other side of the Gilbert coin: the moody worrier who, more than he liked, slipped into a valley of pessimism.

Gilbert shared the two fears of many successful pro athletes: one, that they will be injured and their careers cut short; and two, that the skill they have possessed ever since their youth will vanish overnight, never to return.

"I am a worrier," Gilbert told me one afternoon as he drove his fire-truck red Torino along the curving East River Drive in Manhattan. "I am a pessimist about myself and my career."

He was thirty, a chunky one hundred seventy-five pounds packed on his chesty five-foot-nine frame. Even when he wore a suit jacket, you could see the powerful upper-arm muscles, the gifts of a blacksmith father, bulging the sleeves. His face was dark and sensual, the kind that girls call "sweet" or "sexy." His hair was dark and lapped over his ears, a hair-styling that always reminded me of a World War II German helmet.

As we sped along in the Torino toward a Ranger practice on Long Island, he told me

why he worried that his best skill, his ability to slam pucks into cages, might wither away or suddenly vanish. "I am a streaky scorer. I always have been. If I go three or four games without scoring, I'll tend to pass the puck more. I guess I lose confidence in my shooting when the puck isn't going in. Then I'll stop scoring altogether, you know, because I'm passing too much. But then a shot goes in for me and that will snap me out of it. I say to myself, 'Shoot more, the puck is going in.'"

His medical history had given him more than enough reason to worry about the snapping of a bone ending his career in an instant. In 1961, then a twenty-year-old junior hockey player, he injured his spine. During delicate spinal-fusion surgery, four inches of bone were taken from the tibia in Rod's left leg and used to patch together the spine.

The spine did not fuse well. The leg became infected. For a while the doctors considered amputating the leg. It finally healed, but doctors told Rod that the spine might give way again and at any time. In 1965, during his third year as a Ranger, his spine did give way. He needed a second spinal-fusion operation. It was rare for a hockey player to play again after one spinal fusion; none, as far as doctors could tell, had come back to play pro hockey after two.

The operation was performed by New York surgeon Dr. Kazio "Yan" Yanigasawa. "For weeks in the hospital I stared at the ceiling and wondered if I'd ever play again," Gilbert told me. "Yan would stick that big cigar of his in his mouth and say, 'You'll make it.'"

Gilbert made it back only six months later, a comeback that was hailed as "The Miracle on 33rd Street," the Rangers' home building, Madison Square Garden, being on West 33rd Street. "They're doing a television film of people who made rare comebacks," he told me one afternoon in Il Vagabondo, his face solemn, and he seemed depressed by what he was saying. "One of the people they picked was me." He had seen on those hospital ceilings how suddenly a career in sports could end.

The career had begun in that place so fertile with hockey players—Montreal, home of the then-lords of hockey, the Canadiens. He was born in Montreal on July 1, 1941. He grew up in an East Montreal neighborhood of working people, his father a blacksmith who had come to the big city from a farm. Later his father converted his smithy shed into a garage where he began to build cabs for trucks.

When Rod was fifteen, a Ranger scout noticed him—all of one hundred seventy pounds and built, at five-foot-nine, "like a little bull," the scout told the Rangers. At the time the Canadiens had the rights to every good hockey player within 50 miles of Montreal. Ranger general manager Muzz Patrick wrote to the Canadiens, mentioned the name of an obscure Junior B team that Rod was playing for, and asked the Canadiens if the Rangers could sponsor the team. Apparently unaware of the little bull's potential, the Canadiens said yes. Automatically, for the $1,500 it cost to register and outfit the team, the Rangers owned Gilbert.

He came up to the Rangers in 1962 and by 1967, despite that second spinal-fusion operation which almost ended his career, he was a National Hockey League All-Star. By 1972 he and his linemates, center Jean Ratelle and left winger Vic Hadfield, were among the league's most respected lines. "They aren't scoring thirty-five or forty goals each," Bruin goalkeeper Ed Johnston once told me. "But they aren't giving up thirty-five or forty either."

Agreeing with Johnston was then-Ranger coach Emile Francis, who talked to me about the propensity of hockey forwards for scoring goals while thinking little about the goals scored against them.

"To some forwards," said the diminutive Francis, an ex-goalie who was called the

Cat because of his quickness, "the puck is like a magnet. They are mesmerized by it and it draws them out of position. Rod was like that. He came up from the minors as a big scorer who had the puck all the time. In the NHL he found that other guys also have the puck and he had to do other things. Some wingers never learn that. They are great scorers, period. But Rod is a great scorer and a great defensive player.

"In short, he developed into a two-way hockey player. He not only goes one way to score goals, he comes back—he back-checks—to stop the other guy from scoring. Last season he scored thirty and he was as valuable as someone who scored forty-five because he wasn't letting his own man score. Hockey is not like football where you send in the defensive unit. In a matter of seconds in hockey, you go from offense to defense and then *you* are the defensive unit."

One day, as we sat in a Boston hotel lobby before a game, Gilbert talked about how Francis had changed his thinking about hockey. "He made us realize that on every goal scored against you, there are three mistakes: one by the forward, one by the defense, and one by the goalkeeper. Everyone is responsible. There were lots of one to nothing and two to one games with Francis, and you got keyed up not to make a single mistake on defense. I had to change. I had to sacrifice some of what I used to do on offense to be a better defensive player and stay with this team."

He lived the playboy life away from the grimness and bloodletting of hockey. (His face had been stitched more than two hundred times, six times in the week I was with him, four of the stitches caused by a teammate's razor-sharp blade during a practice session.) Once, while we drove across the 59th Street bridge into Manhattan and a setting sun, he talked about the evening of partying that he was looking forward to. "I love New York," he said. "I have so many different kinds of friends here. Athletes, real-

Rod and his two children during ceremonies welcoming him into the Madison Square Garden Hall of Fame in 1984.

estate people, stockbrokers, university students. That's why New York is so great. You can meet so many different kinds of people."

For a playboy hockey player, it also had beautiful women. That was not always a blessing. "You get spoiled dating so many beautiful women. You see one, she's beautiful, but you know you are going to meet another one next week who is going to be even more beautiful. It's like a wheel that goes round and round." He laughed, talking faster as we crossed First Avenue and turned north toward Il Vagabondo. "Still I want to get married, have children. And I want to be with the Rangers when they win the Stanley Cup. Talk about excitement over the Mets when they won the World Series and when the Jets won the Super Bowl. Imagine how wild New York would be if we won the Stanley Cup."

Rod did get married, and he and his wife, Judy, had two children, a boy and a girl, but the Rangers never won the Stanley Cup during Rod's years as a Broadway Blue. When he retired in 1977, he held or shared twenty Ranger team records. His number 7 was the first Ranger number to be retired. He and Judy still live in Manhattan, where he works for Fundamental Brokers near Wall Street, trading in bonds. Hockey, he says, and bond trading are not that much different. "I'm in a room with fifteen guys screaming," he says. "It's just like hockey." In 1984 he was selected to the Madison Square Garden Hall of Fame.

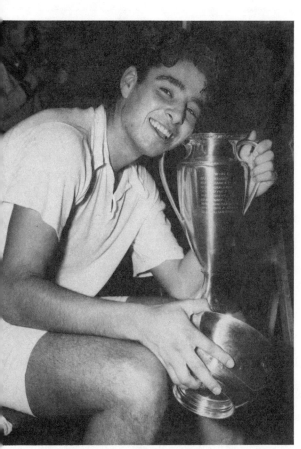

Pancho poses with some winnings in 1951.

Pancho Gonzales

I TELEPHONED PANCHO GONZALES ONE evening in 1957—he was in Iowa somewhere—and I was in New York. A friend, who worked for the A.G. Spalding sporting goods company, for whom Gonzales was then a consultant, had suggested I call Gonzales, who was bouncing from city to city on the pro tennis tour. "He has a lot of interesting things to say about the mistakes that kids make in not playing by the rules—and not only in sports," my friend told me.

I thought that Pancho's ideas on obeying the rules might be interesting since I thought of him as a maverick who followed his own pathways. He had been known to bicker with other players and rant at the officialdom of tennis. At my friend's suggestion, I phoned Pancho late in the evening New York time, thinking it would be late afternoon in Iowa, well before his tennis match that night. I called his motel and when he came on the line, I mentioned the name of my friend from Spalding and told him why I was calling.

He cut me off, his resonant voice impatient. "You guys," he said, obviously meaning the intruding press, "you always call at the wrong time. I'm about to go out onto a tennis court to play a match."

I apologized, telling him I hadn't realized he went onto the court so early. "Suppose I call you about midnight our time," I suggested, "you should be finished and rested by then."

"That's okay, I guess," he said in a grudging way. I thought he wouldn't take my second call—or, if he did, his thoughts on kids and the rules would be curt. I was wrong, and what he told me later that night about his youth was the basis of a magazine article, which I wrote under his byline, titled, "The Game I Wouldn't Play."

"'The Peck's Bad Boy of U.S. tennis today was crowned its king,' that's what a reporter wrote about me after I'd won the National Championship [for amateurs] in 1948," Gonzales told me when I called again. His voice was tired when he began. But as he went on—we talked for almost an hour—his voice grew stronger and more animated. What follows is a condensed and organized version of what he said.

"When I was fifteen I was ranked the best boy tennis player in southern California. Perry Jones of the Southern California Tennis Association, which was turning out scores of fine players, asked me to join his program. But when he found out I'd quit high school at sixteen, he told me I couldn't join unless I went back to high school. I refused. In 1945 I went into the navy. Still rebelling, I spent a week in the brig for going AWOL. When I left the navy in 1947, my father told me to go back to school, take a job, or get out of the house. I got out.

"At nineteen I entered the southern California tennis championships without an invitation and reached the quarterfinals. That led to a number of bids to other tournaments. I knew I was allowed to accept expense money for only eight a year—so, of course, I took money for ten.

"Though I gave back the extra money, I was suspended from amateur tennis. It was then that Perry Jones said to me, 'Pancho, on the court you insist your opponent follow the rule book. So do you. That's the only way tennis can be played. But don't you think rules are just as important for *living?*'

"Gradually I came to realize what he meant. I saw that I'd been pretty foolish, trying to prove I was above the rules. Nobody is. So I began cooperating with the officials. My suspension was dropped. Soon I was invited to better tournaments and played against better opponents. My game improved and I became the national champion. But I'm pretty sure that never would have happened if I hadn't learned that playing the game first means playing ball with the other guy."

Gonzales had won the national championship at the youngest age—he was only twenty—since Ellsworth Vines in the 1920s. Richard Gonzales was born on May 9, 1928, in Los Angeles, the eldest of seven children. His Mexican-born father was a painter of movie sets, his mother a seamstress. When Richard was twelve, his mother, hoping to lure him from the rough-and-tumble of football and toward a sport only the well-to-do then played, gave him a fifty-cent tennis racquet. Richard knew a high-school pal who played tennis. The pal taught Richard the basics of the game, gave him old racquets and tennis balls—and a nickname that stuck: Pancho. In return, Pancho helped the pal to deliver newspapers. "Other than

that," Pancho once said, talking about those casual tips from a schoolmate, "I never took a lesson and I never will. I learned my game by watching other players and working on the shots that suited me best. . . ."

By 1948, matured by his battles with the navy, his father, and Perry Jones, he had become the national champion. His youth and sudden prominence caused some observers to think his rise was a fluke. Sniffed the *New York Times* in 1948: "The rankest outsider of modern times sits on the tennis throne today." He proved he was true royalty by helping to win the Davis Cup and then winning the U.S. national singles title again in 1949, defeating Wimbledon champion Ted Schroeder in an uphill struggle, 16–18, 2–6, 6–1, 6–2, 6–4.

By now the black-haired, olive-skinned Gonzales, a rangy six-foot one-hundred-ninety-pounder, held the U.S. singles grass, clay, and indoor championships, a stranglehold on all the major titles that irritated some amateur-tennis officials. Of Mexican heritage, not from a rich society background, Gonzales was not the typical tennis champion of his time. More typical was tall, jut-jawed, Waspish Jack Kramer, who had turned pro, organizing his own tour. The rivalry between the two was a natural social and ethnic one; and since both men were loud and outspoken, the rivalry was set ablaze later by their angry quarreling. Late in 1949 Kramer signed Pancho to play on his tour, paying him $60,000 for a year of touring. In city after city during the first couple of years of the tour, Kramer demolished the younger Pancho, delighting some tennis traditionalists. Those beatings later may have been the spark that set off violent explosions between the two when Kramer, no longer a player, became pro tennis's number-one tour promoter.

By 1953, however, Gonzales could beat Kramer and any one of a series of ex-amateur "kings of tennis" who joined the tour and were turned into mincemeat in the

Gonzales grinder. From 1953 to 1962 Pancho dominated the pro tour. Pro tennis began an ascendancy that would end with today's open tennis and its millionaires like John McEnroe and Jimmy Connors. Even when he was the game's undisputed king, Pancho talked about retiring. In 1969, at the U.S. Open, he told James Toback, a writer for *Sport:* ". . . I'm not what I used to be. Preparation used to bring me to a point where I could play at 100 percent of my capacity about 85 percent of the match. And I could always call on my best when I had to . . . I have to take one match at a time. I can't take anyone for granted . . . I used to feel less of a man when I lost, but now I have had enough satisfaction that I can lose and accept it. I've satisfied myself that I'm a winner, so now I can accept defeat. I hate it, but I can live with it."

It was at this point in his career that Pancho twice showed that even in his forties there was no one in the world who could beat him when he could put together the game that he had played in his prime. At Wimbledon in 1969, although he did not win, he played the longest match up to then in British history. It went five sets, lasted five and a half hours of playing time, and was split between two days. His opponent was Charles Pasarell, ranked first in America two years earlier. In the first set they battled evenly through forty games. Pasarell finally broke serve to win, 22–20. Darkness was coming swiftly but the referee insisted they play another set. Gonzales raged at the decision, then lost 6–1. The next day he came out the hard-hitting Pancho of twenty years earlier and wore down the younger Pasarell, 16–14, 6–3, and 11–9 to take the match.

A year later, at New York's Madison Square Garden, he met the tall, left-handed Australian Rod Laver, the first (in 1968 and 1969) to win two "Grand Slams" in a row. In a duel still considered by many more than a decade later as the most thrilling ever

played indoors, Pancho won in five sets. I was among the reporters who talked to Laver shortly after that grueling match. He rubbed a hand across his freckled forehead, his hair soaked with sweat, and said, "Thank God I didn't have to play Pancho when he was twenty years younger."

Today Pancho still plays exhibition matches against fellow old-time pros like Bobby Riggs at resorts on the East and West Coasts. He is the resident professional at Caesar's Palace in Las Vegas. He has five daughters by his first wife, and one daughter from his second marriage. To a tennis generation weaned on Jimmy Connors and John McEnroe, Pancho is only a name in the history books when he is recalled at all, but in the 1950s there was only one Mr. Tennis in the world and his name was Richard Gonzales, a.k.a. Pancho.

Pancho is the head pro today at Caesar's Palace in Las Vegas.

Otto Graham

OTTO GRAHAM AND I WERE SEATED IN his car as he turned it onto a wide avenue in downtown Washington on a steamy September afternoon in 1968. We had been talking about Charley Taylor, one of the wide receivers on the team that Graham then coached, the Washington Redskins, and I was speculating on how many passes the speedy, sure-handed Taylor would catch during the 1968 season.

Graham, holding the steering wheel with one hand, rubbed the other hand reflectively across his large chin. "I hope Charley doesn't catch as many passes as he did last season," he said. "If he has to, that means we're in trouble."

I knew what he meant. National Football League championships are not won by teams that have to pass to win. The reasons are many, one being that an incomplete pass stops the clock. "You throw three incomplete passes," former quarterback Bobby Layne once told me, "and you have used up maybe only a minute. Now your defensive unit has to go back into the game with only a minute of rest. You keep doing that over a game and over a season and you are going to wear down your defensive people and see a lot of points scored against you."

Yet, even as I nodded in assent at what Graham had just said, I was struck by the irony of his statement. If you measure the success of a passer by the number of championships he has won, this was the man who was the most successful passer in modern pro football history. His Cleveland Browns had won four straight championships from 1946 to 1949 in the All-Amer-

Otto as the Cleveland quarterback in 1951.

62

ica Conference. He and the Browns moved to the National Football League in 1950 and won its eastern division championship six years in a row and the NFL title three of those six years. Of Graham, Brown coach Paul Brown had said, "He represents the exceptional thrower that you have to have in pro football."

Yet you can't win in the NFL if all you can do is pass, Graham had just said, and while I still agreed with him, I recalled a game in the late 1940s in which his passing turned what had been a humbling pasting for the Browns into a near-victory.

The Browns were playing the New York Yankees in an AAC game at Yankee Stadium. "The game meant nothing to us," Graham later told me, "because we had already clinched our division title and we knew we were going to be in the playoffs. But for the Yankees this was a very important game.

"Football is a game of emotions and the Yankees were way up emotionally for the game while we were not nearly as enthusiastic as perhaps we should have been. You may go out onto a field trying to win, but sometimes you just don't try as hard as other times. This was one of those times when we weren't trying all that hard."

Midway through the second period the Yankees had jumped out to a 28–0 lead. Then they made what Graham told me was "a fatal mistake in a football game. They started to get on us about how they were pushing us around. I remember Buddy Young [the Yankees' squat running back] saying things like, 'Hey, you guys are supposed to be so good and look what we are doing to you.' Other Yankees said the same thing and pretty soon they had us wanting to win that game as badly as we should have wanted it when the game started."

Graham began to play catch-up by throwing passes to his two best receivers, Mac Speedie and Dante Lavelli. "I began to throw from anywhere, even from my own

end zone," Graham told me. "I remember I threw, I think to Speedie, who caught the pass and ran for about sixty yards and then he lateraled to Lavelli, who went on for another twenty or thirty yards. We got a touchdown and went off at the half losing twenty-eight to seven. Then we got three more touchdowns in the second half to tie the game, twenty-eight to twenty-eight, and if that game had just lasted another three or four minutes, we would have won it instead of ending up with a tie.

"That game proved two things to me. One, just how important a factor emotions can be in football. Two, it's never wise when you're way ahead in a game to taunt your opponent. You are much better off slapping him on the back and telling him he's just having an off day and the next time things may be different."

The Browns and their coach had been looking to Graham for that kind of leadership since the team's birth in the summer of 1946. At the time Graham was twenty-four years old, a navy veteran who had impressed Brown both at Northwestern, where Graham had been an All-American quarterback, and as a naval preflight student at the University of North Carolina. "He had the basic requirements of a T-formation quarterback," Brown once told me. "He was poised, and a slick ball handler as he had proved in high school and college as a basketball player."

In Waukegan, Illinois, where Graham was born on December 6, 1921, and grew up, he was an All-State basketball player. In 1940 he went to Northwestern with a basketball scholarship. "We didn't figure him as a football player," a Northwestern coach once said. "At nearly six foot and only one hundred sixty pounds, he seemed too slender."

A coach saw Otto hurl a ball 60 yards in an intermural game and invited him to try out for the varsity. By the end of the 1941 season he had taken the quarterback job away from Bill De Correvont, who had come to

Northwestern from Chicago acclaimed as the best high-school passer in history. In 1942 and 1943 Graham played both basketball and football, setting Western Conference (now Big 10) passing records. In 1943 he made several All-Americas and was chosen the conference's most valuable player.

He enlisted in the navy as an aviation cadet. In 1944 his University of North Carolina Preflight team was matched against Navy. The score was tied 14–14 late in the game. Graham caught a punt on his 45-yard line and angled toward the right sideline. A gang of Navy tacklers descended on him. Graham stopped, wheeled, and tossed a long lateral to a teammate standing alone on the left sideline. The teammate caught the ball and ran unmolested into the end zone for the winning touchdown.

That kind of quick thinking impressed Paul Brown, then the Ohio State coach. Brown was looking for players to join a Cleveland team that would play in a new pro league as soon as the war ended. Brown signed on Aviation Cadet Otto Graham for $7,500 a year, to be paid when the first season started, plus $200 a month from the date of signing until play began. Graham, who was then earning $75 a month as a cadet, signed quickly, using the $200 a month to help finance his marriage to Beverly Jean Collinge, whom he had met at Northwestern.

In the summer of 1946, the war over, Brown brought together the players he had signed. At the time most pro football teams used a single-wing offense that was often a grind-it-out, three-yards-and-a-cloud-of-dust kind of game. Brown decided on the explosiveness of the T-formation, used by the Chicago Bears in their 73–0 rout of the Redskins in an NFL title game just before the war. He thought he had the ideal T quarterback, Graham, who told his receivers: "Just get open. If you are open, I know I have the accuracy to put the ball into your hands."

And Brown had the precursor of today's big and mobile running backs, the two-hundred-dred-twenty-pound Marion Motley, who could run through tacklers like a revved-up tank.

Graham's accuracy forced opposing defenses to spread out to cover his speedy wide receivers. But when they were spread out, the defenses lacked the solidity to stop the rampaging Motley. Graham threw for touchdowns, Motley ran for others, and whenever they came up short of the goal line, the Browns called on Lou (the Toe) Groza to kick field goals. From 1946 to 1949 the Browns won 47 games while losing only 3 on their way to four straight AAC titles.

NFL fans had dismissed the Browns as a team from a minor league. In 1950, the Browns' first year in the NFL, they surprised those fans by winning the eastern division title with a victory over the New York Giants. Then they beat the Los Angeles Rams in the playoff for the title, 30–28, when Groza kicked a last-minute field goal. Years later Graham told me "that game was my all-time thriller. It's the close ones that always thrill you."

No team before or since has so dominated NFL play for so long as the Browns of 1950 to 1955. In each of those six seasons they went all the way to the championship game by winning their division. They lost the championship game to the Rams in 1951, and to Bobby Layne's Detroit Lions in 1952 and 1953. In 1954 they beat the Lions, 56–10, Graham passing for three touchdowns and running into the end zone for three more. After the game, although only thirty-three, he announced his retirement because "I have always wanted to go out on top."

In the summer of 1955, after losing his number-one quarterback to a Canadian team, Brown begged Graham to return for one last season. Reluctantly, knowing his reputation would sink if "I finish on a sour note," Graham came back. He steered the

Otto as the Coast Guard Athletic Director in 1984.

Browns to their sixth conference title in six years, their tenth in ten years. Then he said his farewell to football by throwing two touchdown passes and scoring two himself as the Browns won their third NFL championship in six years with a lopsided triumph over the Rams, 35–14.

In measuring the greatness of the Browns from 1946 to 1955, it is customary to talk about the four AAC titles and the three NFL titles the team won during those ten years, along with the ten division titles and the amazing record of having played in ten championship games in ten years. But perhaps an even better measure of the team's remarkable consistency was its record of having won 106 of 115 regular-season games.

Graham never really left football. He became the coach of the U.S. Coast Guard Academy team and also coached the College All-Stars in their annual games during the 1960s against the best NFL team of the year. From 1966 to 1968 he coached the Redskins. He went back to the Coast Guard Academy, where he retired as athletic director in early 1985. He and his wife plan to live near Sarasota, where he is the part-owner of a golf course on which, he told me, "I plan to spend as much time as I can."

Rocky Graziano

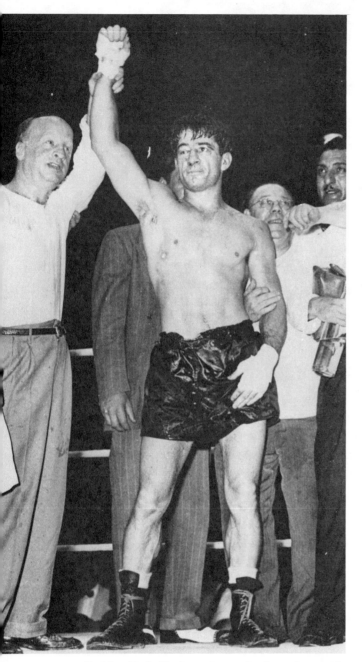

A bloodied Rocky after winning the middleweight title in 1947.

"I HATED THAT GUY," ROCKY GRAZIANO said to me as we faced each other across a glass-topped coffee table. We were seated in the mid-Manhattan office of Rocky's, a chain of pizza stores. "I hated that friggin' guy," Rocky said even more emphatically, but there was a smile of fondness on his face as he talked of the man he said he hated. "I wanted to kill him, you know what I mean?"

I would get to know what he meant about that guy, Tony Zale, during several conversations I had with Rocky in the spring of 1969. We talked about his life in boxing and his later career in television, but mostly we talked about Zale and the three alley fights they had waged some twenty years earlier.

Graziano stood up. "When Zale hit you here," he said, pointing to the lower gold button of his blue blazer, "geez, it made you bend over like he'd stuck something in there inside you, turned it around like it was a red-hot poker, and then left it there, you know what I mean, John?"

His voice, as rasping as sandpaper on steel, was peppered with the *duhs, deze,* and *doze* sounds of a Dead End kid circa 1936. His tailored figure was Beverly Hills Polo Lounge, the blazer falling smoothly from his thick shoulders, the soft gray slacks crisp, the loafers polished. Gold gleamed from wrists and fingers. The blend of lumpy face, slitted eyes, hammered ears, the street obscenities, the fashionable clothes, the flashy look—it was a blend that told you the Rocky Graziano story in an instant. He had come from the stink of Lower East Side street corners to the scented studios and offices of the rich, powerful, and famous, the ex-pug now the highly paid actor in movies and TV commercials. His story was the stuff that East Side dreams were made of in the 1930s.

Rocky Graziano was proof that somebody up there did indeed like Rocco Barbella.

Rocco Barbella was born on January 1, 1922, in what is now known as Manhattan's East Village. He grew up near Avenue A in the tenements that flanked the greasy-dark waters of the East River. At eleven he stared from behind the bars of a reform school. At sixteen he was being walloped by the billies of cops in the back rooms of precinct houses. At seventeen he had been thrown into the blackness of Manhattan's Tombs prison. In the army at nineteen, he had knocked a captain senseless and left the service after a time in the stockade with less than an honorable discharge.

He turned to doing what he had done best for so long—brawling. Fighting under the name of Rocky Graziano, his grandfather's name, he was a chesty, cocky, wild-swinging middleweight of about one hundred fifty pounds who was all fists and fury.

"In those days I wanted to kill everyone," he told me as we sat facing each other in a townhouse on East 38th Street off Third Avenue, the office-headquarters of Rocky's chain of pizza stores. He laughed, remembering that rampaging ring animal that he now impersonated in television commercials. "Geez, I knocked out Freddie Cochran twice, wrecked Marty Servo, and he never fought again." He stopped laughing, the ex-pug's face turning grim. "I always felt sorry about that. Poor Marty."

He looked down at his clenched hands. "Geez, I was a terror. I'd grab 'em by the throat with my left hand and with my right hand I wuz tryin' to knock their friggin' heads off."

In 1946 he took on the middleweight champion of the world, the Man of Steel from Gary, Indiana, Tony Zale, in the first of their three bloodlettings. Those brawls were, arguably, the three bloodiest ever fought inside an American ring. Zale and Graziano met for the first time on September 24, 1946, at Yankee Stadium. The twenty-four-year-old Graziano was nine years younger than Zale, who weighed in at one hundred sixty, six pounds heavier than Graziano. Most of Rocky's kayo victims had been welterweights, whom Rocky had outweighed by four to ten pounds. Rocky's East Side fans wondered how he would stand up against a heavier man's punches.

They got an early answer. A minute into the fight, the Man of Steel lashed a left hook to Rocky's chin. Rocky crashed onto his back, a drunk's glazed-eyed look spread across his face, and immediately the three Zale-Graziano encounters assumed their savage personality.

"I looked up at him and he seemed so tall," Rocky told me. "He always seemed tall to me. I wanted to stuff a friggin' glove down his throat."

The street fighter roared back in the second round, slashing Zale's face. Blood spewed from Zale's mouth, splattering his shoes. Graziano caught Zale's chin with a right cross and the champion went down. He got up and in the third round took more of a beating, Graziano cradling Zale's head in his left glove and flailing the blood-smeared face with his right.

By the fifth the champion was staggering backward on wobbly legs as Graziano nailed him at the bell with lefts and rights. In his corner Graziano was told by Whitey Bimstein, "Zale's head is as hard as watermelon. Go to the body."

Rocky lit a cigarette as we talked, watching the smoke rise. "He said I should go to the body," Rocky told me. "Hell, that was a mistake, I was no body puncher."

In the sixth Rocky leaned forward to throw a body punch and opened up his middle. Zale sent a right-handed rock into Rocky's belly. Rocky sagged against the ropes and Zale slammed a left hook to the jaw.

"It was like I had no feet all of a sudden," Rocky told me, snuffing out the cigarette.

There was a look of embarrassment on his face. "I couldn't feel the ground under me no more."

Referee Ruby Goldstein counted him out. Rocky left the ring with a face that was not even cut while Zale, the winner, looked like the bloodied loser. The next day Rocky heard growls on Avenue A from unhappy gamblers that he had been paid to stay down. "I knew," he told me, "that there wuz only one way to stop that kind of talk—win the second fight."

The second fight was held in a steamy indoor Chicago arena on the hot night of July 16, 1947, and among the sweltering spectators was the stringy crooner, Frank Sinatra. From the opening bell Zale hammered Graziano's face. "All I could see of Zale," Graziano told me, "was a red blur. I couldn't catch my breath. I had pain in both my eyes and Zale was this red blur that came at me and went away."

By the fourth round Graziano could only see through a slit that was his right eye. Rocky shifted his stance so he could see Zale with the one eye. "The stance," he told me, "gave me a better punch with my left hand. It gave me more power."

The 100-degree heat in the packed, humid arena had begun to sap the older Zale's strength. In the sixth the bleeding Graziano landed a right that drove the Man of Steel into the ropes. Zale's knees buckled. A final right spun him upward onto the middle strand of the ropes, where he hung head down as the referee pulled away Graziano, the new middleweight champion. Again, as in the first fight, the winner left the ring smeared with blood, the loser left almost unmarked.

"After I became champion I went the way of all fighters," Graziano told me, a rueful smile on his face. "You know, drinking, smoking, having a good time until all hours of the night. I was the king of the world."

In the third fight, on June 10, 1948, Rocky

paid for that year of fun. Zale knocked him down in the first round, and again in the third. Graziano rose gamely, perhaps hearing the taunts on Avenue A after the first fight, and Zale threw the last punch of this savage feud, a left hook. Rocky toppled backward, his head slamming the canvas, and the referee counted him out.

No longer the champ, Rocky fought Sugar Ray Robinson and lost. He took on Chuck Davey, a fighter who had built up his credentials by winning a number of televised bouts. Davey defeated Graziano in a fight that drew snickers around the gyms on Eighth Avenue where the fighters then trained. In 1951 Rocky retired and soon he was being seen with actress-comedienne Martha Raye on TV comedy shows, usually the ex-pug but never the ex-animal. He also appeared regularly in TV commercials and nightclub acts. In 1955 his highly praised autobiography, *Somebody Up There Likes Me*, written with Rowland Barber, became a movie, a young Paul Newman playing Rocky.

By then, as often happens between fighters who have been rivals in the ring, he and Zale had become good friends. Graziano flew to Chicago to publicize a restaurant opened by Zale. Rocky tried to get movie and TV jobs for the Man of Steel. I brought them together that spring of 1969 for a photograph to illustrate a magazine article I wrote about their fights. Zale was then working as a greeter at a place on Manhattan's West Side. They were affable together, making small jokes. But I sensed a tenseness, both of them knowing that Rocky had been the big success away from the ring, both of them also knowing, as Zale put it to me, that the Man of Steel had been "the boss" inside the ring.

In the 1970s and 1980s, made prosperous by his television commercials and investments in places like Rocky's Pizza Parlors, Rocky was seen often at the East Side of

Manhattan bars where sportswriters and ad executives hung out. Always the laughing buffoon, Rocky drew roaring laughter with stories about his pals in show business and boxing. In 1981 I asked him if he was ever nervous appearing in front of television cameras. "Naw," he said, looking at me as though I had some form of insanity. "Why the hell should I be nervous? It ain't like you get hit in the belly by Tony Zale and you remember it the rest of your life, you know what I mean?"

Rocky and a friend, Margaux Hemingway, at a New York club some thirty-odd years after

Emile in 1960 with former greats Joe Louis and Billy Conn.

Emile Griffith

HE HAD JUST BECOME THE FIRST BOXER to win the welterweight championship of the world a third time. At the moment—five minutes after the fight had ended—that bit of trivia seemed immensely important to me and the dozens of other journalists struggling, shoulder to shoulder, to squeeze through a narrow door into the champion's dressing room in Madison Square Garden. I popped through the entrance and flowed with the stream into the room. I heard a woman—Emile's mother—shouting almost hysterically, "Emile! Emile!" The crowd around the champion parted for a moment and I saw Emile Griffith, seated on a bench, huge beads of sweat clinging like globules

of oil to his chocolate stop sign of a face. I was pushed closer. Like most fighters outside a ring, he seemed lethargic, as though—as psychologist Joyce Brothers once suggested to me—all their brutality was consumed inside the ring. In a numbed voice, he was saying, "The important thing wasn't winning the title again. The important thing is that I proved I could fight again in Madison Square Garden."

Two years earlier, in Madison Square Garden, Emile Griffith had killed a man. He had hammered into unconsciousness the lithe Benny Paret, who died a week later. The Puerto Rican fans of Paret had been unforgiving, and when Emile fought Luis Rodriguez here at the Garden to win back the welterweight title a third time, he had heard the chant "Benny Paret . . . Benny

Paret . . ." Griffith had been reminded that he was a killer, but now he was saying he could fight in the Garden and pound a man to the canvas while not thinking of another man he had seen dying on that same canvas.

I wanted to talk to Griffith about that death in the ring and what it had done to him as a fighter. A few days after the Rodriguez fight I called Griffith's manager, the husky and affable Gil Clancy, who told me to meet him and Griffith at a New York City Parks Department recreation building on the West Side, where Griffith trained. I was talking to Clancy when the champion came into the room. He was trailed by a stream of neighborhood kids, mostly black and Hispanic, and as they pranced around him, like the followers of a muscled Pied Piper, I could see the adoration shining in their eyes.

And mischief, too, for while they obviously admired the champion, they were neither in fear nor in awe of him. They knew well his good nature. One sneaked up behind him and smacked him on the side of his head; another tugged at the tail of his tailored jacket.

"Hey, you!" he shouted, then ran a few steps toward his two tormentors, who ran away, screeching laughter.

The grinning champion turned to face us. Two days earlier, when I had seen him in the dressing room, twin slashes across his cheeks had been oozing blood, but now the wounds were covered by huge wraparound dark glasses. In his smartly tailored Ivy League suit, the lapels narrow, the shoulders natural, he fit the role of the successful man of the 1960s, the suit shaped tightly on his five-foot-seven, one-hundred-fifty-pound body, his wide shoulders and bulging chest tapering to an astonishingly narrow waist that had been measured at 26 inches. Around both wrists dangled heavy gold bracelets. A gold medal, hanging from a chain around his neck, bobbed on his shirt front. I asked about the medal.

"This is the medal I won in the Golden Gloves," he said, the words lilted by the rhythms of his native Virgin Islands. He had won that Golden Gloves medal even at a time when he hated fighting. He had grown up in the Virgin Islands, where he was born in St. Thomas on February 3, 1938. His first ten years had been serene: fishing, swimming, and running free on the beaches. "We threw rocks at each other," he told me as we sat on a bench in the now-quiet recreation center, "but we seldom had fistfights."

Emile was thrown into a much more violent world when he was fourteen and came to Manhattan to live with his mother. They lived in a Harlem infested during the 1940s and 1950s by drugs and killers. But even as gang fights swirled around him, the boy from the Virgin Islands ran clear of the brawls, stabbings, and shootings. At fifteen, overwhelmed by schoolwork, he dropped out of high school to take a job in the garment district as a stockroom boy. He was lifting packing cases one day in a millinery house when his boss noticed Emile's rippling muscles. The boss had a friend in the fight game, Gil Clancy, and the boss told Emile that he might earn more money as a boxer than he ever would picking up women's hats.

Reluctantly, torn between the ambition to make money that would move him and his mother away from the terrors of Harlem and the fear of hitting and being hit, Emile went to see Clancy, who was impressed by his size and speed. Emile joined Clancy's small troupe of fighters. Often, though, he hid out among the swimmers in the pool of the municipal bathhouse, where Clancy trained his fighters, dreading having to go into a ring. More than once, whacking the future champion on the rear, Clancy had to force him into a ring to spar.

Emile learned quickly how to hit while avoiding being hit. By 1957, now nineteen, he was a Golden Gloves champion. He turned professional in the spring of 1959 and won his first twelve fights before losing a de-cision to veteran Randy Sandy.

The defeat created a streak of meanness in Emile. He wanted to beat Sandy and avenge the defeat, which he did. "I began to like the sport," he later said. "There was the money and the fame. Now I was some-body."

On April 1, 1961, he touched gloves in the ring in Miami Beach with Benny (Kid) Paret, at stake the welterweight title. Griffith knocked out Paret to win the title for the first time. In the return bout, Paret took back the title by winning a split decision that was sneered at by newspaper writers and booed by the crowd. After a long delay, hostility building between the two camps, a third fight was arranged. At the weigh-in the hos-tility flared into the open when Paret whis-pered a Spanish word at Griffith that questioned his virility.

They fought eleven bruising rounds. In the twelfth Griffith cornered Paret and ham-mered blow after blow into the Kid's bleed-ing face. As Paret slumped toward the canvas, grabbing a middle strand of the ropes with a limp glove, referee Ruby Gold-stein stopped the fight. It had been stopped too late. Taken to a hospital, Paret slipped into a coma. A week later, his brain tissues soaked in blood, he died.

The boy from the Virgin Islands was sud-denly a killer. He won his next two fights, looking listless, then lost the welterweight ti-tle for the second time in three years, beaten by Luis Rodriguez. I saw him regain the title that record third time by defeating Rodriguez at the Garden. He had left the ring hearing that unforgiving chant: "Benny Paret . . . Benny Paret . . ."

Now, sitting with Emile on a bench in the Parks Department recreation room, I asked him about the memory of Paret. He clasped his hands and stared toward a bare, white-washed wall. "Well, sir, I tell you," he said, the Caribbean accent strong. "The first time I fought in the Garden after the accident, it was against Don Fullmer. And once, when I am punching Fullmer in that same corner that I had Paret, the Kid's face flashed across my mind. And I cannot punch Fullmer any-more. I step back.

"This second time in the Garden, against Luis, the same thing happens. I have Luis in the corner. I am hitting him and then I see the Kid. But I don't pull back. I keep on punching. That's why I said in the dressing room that I was glad I had proved I could fight good in the Garden. I didn't pull back when I saw the Kid. And I think that maybe from now on, I won't see the Kid anymore when I fight."

"That's right," said the gruff-voiced Gil Clancy, his manager, who was listening. "I think Emile has this thing licked. He licked it right there in the ring against Luis, when he kept on punching." Clancy's voice had be-come even more strident than usual, the teacher drilling home something he wanted the pupil to remember.

Emile was living in a $50,000 home he had built for his mother in Queens, he told me later. "I like to come here in the afternoons," he said, looking through the window at a softball game being played on a field out-side. "The kids here call me up at home and tell me there is a softball game that day. I like to catch in softball games, but Clancy is afraid I'll get hurt, so I have to play the outfield."

Clancy said he hoped that Emile would step up in weight and take on Dick Tiger for the middleweight championship. That was what happened and, on April 25, 1966, Em-ile beat Tiger to become the middleweight champion. Later he lost the title to Nino Ben-venuti, regained it, then lost it again. He fought on until 1978, when he retired, both-ered by a torn rotor cuff in one of his shoul-ders. In 112 bouts over close to twenty years he won 84, 23 by knockouts, and lost 21, stopped only once (by Reuben Carter) on a technical knockout. A friend, boxing man-ager Eddie Allen, points out that about two-thirds of Emile's losses happened during his last four years in the ring. Allen adds: "Most of Emile's knockouts were before the unfortunate Paret incident. After that, I think, Emile pulled back on his punches."

Today, still living with his mother in Queens, Emile is a fight trainer for a number of East Coast managers. Among his fighters is Mark Medal, the junior middleweight champion of the word. He also trained Wilfrid Benitez when he won the welterweight championship of the world. "He is very strict with the boxers and is a patient teacher," says Eddie Allen. "I'd rate him on a par with his own manager and teacher, Gil Clancy."

Emile (*far right*) poses in 1984 with a manager and one of his fighters.

Dick Groat

I WALKED WITH DICK GROAT INTO THE spring-training clubhouse of the St. Louis Cardinals on a March day in 1963, and I will never forget the look on his long, pointy face. He was a nine-year veteran of the big leagues, a former All-American basketball player, a former National League Most Valuable Player, a World Series hero, but as he walked into the clubhouse at St. Petersburg, he looked like a kid walking scared into a new school.

I followed him into the wood-raftered clubhouse and watched him shake hands with Stan Musial. He laughed at something Musial said, but the laughter was forced, and a minute later he said to me, "Yeah, I do feel kind of strange." He waved a hand around the noisy clubhouse. "All this, it's all new to me."

Dick Groat was showing me a common experience for athletes when no-trade clauses in contracts were unknown. Groat had been traded to a new team. Judging from what Groat told me of that experience, I decided, it could inflict, albeit temporarily, an unnerving aching in the heart.

I had met Groat earlier that morning in his St. Petersburg motel. He grinned weakly as we chatted about the wet Florida weather; tension had drawn his lean face drum-tight. I said I was often surprised by how most ballplayers seemed so happy-go-lucky in their insecure profession. He said he thought the constant laughter and needling in clubhouses was often a mask to hide worries. He could not hide the concern he felt about being traded. "It's normal to feel you are wanted," he said. "I think that's a need of everybody—in baseball or in anything else. It's just a part of normal insecurity, I guess."

Dick Groat, then thirty-two, was not sure, for the first time in his athletic life, that he

Dick and the author before a 1963 game.

was wanted. Perhaps worse, he *knew* he was not wanted by the team he had idolized all of his childhood life and played for and captained much of his adult life—the Pittsburgh Pirates. He was born on November 4, 1930, in Wilkinsburg, Pennsylvania, and grew up watching games in old Forbes Field. His heroes were Pirates heroes—Arky Vaughn, Elbie Fletcher, Frankie Gustine, Ralph Kiner, Kirby Higbe, Preacher Roe. A high-school star in both basketball and baseball, he was pursued by college basketball coaches and chose Duke. There, called Dick (The Great) Groat, he set scoring records and was a near-unanimous choice on most All-America basketball teams of 1952. Now the Pirates came running, offering money if he'd play pro baseball instead of pro basketball, and Dick chose a large bonus and the chance to play on the field where once he'd watched his heroes.

A tall five-foot-eleven and lean one hundred eighty pounds, he was a nimble shortstop and a strong-wristed right-handed hitter who snapped line drives up the middle and down the foul lines. Fresh out of college, he took over in the spring of 1952 as the Pirates' shortstop and hit .284; all but 8 of his 109 hits were singles, but teams could not defense him by playing shallow because he punched the ball where it could not be caught.

Returning from military service in 1955, Groat was the core around which Branch Rickey, then running the Pirates, began to build a championship team. By 1956 Groat, only twenty-four, was the team's captain. In 1960 he was the National League batting champion with a .325 average, the league's Most Valuable Player, and a member of the world champion team (it included Bill Mazeroski, Roberto Clemente, Bill Virdon, Vernon Law, and Bob Friend) which beat the Yankees (on Mazeroski's last-of-the-ninth homer) in the seventh game of the World Series.

In 1962, Rickey was gone, replaced by general manager Joe Brown, and the team had slipped to fourth. Dick hit only .295 and he heard talk from the front office that he had slowed down as a shortstop and as a base runner. In December of 1962 he was playing golf when he was called to a phone to take a call from Joe Brown.

In St. Petersburg, sitting with me in a motel room some four months later, Dick Groat could recall every word of that brief conversation:

"Dick?"

"Yes, this is Dick."

"Joe Brown. Well, Dick, this is it."

"Where did I go?"

"To St. Louis."

"Good."

"Dick, it's been a nice relationship."

"Thank you."

"I guess you'll want to tell Barbara."

"Yes."

"I'd appreciate it if you didn't tell anybody else for about an hour, until we can call in the reporters and make the announcement."

"Okay."

"Fine, goodbye Dick."

"Goodbye."

That terse conversation extinguished almost a decade of service. Dick called his wife, Barbara, and she told their older daughter, Tracy. "Tracy took it very well at first," Groat told me. "But a few minutes later she was watching her favorite TV show, 'The Mickey Mouse Club,' and they broke into the show to announce I'd been traded. She started crying. She kept saying over and over that she wouldn't be seeing little Debbie Virdon anymore. It took my wife a little time to get Tracy to realize we'd go on living in Pittsburgh, that she'd see all her friends.

"I was as nearly shook up. For weeks my stomach felt like there was an iron ball inside it. I went around telling everybody how happy I was, going to the Cardinals, a contending club. But I was only trying to kid myself. My wife knew there was something wrong. She'd say, 'What's the matter, Dick?' I'd say, 'Nothing, nothing at all, I'm fine.' But you don't live with a person for years and not know that something is eating at them.

"What I was facing was something new—a new manager, a lot of players I didn't know, a new situation—and I guess it's only human to be a little afraid of something new.

"It was stupid to feel badly. But maybe my pride was hurt. Nobody likes to be told they're no longer wanted.

"I remember telling someone a few years ago that in baseball it's a great mistake to get too attached to anything—a ballclub, a city, anything—because it's all so temporary. Someday you know it's going to disappear. Maybe I was too attached to Pittsburgh and the Pirates. Still, how could you blame me? My roots were in Pittsburgh. I've lived there all my life. I work there during the winter. I've been a fan of the Pirates since my brothers took me to games when I was six. I guess I was being stupid or naïve in thinking that I'd be one of those rare creatures—the Untouchables—who stay all their career with one team. It was stupid of me to think that there is room for sentiment in baseball. There can't be; this isn't a game for sentiment."

And so he had come to St. Petersburg worried. Would he be wanted in St. Louis as he had been wanted in Pittsburgh? He arrived in St. Petersburg on a Tuesday evening and phoned Ken Boyer, the Cardinal third baseman, who was a close friend of Bill Virdon, Groat's best friend on the Pirates. Boyer offered to drive him to the ball park. The next morning he followed Boyer into the squat clubhouse, hands stuck stiffly into his pockets. When Boyer stopped to talk to someone, Groat turned to inspect a bare wall, a preoccupied frown on his face, as though he expected to find something of value on the wall.

But the Cardinals had obviously planned to make him feel a part of the team's inner circle. "You're there, Dick," Boyer said, pointing to a wooden dressing stall. A sign above the stall read, 24 GROAT. The one on the right read 6 MUSIAL, the one a stall away on the left read 14 BOYER. Groat shook hands with several of the players, pumping hands a bit too energetically, still obviously feeling awkward in this foreign climate.

A sporting-goods salesman came by. "Hey, Oscar," Groat called out, "I wanted to ask you—"

The lanky, grinning Musial shouted, "Hey, Dick, are you going to Os-ka him now or are you going to Os-ka him later?" Musial let out a throaty laugh.

Boyer groaned. "Dick," he said, "you're now a Cardinal. You've lived through one of Stash's bad jokes."

A few hours later I thought he had become very much a Cardinal. As a circle of new teammates sat around him in the clubhouse, he told of the winning of a pennant by the 1960 Pirates. "It was a funny thing," he said, "but a different guy was always getting the big hit for us. Take Hal Smith. I don't think he hit ten home runs that season. But at least eight of them must have won ballgames. Once we were playing the Dodgers and we're down, three to nothing, with two out and nobody on in the ninth. Someone hits a dribbler and gets on. Gino Cimoli's up next, and the Italian hits a seventeen-hopper through the middle that nobody touches and now there are two on. Smith steps in, home run and we're tied.

"In the eleventh up comes Smith again. Ooops! Another home run. In the last half of the eleventh, we put in Elroy Face, one-two-three they're out, and let's go home. That's the way we were winning all year—a different guy picking us up every time."

The Cardinals nodded, fascination glinting in their eyes. And maybe more than a little ambition showing as well. The Cardinals had finished sixth in 1962 and were picked for no better than third or fourth in 1963. But here was Dick Groat, once a world champion, telling the Cardinals that in baseball anyone can be a hero.

I saw the Cardinals later that spring when they came to the old Polo Grounds to play the Mets. Groat was hitting .340 and the Cardinals were two percentage points out of first place. The Cardinals had made him their unofficial batting instructor. He watched young catcher Tim McCarver poke a pitch during batting practice into the nearby right-field stands.

"That's the way, Mac," Groat yelled. "Dip that left shoulder." A worried-looking Mc-Carver came out of the cage and asked, "What was the matter with my left shoulder, Dick?"

Groat laughed. "Aw, I was just kidding. We used to say that all the left-handed hitters walked into the Polo Grounds with that back shoulder dipped way down, 'cause they were trying to flip that ball into those right-field seats. Like this." Grinning, he tilted one shoulder and began to duck walk.

Ken Boyer watched him. "You'd never think he was a born worrier, would you?" Boyer said to me. "You have to talk to him a while to find out." But I knew that Groat worried. That spring he had told me: "I'm worried about doing a good job for the Cardinals. I want real bad to live up to everything the Cardinals expect of me."

Boyer laughed when I told him what Groat had said. "He has no reason to worry. It's always easy for a ballclub to accept a guy who can hit the way Dick can. But it was even easier in his case because of the kind of guy he is.

"The hitters go to Groat and they say, 'How do you do this?' And the pitchers go to him and they say, 'Hey Dick, how was I throwing today?' He knows the answers because he has made it his business to know them. He thinks about this game. Someday he'll be a manager."

In 1963 the Cardinals jumped to second and Groat hit .319, tops on the team. In 1964 the Cardinals won the pennant, Groat hitting .292. In the World Series he got five hits, including a double and a triple, as the Cards beat the Yankees in 7 games. Groat goes into the trivia books as one of the few to have been on two different teams that beat the Yankees in two 7-game World Series.

By 1965, now thirty-four, he was drilling fewer line drives over infields, his average dipping to .254. In 1966 he was sent to the Phils and in 1967, after a brief stay with the Giants, he retired. He never became a manager, although there was talk for a time of his becoming the manager of the Pirates and, later, the Giants. Today he still lives in Pittsburgh. He operates Champion Lakes Golf Course in Ligonier with former teammate Jerry Lynch and is a representative for four industrial companies in the Pittsburgh area. He is also a commentator on telecasts of University of Pittsburgh basketball games.

◄
Dick waves to the crowd at a 1983 old-timers game.

The Hawk shows his finery to a doorman in Boston in 1968.

Ken Harrelson

WHEN I BEGAN TO INTERVIEW BASEBALL players, an editor gave me tongue-in-cheek advice. "Always carry a fake microphone with you," he said. "Ballplayers will talk to you if they think they are going to be on radio or television. They are not as interested in seeing their words in type."

He was chuckling after he said that, but there was truth, I discovered, in his observation that some ballplayers of the 1950s and 1960s seemed willing to talk until their jaws ached in front of a microphone while giving a man with a pad and pencil only monosyllabic grunts. A singular exception to this phenomenon, I discovered during the summer of 1968, was Ken Harrelson.

"I don't like to talk a lot," the lanky Harrelson told me one afternoon as we sat in the shade inside the Red Sox dugout at Fenway Park. That caused me no alarm because he

had been talking nonstop for almost a half-hour and would keep on talking for much of the next 30 minutes. Along with another athlete, who was prominent in boxing and named Cassius Clay, The Hawk, as Harrelson was called, had confidence that he was among The Greatest. "The Hawk," Boston coach Bobby Doerr told me, "has got more confidence than the law allows." One reason that The Hawk talked a lot, even to people with notebooks, was to make sure they understood in just what areas he was so great.

"I always give honest answers," he told me in the dugout. "A reporter asks me how far can I hit a golf ball. As I say, I don't like to talk a lot. It saves a lot of conversation if I say, 'I can hit it out of sight.' Or the reporters ask, 'Who is the best golfer in baseball?' I say I am. I don't hem and haw. What should I say? Should I say, 'Well, I won the golf tournament for baseball players three years out of four.' Everyone knows I did. But a lot of the writers, they write up what I say like I'm putting the dog on.

"Same thing with arm wrestling," he said without much of a pause. "I always said that no one had ever beaten me in arm wrestling. I never said no one *couldn't* beat me. I just said I'd never been beaten. In fact, I did say that some pro football player had beaten me. Curt Merz (then of the Kansas City Chiefs) did beat me. But the reporters wrote stories about my arm wrestling that gave the impression I was bragging."

He shook his head, seemingly mystified by the inability of reporters to give the proper impression of The Hawk. "They write that I am nutsy, that I am a flake. I'm anything but a flake, I'm really a conservative guy."

I nodded sympathetically. And as I later wrote about The Hawk: "A flake? What kind of person would consider calling Ken Harrelson a flake? Just because he was often seen wearing a hip-length silky green Nehru jacket with a heavy gold cross dangling from a chain around his neck? Just because he wears tight-fitting white pants, no socks and white moccasins? Just because he likes to play some bizarre pranks on his teammates?"

I had watched The Hawk come into the Red Sox clubhouse one evening. He saw a pair of old black sneakers that teammate Joey Foy wore most every day to the ball park as a kind of good luck omen. The Hawk beckoned to pitcher Juan Pizzaro. They whispered to each other. A grin spread across The Hawk's face as he watched Pizarro, a slender pitcher, pour rubbing alcohol over the sneakers, drenching them. Then Pizzaro lit a match, dropped the sneakers onto the floor, and put the match onto the sneakers.

Poof! A ball of blue flame enveloped the sneakers, then came black smoke and the acrid smell of burning rubber.

The Hawk ran to the trainer's room. "Joey," he yelled to Foy, "come quick!"

Foy hurried from the room just in time to see his beloved black sneakers being stomped on by Red Sox fire-fighters; the fire was quickly put out but nothing was left of the sneakers except a trampled pile of black ashes and hunks of charred rubber. A pained look had spread across Foy's face. The Hawk put a brotherly hand on his shoulder, "Gee, Joey," said The Hawk, "what rat would do a thing like that?"

A little later, still relishing what had happened, Harrelson realized I might write the story of the burnt-out sneakers. "Now look," he said, "when you write about me, don't make me sound like I'm some sort of flake."

The Hawk spoke with a charming southern drawl that made "head" sound like "haid." Tall (six-foot-two) and lean at one-hundred-ninety pounds, he had a beak-like nose that looked even more prominent on his slim, fair face. As a rookie with the Kansas City A's, he'd been known as Chicken, the bird-like beak rather than any lack of courage having won him the nickname. Over the years he had managed to adopt a tougher bird as his middle name. The improvement in his hitting may have made opponents think of him more as a hawk than a chicken. A righthanded swinger, he had never hit better than .255 and 23 home runs until 1968, when, midway through the season, he was leading the American League with a .301 average and was on his way to hitting 35 home runs. The year before, the Red Sox's leftfielder, Carl Yastrzemski, had won the Triple Crown; in the summer of 1968 there were Bostonians hoping that Harrelson, a rightfielder and first baseman, might also lead the league in average, home runs, and runs batted in.

"This year he is concentrating on baseball," Yastrzemski, one of his closest friends, told me. "Before he played golf in the mornings of a night game, he fooled around shooting pool. There is none of that now. Now it's baseball."

The Hawk nodded meaningfully when I told him what Yaz had said. He agreed that he had funneled too much of his energies into trying to shoot golf in the low 70s, bowl in the 200s, beat anyone in arm wrestling, and knock eight balls into side pockets. "And I used to sulk when I struck out," he added helpfully.

He had a reason for this sudden concentration on baseball. A year earlier The Hawk had discovered how rich the pickings could be in baseball as he became the first of the sport's highly paid free agents. Up to then, he told me, "I liked golf better than baseball. Baseball was just a job to me."

Kenneth Smith Harrelson was born on September 4, 1941, in Woodruff, South Carolina. At twelve he won an athletic scholarship to the Benedictine Military Academy, where a coach wanted him to play football. His mother, whom he once called "the driving force in my life," said no—she was afraid he might ruin his chances to play big league baseball.

He played baseball, basketball, golf—and he boxed. "There would be three, four fights a day," he told me with a fond smile of recollection. "I was the second toughest guy in the school. The toughest guy was my best buddy."

At his favorite sport, golf, he was winning local tournaments. A number of colleges offered him scholarships to play basketball. ("Oh, I was a gunner in basketball," he told me. "I had no qualms at all about putting that spheroid in the air.") But he chose baseball when the Kansas City A's (now the Oakland A's) offered him $30,000 to play baseball. He immediately bought his mother a brand-new Pontiac with some of the money. In the minors he hurt his arm as an outfielder and for the rest of his career would shuttle between the outfield and first base.

When The Hawk joined the Kansas City A's in 1963, he batted only .230 with his bat but at least .300 with his mouth. Once he challenged the strong-throwing Rocky Colavito to a throwing contest. To no one's surprise except perhaps his, he lost—but only the contest, not his confidence that he was the better thrower. Five years later he was playing bridge against other Red Sox—and nearly always losing. "I don't understand it," he once told me. "Yaz and I are the best bridge players on the team. I don't understand why we always lose." That Yaz and Mr. Confidence might not be the best bridge players on the team apparently never occurred to him.

In 1966 the A's impetuous owner, Charles O. Finley, traded him to Washington, but he was playing again for Finley's A's by the 1967 season. Harrelson had come to admire the A's manager, Alvin Dark, and when Finley suddenly fired Dark late in the 1967 season, The Hawk—batting .305 at the time—spoke as loudly with his mouth as he had been with his bat. He told reporters that Finley was "detrimental to baseball."

An infuriated Finley did what few if any owners had ever done before: He fired a player of value instead of trading or selling him for dollars or talent. At first Harrelson was stunned. "I thought I was finished in baseball," he told me. "I thought that Finley would talk to the other owners and I would be blackballed."

Instead four owners, fighting for the American League pennant, offered Harrelson, who had been paid $13,000 a year by Finley, at least five to almost ten times that much money to sign with them as a free agent. At the time Harrelson was almost $20,000 in debt—for a house, a car, furniture, appliances, and his favorite investment, clothes. Harrelson accepted the Red Sox offer of somewhat more than $100,000 a year, played for them in 23 games (in which he hit .200), and the Red Sox won the pennant. "Suddenly," the Hawk told me, "I was making more money than I could count."

Unwittingly, Finley and the Red Sox had started other ballplayers on a road toward more money than they could count. Seeing the Red Sox happily shell out $100,000 a year for a hitter of unproven quality, proven hitters like Johnny Bench, Pete Rose, and Carl Yastrzemski began to weigh their true worth in dollars and talk about piercing the $100,000 ceiling in sports. By the early 1970s, free agentry had become a possibility for anyone with more than five years of big league service. Ballplayers talked of breaking the $200,000 ceiling—and forever gone were the days of $13,000-a-year big leaguers.

The Hawk hit .275 and 35 home runs for the Red Sox in 1968, but he was never a top fielder. In 1969 the Red Sox sent him to Cleveland. He broke an ankle in 1970 and by 1971 he was beginning to look with longing at an old love—golf. He took lessons with professional Bob Toski, put together "a lot of rounds under 70," he told friends, and decided in 1971 to quit baseball and try to join the Professional Golfers Tour.

"A wealthy New Yorker helped me a lot," he said shortly after making his decision. "We played every Saturday and Sunday. He made me play for real big money, and I had to give him his handicap. Sometimes I was putting for as much as $10,000, which was what he wanted me to do. He knew the crowd pressure would never get to me on the tour, but he was afraid the money pressure might. Playing with him week after week for big money—usually in four figures—got me used to going for the heavy dough."

But The Hawk could not pluck even light dough off the fiercely competitive pro tour. He came back to baseball as a radio and television announcer. In 1984 he was a broadcaster for the White Sox in Chicago, where he now lives. Late in 1983 he proved he could still bat .300 with his mouth. The White Sox and their highly rated second baseman, Julio Cruz, could not agree on a contract. Harrelson called up Cruz, then phoned Sox chairman Jerry Reinsdorf. He talked both men into meeting. The result: Cruz signed a long-term contract to stay in Chicago, Reinsdorf smiled, The Hawk preened.

The Hawk today is a baseball broadcaster.

Bill weighs in after a 1958 race.

Bill Hartack

"WE WANT TO TAKE A PICTURE OF YOU today in the winner's circle if we can, Bill," I said. Bill Hartack nodded. We were sitting on folding chairs in the jockeys' recreation room at Monmouth Park in New Jersey on an early afternoon in the fall of 1958. The diminutive, leathery-faced jockeys clicked Ping-Pong balls back and forth while shouting shrilly at each other in English and Spanish.

"I have only one photographer with me for this story," I said. "He wants to get pictures of you in action and also at the winner's circle. But he can't get from where he's stationed for the action pictures to be at the winner's circle in time. He'll stay at the winner's circle for one race. Can you tell us in

what race you are most likely to be in the winner's circle?"

He thought for several moments, his knife-slim body erect in the chair. Bill Hartack was a proud athlete and the pride showed in his square-shouldered military bearing. He was twenty-five years old, his hair dark and curly, the face high-cheekboned and handsome. (He looked like singer Eddie Fisher.) He said he thought he was most likely to have a winner in the fourth race.

I told him I would stop in to talk to him again after the fourth race. I walked out of the recreation room, found the photographer, and told him to be at the winner's circle for the fourth race.

I was having a beer and a sandwich minutes later when I suddenly realized that the photographer and I were the owners of a most valuable tip. "Do you realize what we have?" I told the photographer, Ben Ross. "Bill Hartack, the winningest jockey in America, has just told us the race he thinks he's most likely to win. Who else would be better suited to pick a winner?"

Hastily, we pulled out our wallets and bet most of what we had—about $20, as I recall. We put it all on Hartack to win the fourth race. We went back to our beers, all but rubbing our hands with glee as we watched the ordinary horse players thumbing through their *Morning Telegraphs* and the tout sheets. What did they know? We had a tip, so to speak, from the horse's mouth.

The horse, of course, finished far back—last or next to last. Later that day I talked to Hartack about the horse in that fourth race, without mentioning—I was too embarrassed to do so—that I had bet on the race. Anger lit his dark, deep-set eyes, and his voice, always shrill, was like a whistle blast. "That horse wasn't as ready as I'd been led to believe," he snapped. "And I'm going to let that trainer know that the horse wasn't as ready as I'd been led to believe."

Nothing, he told me, infuriated him more than to ride a horse that wasn't ready to win. "I'm out to win every race that I'm in," he said. "I don't want anyone to tell me that the *next* time the horse will be ready to win it. When a trainer tells me to take it easy with the whip because a horse isn't yet at its peak, I tell him to get another rider. I want to mount only running horses—horses ready to run to win."

His pride often triggered his anger, he told me. "I'm always after some goal. Like a record for riding the most horses, winning the most races. And the closer I get to the record, the harder I work—and the worse my temper gets."

Trouble was, in racing for records, Hartack never felt any joy in passing the finish line. "Nothing I have accomplished in racing has given me an absolute, pure thrill. So

far there's been nothing, absolutely nothing, I can rest on.

"I know I'm sometimes hard to get along with. I can't go on like this. I'm lucky I never got married. I don't pretend to think I'd make anybody happy the way I am right now. The biggest problem I have is to learn to relax and get along with people."

During his racing career in the 1950s and 1960s, however, he was constantly feuding with owners, trainers, the press, even his own agents. "When someone asks me a question I think is stupid," he told me on that afternoon in 1957, "I say, 'That's a stupid question.' Then we fight.

"I'm a funny guy. Sometimes I'll go home after winning a big race and just sit by myself. Then two weeks later I'll go out and celebrate. Other times I lose and go out that night and enjoy myself. I don't like to plan ahead. I hate to accept invitations to parties in advance. You keep thinking about the party till all the freshness is gone, and then you don't enjoy it.

"When people invite me to their homes, I decline when I know I won't have fun. I refuse to put up with something I'm not enjoying just to be polite. I like to go anywhere— movies, theaters, nightclubs, wherever there is a lot of action—but only when I'm in the mood. I don't go because someone else wants to go."

His voice rose again to a shout when I asked him about a charge I had heard concerning him: that he was only concerned about riding mounts for rich stables that entered horses in the big races. "Look, I started out riding in cheap races for people who needed the purse money to pay the feed bill and get out of town. I haven't forgotten them. It hurts me, really *hurts* me, to hear people say I don't care about the poor people in racing."

Hartack was born on December 9, 1932, near the coal-mining town of Black Lick, Pennsylvania. His mother died when he was four. His father, a coal miner, raised Bill and his two sisters. (Years later he brought his father to live with him on a farm he bought in West Virginia.) An honor student, he was valedictorian of his class, a drummer with a local band, but not overly skillful as an athlete.

"I had no desire to be a jockey," he told me. But since he was only five-foot-four and about one hundred ten pounds when he graduated from high school, he knew he was the right size to ride horses for money. A friend persuaded his father to let Bill go to the Charles Town track to walk horses. "I still wasn't thinking at all about being a jockey," he said. "But I decided all the same I would learn everything I could about it." Characteristically, he first learned all about being a jockey, then decided to be one.

Riding the cheapest horses at the track, he learned how to get his horse quickly out of the gate, and within a year he was among the best in the country at jumping into the lead. He began to study the temperaments of each horse he rode. "By now," he told me in 1958, "I have an image in my mind of each of the seven thousand horses I have ridden, not what they look like, but what their traits are, and what they can and cannot do."

In 1955 he was the winningest jockey in the United States. He led again in 1956 and 1957, the first jockey ever to be the leading winner three years in a row. He was the first jockey to win $3,000,000 in purses in a single year (he kept 10 percent). And in 1957 he won his first Derby aboard Iron Liege.

His success surprised some trainers and riders. One jockey told me at Monmouth Park: "Willie sits poorly on a horse. He rocks side to side instead of pushing forward the way you should."

"That's crazy," Hartack snapped when I repeated the critique to him. "I've seen jockeys who sat well on a horse and won and I've seen jocks who sat well and lost. Do you think I wouldn't change the way I sit if I thought it made any difference?"

Hartack lived in Miami, not far from the airport, and once a year he took a month off from racing to relax at home. "I do a lot of swimming, water skiing, fishing, and hunting," he told me. "I feel relaxed. But soon I start getting restless—I'm tearing to get back to the track—and then I'm as tense as ever."

He explained why he was so tense as a jockey. "I bat my brains out all day long concentrating on every race. To do anything well, you have to concentrate. Ability will get you so far—but if you don't put your whole mind into what you're doing, you don't succeed. So I put every last ounce of my body and mind into a race. Then what happens? Some wise guy comes up and says, Why did you do this or why did you do that? I can't stand people bugging me like that. They change me from one kind of person to another. They get me so worked up, I can't settle down all evening. If people left me alone, I'd be all right."

I talked to one of his closest friends, turf writer Joe Hirsch, who told me: "First of all," he said. "Bill is one big bundle of nervous energy. The second thing you've got to remember about Bill is that he's always got to be the winner. No matter what he does—Ping-Pong, water skiing, cards—he has to be the best. If he's not, he'll have nothing to do with it."

"I am very serious about my work," Hartack told me. "I don't kid about it and I don't like other people to kid about it. Some people can laugh off their mistakes. I can't. And I'll tell you something, I *want* to worry. If I don't, someone else will—and I won't be winning anymore."

He won all the major races. He won the Preakness twice, in 1956 aboard Fabius, in 1964 on Northern Dancer. He shares the record with Eddie Arcaro for the most Derby winners with five: Iron Liege in 1957, Venetian Way in 1960, Decidedly in 1962, Northern Dancer in 1964, Majestic Prince in 1969.

He feuded with reporters, especially those who called him Willie, a name he disliked. He was critical of racing officials. He argued that suspensions of jockeys for minor infractions like so-called "careless riding" was unconstitutional. Most stewards, he said, did not understand the problems of trying to steer a half ton of racing animal through a cluster of frantic horses, each galloping toward a finish line. "They can't possibly say they understand how a horse reacts if they've never been on one. . . ."

By the early 1970s he was racing in the Orient. When he retired in the middle 1970s, he lived in Miami near the Hialeah track. In 1983 he joined ABC-TV as a commentator at big races like the Derby. Just before the 1983 race, the track was drenched by rain. Hartack told his partner, Howard Cosell, that the rain should be no problem to the horse that jumped out in front from the start. And who would win? Cosell asked Hartack. "Sunny's Halo," Hartack said. I still recalled the tip from Hartack that had failed some twenty-five years earlier and so I bet on another horse. Sunny's Halo jumped out in front, led all the way, and won.

ABC-TV's Hartack (*right*) and Jim McKay in 1984.

John Havlicek

JOHN HAVLICEK, WHO WAS CALLED Hondo by his Boston Celtic teammates, and I were flying in a jet plane to Milwaukee, where the Celtics were playing a game in 1968. His large, rectangular face was flushed, a red tide creeping up his forehead, as he talked about the only significant defeat of his athletic career. A proud man, he believed he had lost that once and only time because he hadn't been given a fair fight.

He was talking about the summer of 1962. He had graduated that June from Ohio State, where he had been a member of a Buckeye basketball team that had won one national championship and come within two games of winning two others. At Ohio State the swimming coach had told him he could have won medals at the Olympics. The baseball coach said he could have gone to the big leagues with two of his former high school teammates, Phil and Joe Niekro. The football coach, Woody Hayes, said he could have been the Big 10's best quarterback.

In the spring of 1962, Havlicek listened to offers from football's Cleveland Browns and basketball's Boston Celtics. Havlicek decided to try to make a pro football team without having played a minute of college ball. "I did things in basketball that pro football coaches thought would carry over to pro football," he told me over the roar of the jet plane. Most of the other Celtics, including their coach, Bill Russell, were slumped in their seats, sleeping. "The coaches with the Browns thought I could be a wide receiver. I was quick, I had good moves and good hands. Several pro teams sent me questionnaires. I began to think I might like pro football. I figured that if I could play for the Browns, I'd stay in Ohio and I like Ohio. The football season was short, the pay was the same as basketball, and football is not as

Hondo as a Celtic in the 1960s.

demanding as basketball. And I knew that if I didn't make the Browns, I could go back to basketball and try to make the Celtics."

That summer he reported to the Browns' camp at Hiram, Ohio, and ran wind sprints as Paul Brown, then the Browns' coach and the team's founding father, watched. "When we ran the 40-yard sprints," Havlicek told me in his quiet, reserved way, "I had the fastest time. I didn't have the college experience, but that was something I knew I could have learned.

"Paul Brown put me in for only a few plays in an exhibition game against the Steelers. On the first play I was flanked to the right."

Havlicek was staring out the window of the plane, seeming to look at a film of that game flickering on a screen. "It was an end sweep for Jim Brown. It was one of those picture things. I cut down the defensive halfback and Brown went 48 yards to the 2-yard line.

"On the next play, from the 2, I was the tight end. The play was to come off my left hip. I looked across the line and there, facing me, was Big Daddy Lipscomb." (The late Big Daddy was a three-hundred-pound defensive tackle with hands, coaches said, as big as toilet seats.)

Havlicek turned to face me, face still impassive. "I sort of blasted straight ahead. I ended up at the bottom of the pile, my helmet knocked half off. But on the next play we passed for a touchdown.

"The next time we had the ball, I was a decoy on the flank. I ran my patterns, but no one threw to me. And that was it. I didn't play any more."

The flush lingered on his forehead as he spoke of that rejection, a rare show of emotion in someone who usually seemed placid. "That was it," he said again, and this time there was anger in his tone. "Paul Brown told me he had enough receivers. Other pro teams asked me to come to their camps, but I had thought all along that if I didn't make the Browns, it would be an omen to go back to basketball."

At the Celtic camp that fall, he astonished the veterans with his seemingly endless endurance. "In some of the intrasquad games," he said one day as we lunched in a restaurant near Boston Garden, "Jim Loscutoff went over my back. I figured that a referee would call that a foul in a game, but I said nothing. If he wants to do that, I figured, I'll run him to death. One day he said to me, 'Man, you run too much.' I said, 'You keep climbing on my back, so I got to run to keep away from you.' He didn't climb much after that."

During that 1962–63 season, however, the Celtics discovered that the rangy six-foot-five, two-hundred-twenty-pound Havlicek, playing both guard and forward, could not score a great deal of points at either position. He averaged only 14 points per game and one day his old rival, Loscutoff, warned him: "You got to score more if you're going to last much longer in this league."

He had never been called upon to be a scorer during his years at Ohio State. "In college," he told me, "our job was pretty much to get the ball in to Jerry Lucas (the team's high scorer) in the pivot. At practice we spent seventy percent of our time on defense. It was always my job to guard the other team's high scorer. When I got to the Celtics I realized I had to develop my offense and score more points."

In the summer of 1963 he went back to Columbus and the Ohio State gym. All summer long he lobbed one handers at the basket from 10 to 15 feet away, the bracket in which pro shooters are expected to hit at least 50 percent of their shots. "They say you can't learn to shoot—that you either can or you can't," Tommy Heinsohn, one of Havlicek's Celtic teammates in 1963, once told me. "But when John came back that second year, he was knocking the eyes out of the basket."

From 1963 until his retirement in 1978, Havlicek, often the team's "sixth man" who came off the bench to pour in a flurry of points, averaged 20 points a game. Almost every season he played, he was second or third in both rebounds, a forward's responsibility, and assists, a guard's responsibility. And all during his career he left defenders panting in his wake. "He is the only guy on this club capable of going forty-eight minutes, an entire game, at full speed," Bill Russell once said. "He runs so much on offense," Detroit's muscular guard, Eddie Miles, told me, "that you're always moving trying to guard him. That's bound to slow you up when you get the ball." And Celtic general manager Red Auerbach looked back on more than thirty years in basketball and said to me, "He is probably in the best shape of any athlete I have ever seen."

Havlicek was quicker than most forwards who tried to guard him and taller than most guards when he played the backcourt. When he bounded off the bench to come into a game as the sixth man—the first substitute in the starting lineup—he always had one thing in mind, he told me: "To get the team running again. And what I would try to do was work a pressing defense, steal the ball, then throw a long pass for a quick basket. One of the most demoralizing things you can do to another team is score a quick basket on a turnover after they have worked hard for 2 points. And nothing will get your team running again like a quick 2 points."

Friends and teammates called him Hondo because he resembled the late John Wayne, who had made a movie with that title. Bill Russell called him Farmer John because he had grown up in a small town in Ohio. He was born in Martins Ferry, Ohio, on April 8, 1940. Two of his Martins Ferry pals were Phil and Joe Niekro, later big-league pitchers. John played shortstop for the high school team and was the quarterback of the football team. The team had such a tiny bunch of players on the line—they averaged only one-hundred-thirty-five pounds—that it was known as Big John and the Seven Dwarfs. Big John also ran the quarter-mile on the track team and was an All-State forward on a basketball team that won 17 of 18 games in his senior year. He became friendly with two other Ohio high school stars, the six-foot-eight Jerry Lucas, a high-jumping center, and Larry Siegfried, a quick guard. The trio decided to enroll together at Ohio State. All three, along with another guard, Mel Nowell, became NBA players, perhaps the most pros ever produced by one college team. In three years Ohio State won 78 games, lost only 16, and won the NCAA championship in 1960. In 1961 and 1962 it went into the NCAA championship final game, but lost both games to the University of Cincinnati, the second time when Lucas had to play with an injury. Most basketball historians rank that Buckeye team among the ten best college teams ever.

He joined the Celtics in 1962 and, as a guard, helped the team win its fifth straight title and its sixth in the previous seven years. In 1963–64, the team played without the retired Bob Cousy and won its sixth straight title, the most ever won in successive years by a big-league pro team. As a rookie and, later, as a veteran, Hondo always seemed imperturbable. While I was with him during the 1968 season, we met after a game in Milwaukee and went to the cocktail lounge of the motel where the Celtics stayed. He ordered a beer in the same impassive way he had played against the Bucks that night.

"You never seem to get excited or involved," I said. "Whether you win or lose, whether you make a shot or miss it, even when a foul is called on you, your expression never changes."

He smiled and I thought to myself: Well, *sometimes* your expression does change. "I have a very simple approach to life," he said. "It's this: Do the right thing and eliminate the wrong things. If you can get a good percentage of the right things on your side, you will be successful."

But he was not as placid on the inside as he seemed on the outside, he told me. "Until a few years ago I got terrible stomach pains after a game. A doctor told me to have a beer or two after a game, that the alcohol would relax me. I do, but every once in awhile I still get those pains and they double me up."

"Maybe you get the pains," I said, "because you bottle up all those emotions inside you."

"I think that's true. Because I can get very excited. Occasionally I will yell at a referee after a call. And I'll tell you, if I'm watching a game as a spectator—even a high school game—I get all pysched up. My hands sweat. I'm jumping up and down, the whole thing. What it is, I hate to see anyone make a mistake out there, you want to see everyone do it right."

As a Celtic, he would make hardbitten veterans like Heinsohn shake with laughter during a timeout when he shouted in his high-pitched voice, "Come on, guys, let's do it *right*." The Celtics did it right often enough to win eight championships from 1963 to 1978, when he retired. In 1968 he was the NBA's Most Valuable Player. From 1968 to 1978 he was the team's captain. He played in 1,270 NBA games, more than any player

before him (the record was broken by Elvin Hayes in 1984). In 1980 he was picked for the NBA's 35th anniversary All-Time team, and in 1984 he was named to basketball's Hall of Fame. A few months earlier he had visited the Celtics' training camp during a get-together of former Celtics. While the other oldtimers watched from the sideline, Havlicek scrimmaged against the 1983 Celtics. Later Red Auerbach told someone, "All John needed were a couple of more workouts and he could have started the season for us." He lives now in Weston, Massachusetts, where he is involved in office-product businesses.

Hondo plays in an old-timers game in 1983. Guarding him is ex-NBA star Bob Pettit.

Connie as an Iowa freshman in 1958.

Connie Hawkins

THE DAY I FIRST SAW CONNIE HAWKINS do all those things that he could do with a basketball, I had lunch with one of the people, Roger Brown, who would be matched against him that evening. Roger had played against Connie in Brooklyn schoolyards and in Madison Square Garden when both were high school sensations during the late 1950s. "Connie can do everything," Roger told me. "He is the best all-around basketball player in this league."

A few hours later, on an evening in 1968 in Indianapolis, I saw the truth of that appraisal. By the first period Connie had four personal fouls against him and his Pittsburgh Piper team was losing to Browns' Indiana Pacers, 28–24. Then The Hawk, as the players called Connie, took off in full flight. He threw in a long one hander. He led a fast break like some high-stepping greyhound for another two points. He flipped a pass the length of the court to set up another Pittsburgh basket. Roaming the middle of the Pittsburgh defense, he soared to block one shot, then a second. A minute later his six-foot-eight, two-hundred-pound body sprang off the floor, elbows close to the rim of the basket, as he slam-dunked. By the end of the night he had dropped in ten of sixteen shots and eight of ten free throws for a game-high 28 points. And his Pipers were easy 137–101 winners. It was almost five years before I saw another player perform in that same soaring, swooping fashion—that player was Julius (Dr. J) Erving.

Yet The Hawk was not allowed to play in the National Basketball Association. In 1961 the Manhattan District Attorney said that Jack Molinas, a former Columbia University player, had bribed college players to fix the results of games. Connie Hawkins, with several other New York City high school players, had known Molinas. No charges were ever filed against Connie or the others, but the University of Iowa, where Connie was then a freshman, asked him to leave and the National Basketball Association announced that "anyone who was named in the investigation cannot play."

I thought, as I wrote in *Sport* in 1968, that Connie and the others "had been victims of clumsy justice." In the 1968 season I talked to four of the players who had been banned by the NBA—Doug Moe (later an NBA coach), Tony Jackson, Roger Brown, and Connie. All four were playing in the new American Basketball Association. I talked to Roger in Indianapolis over lunch and asked him if he had ever taken money from Molinas.

"Are you going to pay for this lunch?" Roger asked in his understated manner.

"The magazine is."

"Well, that's the way it was done. Molinas bought a lot of things for us—not just for Connie and me but for all the ballplayers. We'd play a schoolyard game down at the beach, he'd buy dinner. The DA added it all up. It came to $250 or so, and the DA said we accepted that sum for, as he put it, 'our good offices.' Hell, what could we do for the fixers? We were still in high school."

That night I talked to Connie after the game. He was dressing with his Pittsburgh teammates in a small room in the arena. Their street clothes were hanging on nailheads hammered into walls. Several players shouted that their showers were running only cold water.

When I introduced myself, Hawkins smiled—a quick smile replaced instantly by a somber, distant frown on his long equine face. As he pulled on a sportshirt, I could count the ribs that made his side look like a washboard. He looked even skinnier than someone who had his build. "My biggest weakness," he told me with a faint smile as we talked about his skinniness, "is I'm weak."

The next morning I flew with him and his teammates back to Pittsburgh. Boarding the plane, most of the players were dressed in slacks and sports jackets. The Hawk looked like a banker. He wore a double-breasted gray pin-stripe suit with a matching foulard tie and handkerchief. His expression was somber and dignified, like someone on the way to a funeral and thinking of a friend now gone.

I told him I had expected to meet an angry man, his world suddenly turning nightmarish after being punished for nonexistent faults. He smiled. During the next hour, he gave me a lesson on being a survivor when a world collapses around you.

Only eighteen, he had come back to Brooklyn from Iowa and stared for weeks at the wall of his mother's tenement apartment. (Connie was born in Brooklyn on July 17, 1942.) "Connie," a friend later told me, "knew nothing except how to play basketball." A Pittsburgh promoter came by and offered him $7,000 to play for a Pittsburgh team in a minor league. He led the league in scoring, but it collapsed after a season. In 1963 he got a job touring the world with the Harlem Globetrotters, which meant long separations from his wife, who stayed in Pittsburgh.

"I played four years with the Globetrotters," he said above the drone of the airplane's engines. "You couldn't pay enough to get all that experience. You played every day. You learned ball control doing all those Globetrotter stunts. You learned how to travel without getting too tired to play.

"We went to Europe four times. I learned a little of the language of every country where we played. In Czechoslovakia we traveled with a dance group. Two of the dancers taught me Czech and I learned to speak it fluently. I can speak French, German, Italian, Spanish. I have a good ear for language. I enjoy learning a new language. It used to bother me when people came up to us in Europe and I couldn't understand what they were saying. It felt good to be able to have conversations with people and know what people were saying about us.

"Have you ever been to Europe? There's a difference of night and day between the people there and the people here. Especially in Germany. Two or three of us Globetrotters would walk down a street and people invited us into their homes."

As Hawkins talked I wondered if the education he had received as a Globetrotter might have been superior to what he would have gotten as a basketball-playing jock at the University of Iowa.

By 1967 he no longer wanted to be separated from his wife and two children. He left the Globetrotters. On weekends he flew from Pittsburgh to New York to play "fooling-around" basketball with the Harlem Wizards, minor league Globetrotters. During the week he went to a schoolyard in north Pittsburgh, where he and his family were living, a basketball tucked under his arm.

"I'd shoot around for an hour or so by myself," he told me. "The trouble was, I had no one to play against."

"You must have been concerned about supporting your family," I said.

"Sure I was worried. I was twenty-four and getting on in age as far as a career was concerned in or out of sports. I had a family to support, as you say. But my mind was infected with basketball. Always has been. I couldn't get interested in doing anything else."

Then came the ABA in 1967. He was asked to play for the Pipers. "They had no trouble signing me," Connie told me, with a soft, sardonic laugh. "Actually, I was surprised they wanted me. I didn't think anyone in the new league would know who I was or what I could do."

The league soon found out what the NBA had been missing. In that 1967–68 season Connie led the ABA in scoring with 26 points a game. He was voted the league's Most Valuable Player. And the Pipers won the ABA championship. A year later, the team now playing in Minnesota, Connie talked to a *Life* magazine writer, Dave Wolf, who wrote a book, *Foul!* that spelled out the flimsy reasons the NBA had used to bar Hawkins, Jackson, Moe, and Brown. A lawyer, meanwhile, had filed a $6 million damage suit on Connie's behalf against the NBA. The NBA settled out of court. It gave Connie more than $1 million and a contract to play with the Phoenix Suns at the start of the 1969–70 season. In that first year in the NBA, Connie showed what he would have been like during his prime years as he scored 24 points a game, tops on the Suns.

His swoops to the basket along the baseline astonished veteran NBA stars. Years later one seven-foot center talked to a *Sports Illustrated* writer about the kind of thing that The Hawk did as he floated toward the basket with the ball held in the palm of his stretched-out right arm.

"Connie got the ball in the corner," said

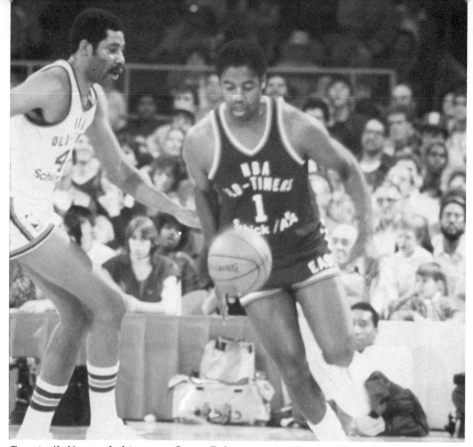

Connie (*left*) guards his man, Oscar Robertson, during an old-timers game in 1983.

the center, "and as I started to come out at him, he put the ball on the floor and drove at me. I took a step backward to protect the basket, knowing that eventually he'd have to go up at me, and after one dribble, he did. Now you have to remember that this is my home court, and I am ready for him. I prided myself on being The Man under the basket, and he knew who he was coming at. So he's up, and now I'm up. And then suddenly, he goes around me in midair. He twists completely around, goes under the basket, comes out the other side, and puts it up backward and in. He not only has to make a great move to score, as far as I'm concerned, he has to make the *greatest* move ever, because he's doing it against me! No way in my mind does anybody—not even King King on a ladder—make that play. It's the most awesome play I've ever seen, and I'm awed by it still."

The awed player, who was not easily awed by anything or anybody on a basketball court, was, arguably, the greatest defensive player of all time—Wilt Chamberlain.

With those kinds of moves, Connie averaged from 16 to 20 points a season for Phoenix from 1970 to 1973. He played for the Los Angeles Lakers for two seasons before retiring after the 1975 season. He returned to the NBA for its 1984 old-timers game in Denver and brought the crowd to its feet by doing a Dr. J-like swoop, taking off from the foul line to float through the air for a lay-up. Now involved with a number of businesses in the Pittsburgh area, Connie lives with his family in Wilkinsburg, Pennsylvania. During the spring of 1984, still lured by faraway places, he toured the Orient with a team of former NBA stars led by Earl (The Pearl) Monroe. In the Hawk's mind, obviously, there is still that infection called basketball.

Carol Heiss displays the form and grace that won the 1959 world championship.

Carol Heiss

I MET CAROL HEISS FOR THE FIRST TIME in the fall of 1955 when she was fifteen years old. She lived with her family in the Ozone Park section of New York City's borough of Queens. Her father, a baker, and her mother had come to America from Germany before the war. Carol, born on January 20, 1940, was the oldest of three children. Her sister, Nancy, was fourteen, her brother,

Bruce, twelve. Although neither Marie nor Edward Heiss had ever been ice skaters, their three children had won skating championships. Their talent had been discovered and encouraged by their tall, dimpled, and energetic mother—but at a cost in time and money that to me seemed staggering.

"There is talent in every child," Marie Heiss, a woman in her forties, told me as we sat in the living room of her apartment in a quiet middle-class neighborhood. Her three children were seated in a row on a nearby couch. "It is up to the parents," she said with a slight German accent, "to find that talent and help it grow. The best way to find it, I think, is to play with your children as often as you can."

She told me how she had spotted that talent in Carol, her oldest, whose straw-blond hair was neatly pony-tailed. "When Carol was about two and a half, I bought her a pair of roller skates. I was astonished; she could skate as well as any teenager. Then, about two years later, she and I went to an ice-skating rink and without any instructions at all she went skimming beautifully across the ice. Right then I decided to get Carol professional instruction. And when my two other children got to be about five and I could see that they also were natural skaters, I got instruction for them too."

Some ten years later the five-foot-two, one-hundred-ten-pound Carol was America's second-best figure skater, second only to Boston's Tenley Albright, then twenty, who was world champion. Nancy, fourteen, was the U.S. National Junior Champion, and Bruce, twelve, had skated with Nancy to win the 1955 Eastern Junior Pair Championship.

Mrs. Heiss and her children then began to tell me what those titles had cost. Each morning all three children arose at five thirty and rode, sleepy-eyed, by subway into Manhattan. At six thirty or so, in wintry darkness or the mugginess of summer, they arrived at the New York Skating Club on

Manhattan's West Side. Obeying the orders of instructor Pierre Brunet, a former Olympic gold medalist, they skated from seven thirty to ten or later. Then they hurried over to the Professional Children's School for several hours of reading, writing, math, and all the other things that less talented kids did from nine to three. From three to five or six the Heiss kids skated or attended ballet class, which is a must for figure skaters. Home by seven or eight, they studied until ten and flopped into bed.

The parents had to make their own sacrifices. Brunet's lessons were $6 a half-hour for each child and ballet lessons were $10 an hour. Skating costumes cost $60 to $80 and then there were traveling expenses. By 1955 Carol had traveled twice to Europe to skate in international meets, the costs paid by her father and mother. Mrs. Heiss told me that she figured that the skating bill for Carol alone had come so far to more than $15,000.

I asked her if she thought the results had been worth the expense. "Oh, of course," she said with a proud look. "Don't you think that these children"—she pointed to her trio of champions—"are the better for having done something with their God-given talent?" I looked at the children, their pride in themselves and in their mother radiating from their faces, and I told Marie Heiss that I agreed.

A few months later Carol went to Cortina d'Ampezzo in Italy for the 1956 Olympic Games. Her mother, although by now suffering from cancer, accompanied her, as usual paying her own expenses. Tenley Albright won the gold medal, Carol the silver. A few weeks later, however, Carol topped Tenley to win the world championship. And the pony-tailed girl who had never cried in defeat, she later told me, cried happy tears in victory. Carol's victory was especially important to her because it became a final prize for her mother, who died eight months later.

During the next two years I saw Carol occasionally when she skated at Grossinger's Country Club, a resort about an hour's drive from New York City, which often invited sports celebrities to perform. I went there in the fall of 1958 to interview Hayes Alan Jenkins, who had won the gold medal in men's figure skating at the 1956 Games, and his brother David, who had finished third. Hayes had retired from amateur skating, performing as a professional in an ice show while studying law at Harvard. David had replaced him as world champion and hoped to succeed him as Olympic champion at the 1960 Games. While interviewing the Jenkins family, I was struck by the fact that it was the boys' mother, Sara Jenkins, who had discovered their talent and then encouraged them to become champions, despite the burdensome costs. Like Marie Heiss, Sara Jenkins was very much the ambitious and dreaming "skating mother," a type I would meet a third time some twenty years later when I interviewed 1982 world champion Elaine Zayak. It was Elaine's mother, I learned, who had first put her into ice skates and who had then been willing to spend as much as $20,000 a year for lessons and costumes to see her daughter become a champion. In almost the same words that Marie Heiss had used in 1955, Gerri Zayak said to me at her Paramus, New Jersey, home in 1983: "It was expensive, but what choice did we have—we couldn't let all that talent be wasted, could we?"

In talking to Hayes and David Jenkins at Grossinger's in 1958, I discovered that the twenty-four-year-old Hayes, while traveling around the country, had been corresponding with his former Olympic teammate, the eighteen-year-old Carol, who was attending New York University while training with Pierre Brunet for the 1960 Games. (Her brother and sister had taken very early retirement.) My wife Barbara asked Hayes what Carol was like and in his best good young lawyer's firm voice he said something to the effect that she was very young. Nei-

ther Barbara nor I suspected there could be a romance between the two.

In 1960, just before Carol left Manhattan for Squaw Valley, California, and the Olympic Games, I interviewed her and she told me this story about a fellow skater, Holland's Sjoukie Dijkstra.

"I want to be an Olympic champion very badly—this could be my last chance," Carol told me. "But if I can't win then I hope the winner will be Chokey, which is how I pronounce Sjoukie. Though she is my age, twenty, and though I have finished ahead of her in four world championships, she has become something of an idol to me.

"I've known her since we were fifteen. I remember Chokey best for something that happened when I defended my world championship last year at Colorado Springs. She was really eager to beat me. Once she walked into the dressing room with a woebegone look. 'I was just awful doing my figures for the judges this morning,' she said. 'Oh, cheer up,' I said. 'You said the same thing yesterday'—I was teasing her—'and look what a high score you got. Why, Chokey, I think you're just trying to make me overconfident.' She burst into laughter.

"The next day Chokey made me laugh over something. We teased each other constantly, helping each other to forget the dressing-room jitters that can ruin a skater before an event. Never once did we say so, but I know that both of us had the same thought; 'I am going all-out to beat you on the ice—but I'll do all I can to help you off the ice.'

"Chokey finished third while I was first. When we stepped up to the platform to receive our medals, Chokey leaned over to me and whispered: 'I am proud to be standing on the same platform with you.'

"I only wished I had said it first for I was prouder to be on that platform with Chokey. Previously I had read thousands of words about how international competition can help people of different nations to cooperate and to know each other better. But Chokey, in a dozen simple words, had made me understand."

At Squaw Valley a few weeks later, Chokey finished second and won the silver. Carol stood on the top platform to receive the gold. Later she congratulated another gold-medal winner, David Jenkins, who had succeeded his brother as Olympic champion. And shortly after the Olympics Carol and Hayes had an announcement to make—they would soon be married.

They were married in New York on April 30, 1960. Carol had promised her mother that she would not turn professional until she won an Olympic gold medal. The medal won, she toured with an ice show. She also appeared in a movie, *Snow White and the Three Stooges*, with the slapsticking trio,

and occasionally you will see the movie on late-night television. She and Hayes settled down in Akron, his hometown, where he became a corporate lawyer for a tire manufacturer. They raised three children, all athletic, says Carol, but none showed any interest in ice skating. Their parents were relieved. "We'd hear people say to them when we went ice skating on a pond," says Carol, "'Oh, will you be as famous as your mother and father?' Hayes and I said nothing to each other, but we had a silent agreement to do nothing to push them into a sport that was very good to us but very demanding." During the past few years Carol has been teaching aspiring Olympic figure skaters from across the nation at an Akron rink. She was a commentator for ABC radio at the 1984 Winter Olympic Games.

Hayes and Carol Jenkins in Akron in 1984.

Hogan flashes a rare smile during a 1941 match.

Ben Hogan

I WALKED TOWARD THE WEE ICE MON, as the Scots called Ben Hogan after he won the 1953 British Open at Carnoustie. He had just stepped out of his car on the curving driveway at the Seminole Country Club near West Palm Beach on a cool March day in 1958. He was wearing chocolate-brown slacks, a wine-red sweater, and a checked sportshirt open at the neck. His famous white cap was set squarely above his broad forehead. A bantam of a man at about five-foot-eight and one hundred sixty-five pounds, he had the I'm-part-of-this-elegant-world assurance of the millionaire club members here at Seminole. Yet, I sensed, he stood out from them like a pickup truck among a fleet of limousines. The chesty body, the hard face, the blocky chin, and the bullet-hole eyes flashed the message that here was a working man.

I introduced myself, explaining that I and a photographer had come here to take pictures of him for an article I was editing on his chances of winning the 1958 U.S. Open. "Fine," he said, "but if you don't mind waiting for about an hour, I'd like to get in some practice." I thought the drawl was remarkably gentle for someone who looked so much like a gunfighter.

"Can we watch you practice?"

"I know of no law against it, do you?" he said, a trace of a smile forming around his thin lips. He turned to say something to a short black man, his caddie, who had suddenly appeared at his side, and that was the last smile I would see on the face of Ben Hogan for two hours. Hogan, I learned, never looked at a clock when he practiced, and so what he said would be an hour stretched to almost two.

During those two hours I stood behind Hogan as he whacked what surely must have been at least two hundred balls. Before each shot he stood solemnly over the ball, looking down at it, then looking out to where he had positioned the caddie, anywhere from 50 yards away to more than 250 yards, depending on the club he was swinging.

He drew back the club and—*whoosh!*—the ball streaked away like a white rope shot from a gun, leaped upward with that second liftoff the pro golfers give to their shots, then seemed to hang forever like a white pinhole in the blue sky. When it came down—50 yards away, 150 yards away, 250 yards away—the caddie, positioned before the shot by Hogan with a wave of his arm, never had to walk more than a dozen steps to pick up the ball. If Hogan had placed a blanket out there on the grass where he signaled the caddy to stand for each shot, I am sure that nine out of ten of his shots would have rolled dead on the blanket.

I stood amazed by such accuracy. For the first time I became aware that the pro golfer plays a different game from the rest of us who consider dropping a ball on a huge green from a hundred yards away a major accomplishment. Here was a man dropping a ball from more than a hundred yards away onto an area no bigger, compared to an ordinary green, than a handkerchief.

And not all that pleased, I surmised, by what he was doing.

That was the second surprise I got that day while watching Hogan practice. He obviously thought that he could be doing at least a little better. After each shot he seemed to study the distance between himself and the caddie, frowning, his expression that of a man isolated in a booth and trying to work out a complex mathematical problem step by step. As he stared into space, he smoked a cigarette that he dropped onto the grass before the next shot. He never said a word to me or the half dozen others who were watching, and we never spoke to him, in my case partly out of fear of irritating him, but also because I sensed he was so locked inside that invisible booth that he probably would not hear what anyone said to him. A few years later I read something he had once told writer Bob Bumbry: "I never hit a careless practice shot." I could testify to the truth of that.

Finally he finished. As the caddy, only a speck in the distance when Hogan took his final wood shots, trotted in to take care of Ben's clubs, Hogan walked toward the photographer and me. There was a faraway look in those small eyes, and I wondered for a moment if he would remember having promised to pose for the magazine photographs. He nodded absently when I reminded him who we were and why we were here. We walked to a nearby practice green. He said we could take the pictures in a few minutes; first, he wanted to do some putting. He putted on the practice green for almost a half-hour. Then, smiling agreeably, he asked us what we wanted him to do.

We posed him on the ninth green, the pin's flag fluttering behind him. I had heard he could be impatient with photographers and interviewers, but he wasn't on this day, asking us at the end if we were sure we had all the pictures we wanted.

Only once did I see anger flash from those small eyes. I asked him if we might take a series of sequence photographs to show the legendary Hogan swing.

He glared at me for several moments, face stony, but then a smile began to move the square chin. "Oh, no," he said in his pleasant Texan's drawl. "Oh, no. I don't give away for nothing what's my stock in trade."

I had realized my mistake immediately. Publishers paid him a great deal of money to show that Hogan swing. Why should they pay him money if he gave away that swing's secrets for nothing?

"Of course," I said, "you're right." Later, after I had said goodbye and watched him walk in that confident, head-down fashion of his toward the clubhouse, I thought to myself, There goes a man who knows the value of what he owns and plans to squeeze every last dollar out of what he has. Years later I understood him better when I read what he had once said to a writer: "I know a lot of people don't like me. They say I'm selfish and hard, that I think only of golf. Maybe I do. But there's a reason. I know what it means to be hungry. I sold newspapers around the Fort Worth railroad station when I was twelve. I never intend to be hungry again . . ."

William Benjamin Hogan was born in Dublin, Texas, on August 13, 1912, the son of a village blacksmith. He grew up with his father's blocky build and muscled arms, but at twelve he was small for his age. The family had moved to Fort Worth and Ben, wondering if he could carry the players' heavy bags, took a job as a caddie at the Glen Garden Golf Club. Club members called him Little Ben.

Each afternoon after work the caddies hit balls from the practice tees. The caddie who hit the shortest drive had to pick up all the balls hit by the others. Club members, departing late in the evenings, chuckled as they watched Little Ben scurrying up and down hills to pick up balls.

He decided to try a longer swing. He brought back the driver as far as he could bring it, the clubhead dipping close to the ground. He swung and hit the longest drive of his life. Within a week of practice he was among the longest hitters among the caddies.

"What happened, Hogan?" a member asked.

"My rule, sir," said Ben, "is if you can't outplay them, then outwork them."

At fifteen he won the club's caddie championship, succeeding another golfer who also would give an era of American golf his name: Byron Nelson. In 1931, just out of high school, he drove to California to join the pro tour. Three months later he came back to Fort Worth penniless. For four years he "outworked" them, practicing while teaching at a country club. In 1938, his wife Valerie at his side, $1,400 in his pocket, he drove to California to try the tour one last time. Four weeks later, failing to win even a dime in three tournaments, the Hogans drove into Oakland in their wheezing car, $85 left. If they didn't win here, they knew, they would have to go home and forget about tournament golf. "The night before the first round," he once recalled, "I didn't sleep at all."

He shot a 66 on the first round, then hung close enough to the leaders to win $380 and stay on the tour. By 1939 he was among the tour's biggest winners and by 1942 he was golf's biggest winner, earning close to $30,000 at a time when first-place purses were as paltry as $5,000. But this was the Byron Nelson era, Nelson winning all the major tournaments—the Masters, the PGA, the Open—while Hogan had yet to win one.

The Nelson Era continued until 1946, Lord Byron a civilian while Hogan, Sam Snead, and other prewar pros were in the service. In 1946, out of the service, Hogan won the PGA championship, his first major title, and in 1948 the Open. Nelson had retired and the Hogan Era had dawned.

Fellow pros called him the Hawk. "With those cold eyes and tight jaw," said one pro, "he comes down those fairways looking like he'll swoop away with anything and anyone that gets in his way." Valerie seldom followed him on the course. "It doesn't make any difference whether Valerie follows him or not," another pro said. "The way Ben concentrates, he couldn't see her anyway."

Early in 1949, racing on a Texas highway with Valerie in an early-morning fog, his car was rammed front-on by a bus. Valerie was hurt only slightly. Hogan's slim body was crumpled, a pelvis bone fractured, a collarbone broken, his left ankle splintered. Doctors said he would live but never again play tournament golf.

Three months later he walked for the first time since the accident. Six months later he was gripping a club. Eighteen months later he came to the Merion club outside Philadelphia for the 1950 U.S. Open. He was among the leaders the first two days. On the final day he had to play 36 holes. He came to the thirty-second hole needing only four pars to win. His drawn, pale face showed the exhaustion of having to walk some 10 miles so far today on those recently mended legs. He missed a putt on 32, then another, and finished two over par with a 74. He was tied for the lead with Lloyd Mangrum and George Fazio. Tomorrow there would be an 18-hole playoff. "He can't play eighteen more holes," people said at Merion that evening. "You can see he's a wreck."

He played the 18 holes, stroked in a 50-footer for a birdie on 17, and walked away from the playoff with his second U.S. Open.

In 1951 he won his third Open on a tricked-up course, Oakland Hills, in Birmingham, Michigan. Not one in the field of 162 of America's best amateurs and pros could break par during the first three rounds. On the last round Ben shot a 3-under-par 67 to clinch victory. He delivered a memorable victory statement that summed up every man's secret mission on a golf course: "I'm happy because I brought the beast to her knees."

He would win four U.S. Opens, tying the record then held by Bobby Jones. In 1953 he won the Masters, the Open, and the British Open, a grand slam. In 1955 he seemed to have grasped his record fifth Open only to lose to an unknown, Jack Fleck, who shot a birdie 3 on 18 to tie Hogan and then beat him the next day in a playoff.

By the late 1950s he had lost his putting touch. "I can do all the things I could ever do from the tee to green," he said, "but then I have trouble putting the ball in the hole." He added, eyes twinkling, "You would think that putting a ball in a hole two feet away would be easy, wouldn't you, but it's not easy for me anymore."

The yips, as Sam Snead called aging's attack on the nerves, had brought down the Hawk. He tied for second at the 1959 Open and came close to winning the 1960 Open, but lost the lead to the eventual winner, a rangy golfer from Latrobe, Pennsylvania—

Arnold Palmer. The Hogan Era had ended, the Palmer Era had begun.

In the late 1960s Hogan appeared only at the major tournaments. At the 1967 Masters he thrilled thousands by shooting a 30 on the back 9, and millions more hoped to see him (and, of course, themselves) replay a triumph of youth. It would not happen then nor ever again for Bantam Ben, and his only appearances on the tour during the early 1970s came when the pros arrived at his home course, the Colonial, near where he lived in Fort Worth. In the 1980s, TV sponsors hoped to lure him into appearing at a Masters of Golf tournament for over-fifty golfers, but Ben stayed home in Fort Worth, where he was busy overseeing the production of Ben Hogan clubs for golfers unafflicted by the yips.

Ben (*left*) at the Masters in 1980 with two former pros, Gene Sarazen (*center*) and Jack Burke, Jr.

Carl Hubbell

HE WAS STANDING ALONE IN THE HOTEL lobby in St. Louis. He was as tall and gaunt as I had remembered him from the 1940s when I'd watched him as I sat in the Polo Grounds bleachers. His left arm, his pitching arm, dangled at his side, twisted so that the palm of the hand faced outward. His sparse, iron-gray hair was combed straight back, 1930s style. As I approached him I saw

King Carl warms up in 1941.
←

that though the long, rawboned face was deeply lined, it was the same Gary Cooperish face that I'd seen in newspaper photos when Carl Hubbell was my first sports idol. I'd listened on a radio when he had triumphed over cold and rain and Yankee bats in the first game of the 1936 World Series, and now I was walking toward King Carl, as we called him, to ask about that game.

"I am swinging a heavy schoolbag home from St. Jerome's school on a windy, rain-swept day in early October of 1936," I once wrote in a book about the World Series. "Stopping some fifty yards short of the corner of Willis Avenue and 138th Street in the Bronx, I see three or four men clustered around a radio perched on a chair outside what I remember was a shoe store. The radio announcer is describing a Series game at the Polo Grounds, only an hour's walk from where I am standing but a place I have never seen. He is talking in excited tones about a man named Carl Hubbell, who is pitching gallantly, the announcer tells us, in the rain and the mud at the Polo Grounds. I drop my schoolbag between my legs. I stand there for an hour or more in the gusty, dripping autumn wetness, sharing the discomfort of Hubbell who has become, within an hour, a hero to me. Hubbell and the Giants beat the Yankees that day, 6–1—I have never forgotten the score—and after the game I walk with a swagger along Willis Avenue, glowing inside, proud to be a Carl Hubbell fan and a Giant fan."

Now, in 1967, some thirty years later, I was standing next to this gray-haired, six-foot, one-hundred-seventy-pound man whose pitching that day had made me fall in love with baseball. I introduced myself and told him how thrilled I had been listening to

that game. How difficult had it been, I asked, pitching against a team like the Yankees with a cold rain blowing in his face?

"Well," he said, slowly with an Oklahoma drawl, staring at the floor and obviously both pleased and embarrassed, "you know, it was raining, but it was as hard for the other guy, the other pitcher, as it was for me."

I was disappointed by his reply—I suppose I had expected to hear something more heroic—but I was to discover in this and other conversations with Hubbell that he was a plain man. He looked back on his accomplishments with a pride he locked within himself. And he talked of baseball in simple no-nonsense fashion. "We had a book on all the Yankee hitters," he told me, speaking of that 1936 Series that the Yankees won, 4 games to 1. "Our scouts had watched the Yankees and they told us the usual things: pitch so-and-so inside, that sort of thing. But I have always thought those World Series books on hitters were vastly overrated. Before every World Series you will hear how one team is going to pitch so-and-so high and tight, and this other guy low and away. But no two pitchers can pitch alike. A book could have told me and Fred Fitzsimmons to pitch tight to a certain hitter. But a hitter might murder a tight pitch by me while a tight pitch by Fitz might get him out."

Hubbell's best pitch was the screwball, or screwjie, as today's ballplayers call it. In effect, it is a reverse curve. A left-hander throws a curve by twisting his wrist to the left—that is, away from him, or counterclockwise. A left-hander's curve breaks in on a right-handed batter, away from a lefty hitter. The screwball is thrown by twisting the left wrist to the right, a clockwise motion. The screwball drops down and away from a right-handed hitter, down and in on a lefty hitter. It also pulls, tugs, and jerks muscles and tendons in the lower arm, a corkscrewing effect that changed the direction of Hubbell's arm. Los Angeles sportswriter Jim

Murray once wrote that "Hubbell's left hand turned out instead of in. He almost looked as if he was trying to slip you something behind his back. From the looks of his arm, they could call the pitch the corkscrew ball."

By any name the pitch bought Hubbell's passage from the minors to the big leagues. He was born in Carthage, Missouri, on June 22, 1903, but grew up in Meeker, Oklahoma. Pitching for a minor-league team in Oklahoma, he developed the screwball while he was trying to find a way to make his curveball sink.

The Detroit Tigers bought his contract and took him to spring training in 1925. The Tiger manager, Hall of Famer Ty Cobb, told Hubbell to give up the screwball or "it'll cripple up your arm." The twenty-two-year-old lanky kid from Oklahoma followed Cobb's advice, ducked line drives that zoomed by his large ears, and was dropped to the minor leagues. There he labored without either the screwball or much success for the next three years. In 1928 the Tigers sold him to Beaumont in the Texas League. A manager encouraged him to throw the screwball. The pitch raised the eyebrows of a Giant scout. The Giants paid $30,000 for Hubbell early in the 1928 season.

At first he was leery about trying to throw the screwball against big-league hitters. When he did, striking out future Hall of Famer Chick Hafey of the Cardinals, his astonished catcher, Frank (Shanty) Hogan, told him: "I don't know what the hell that pitch is, kid, but keep throwing it."

In 1929 he pitched a no-hitter against the Pirates, the first in the majors in eleven years. In 1933, the Giants locked in a pennant duel with the Cardinals, he went to the mound against the Cardinals' Tex Carleton in a game at the Polo Grounds. For seventeen innings he and Carleton did not allow a run. In the eighteenth the Giants scored to win a marathon four-hour 1–0 battle. In pitching the equivalent of a doubleheader,

Hubbell struck out twelve, walked nobody, and gave up only six hits. He won 23 games that year, lost 12, posted a league-leading 1.66 earned-run average, and was named the league's Most Valuable Player. The Giants won the pennant and beat the Washington Senators in the Series, King Carl winning 2 games.

He is best remembered today, however, for strikeouts that never counted in the official record books. Pitching in the 1934 All-Star Game, the second to be held between the two leagues, this one at the Polo Grounds, King Carl struck out five men in a row. The five men were named Babe Ruth, Lou Gehrig, Jimmy Foxx, Al Simmons, and Joe Cronin, all five now members of baseball's Hall of Fame.

"There was a World Series air as the game began," a *New York Times* reporter wrote of the game, played on July 10, 1934. The pregame ceremonies—and the tension of a World Series atmosphere—rattled the usually imperturbable Hubbell. "There was a lot of picture taking and stuff before the game," he told me in 1983. "I kept saying to myself, 'Let's get going with this thing, let's get it started.' I was so pumped up that when the game began, I was throwing too hard."

Pitching without his usual smoothness, Hubbell was tagged for a single by the American League's leadoff man, Charley Gehringer, and he walked Heinie Manush. Toward the plate, the crowd of 50,000 screaming, stepped Babe Ruth.

The National League infield huddled around Hubbell at the mound. He was given expert advice on how to pitch to Ruth; three of the four infielders were National League managers: first baseman Bill Terry of the Giants, second baseman Frank Frisch of the Cardinals, and third baseman Pie Traynor of the Pirates. The advice fell on the numbed senses of Hubbell. "I never heard what was said," he told me. "I was too busy having a meeting with myself. I told myself, 'You're not going to be around here long if you don't settle down.'"

He reminded himself, he told me, to throw only screwballs at Ruth and the succeeding American League hitters. "They'd seen better fastballs than I had," he said, "but none of them had ever seen my screwball."

A screwball struck out Ruth, who "looked decidedly puzzled," a reporter wrote. Next to bat was Lou Gehrig. On a three-and-two count, he waved at a screwball and struck out. Boston's Jimmy Foxx lunged at another screwball for a third-straight strikeout that ended the inning.

In the second inning Hubbell struck out Philadelphia's Al Simmons, a lifetime .344 hitter, and Washington's Joe Cronin, a .301 hitter. The Yankees' Bill Dickey ended the five-strikeout skein by slapping a single. Hubbell then struck out New York pitcher Vernon (Lefty) Gomez to end the inning. In two innings he had faced nine future Hall of Famers and struck out six of them, five in a row.

"It was something you always remember," Hubbell told me in 1983, "because it was unexpected and you always remember the unexpected."

Hubbell again won the Most Valuable Player prize in 1936, leading the league with 26 victories, as the Giants won another pennant. He won 16 in a row from July 16 to the end of the 1936 season, then won 8 in a row in the early part of the 1937 season. Those 24 straight victories are 5 more than the big-league record of 19 set in 1912 by Rube Marquard, but do not constitute a record since they were set over two seasons (and broken, as Hubbell always pointed out, by a loss in the 1936 Series to the Yankees). He won 22 in 1937 as the Giants won a second straight pennant, then beat the Yankees once in the Series while losing once. The Yankees also won that Series to begin a string of four straight championships from 1936 to 1939 and six over the eight years from 1936 to

1943. In that stretch of time only one other pitcher, the Cardinals' Johnny Beazley, matched King Carl in beating the Yankees twice in Series play.

Hubbell's twisted left arm began to ache in 1938 and never again was he the pitcher he had been. He retired in 1943 with a record of 253 wins and 154 defeats, an earned-run average of 2.98. He became the director of the Giants' farm system and directed scouts who sent to New York and San Francisco some of the greatest black and Hispanic players of the 1950s and 1960s, notably Willie Mays, Monte Irvin, Juan Marichal, Felipe Alou, and Willie McCovey. He was elected to the Hall of Fame in 1947. A part-time scout for the Giants, he now lives in Mesa, Arizona, and was a frequent spectator at Arizona spring training games in the 1980s. He always frowned on opposing players fraternizing before a game. "I never believed in it," he told me in 1983. "Suppose a fan saw me talking to Lou Gehrig before a game. Then in the game Gehrig hits one up into the seats off me. The fan, he's got to think, Is there something going on here or what?"

Today Carl is a part-time scout with the San Francisco Giants.

The Golden Jet as a Black Hawk in 1965.

Bobby Hull

THE GOLDEN JET SAT ON A GREEN BENCH in a dressing room buried under Madison Square Garden. He glared at me, resentment flaring in his sky-blue eyes. His thick legs were stretched out in front of him. He wore only gray gym shorts and a towel draped around his muscle-slabbed shoulders. A Chicago Black Hawk equipment man was picking up soiled towels and toss-

ing them into a laundry wagon. The only sound in the vaultlike room was the scuffing of the man's shoes on the concrete floor.

"What's in it for me? What's in it for Bobby Hull?" Bobby Hull said again to me. He had asked me if I would pay him to be interviewed, and I had said I couldn't. I suspected he was sorry he'd asked, because, after all, I was a fan as well as a writer and Bobby Hull, believe it, would do most anything for a fan.

The equipment man left; we were alone. I decided to ignore his request for pay, and I soon found that he was more than willing to talk for no pay. At this point in his career, the winter of 1972, he had scored almost 600 goals over fifteen National Hockey League seasons. He had a chance to top Gordie Howe's record of 786. "Do you think much about Howe's record?" I asked.

His gnarled, thirty-three-year-old face, crowned by a sparse field of blond hair (some of it recently transplanted), twisted into an expression of contempt. "If I was told that I could own all the records that have ever been set if I quit tomorrow, I wouldn't do it," he said in a harsh voice. "Records don't mean that much to me. Hell, they will be broken. Look at all those big young fellows coming into the league, big guys whose mothers have been giving them vitamins all their lives. Look at Phil Esposito. If he plays a few more years, he will have every scoring record there is. So what will it mean if I hold them a short while?" He shrugged his thick shoulders.

Then he remembered what he loved best next to hockey and his fans—his kids. "Sure," he said in a voice that had lost the contempt, "it would be nice if my daughter could say, 'My dad did this or that.'" The look of cynicism that had appeared on his face faded as a dad imagined his little girl bragging about him. "But, hell, I just enjoy scoring goals. That's why I play hockey—to score goals, the kick I get out of scoring goals. If I set a record, fine. But the goals themselves, they give me all the satisfaction I need."

Swiftly, like an oncoming summer storm, the cynicism and contempt returned. "Let those younger guys have all the records," he said with a growl that seemed to come from deep within his five-foot-eleven, one-hundred-ninety-pound body. "They're welcome to them all. Let *them* feel that pressure." He laughed, a cold, barking laugh. "Let them hear people tell you every day, before every game—the management, the press, the players—Go out there and *do* it, score one or two goals for us . . . do it . . . do it . . ."

He rubbed a towel briskly across his thick, hairy chest. He glanced at me, seemingly embarrassed. "I need the towel for the sweat," he said. "I always sweat like this when the game gets closer. I can feel it inside me, in the pit of my stomach, the adrenaline's flowing already and what's the time—only one o'clock in the afternoon. When I get out there at seven thirty tonight that old adrenaline will really be flowing. It's not good; it's hard on the nervous system. But you can't play any other way.

"Ten, fifteen years ago I just wanted to play hockey." The cynical smile turned to a boyish grin. "I loved hockey. Just give me that old thisket and let me shoot it, let me go. I just wanted to chase after that puck, race all over that ice." He had been speaking quickly but now the pace of his voice slowed down. "Now it's less racing around. Maybe there is less enthusiasm and I am more . . ." He stopped.

"Professional," I suggested.

"Yes," he said tiredly. "It's more of a business now, scoring goals to win games. Instead of the legs I use more of upstairs."

He was still using the same shot whose velocity had terrified NHL goalies for more than a decade. Once, in a game against Montreal, he drove the puck into the skull of Johnny Bower, knocking him unconscious. Bower was replaced by Terry Sawchuk. A minute later Hull drove another puck that kayoed Sawchuk. The speed of the shot had been estimated at 119 miles an hour.

I mentioned that figure and the contemptuous smile curled his lips. "I don't know where they got that," he said. "I know that no one ever measured it. But if they say a pitcher's fastball has been measured at a hundred miles an hour, then I'm sure I hit a puck at least one hundred nineteen miles an hour. When I shoot a puck from sixty feet, it gets to the cage faster than any pitcher's fastball, I know that."

For much of the next week, I traveled with Hull and the Hawks on a road trip that took us from New York to Montreal to Detroit and then back to Chicago. On planes, in hotel rooms, buses, and dressing rooms, we talked about his past, present, and future. He was born on January 3, 1939, in Point Anne, Ontario. A high-school teammate was a skinny, bone-hard center, Stan Mikita; the two eighteen-year-olds were invited to the St. Catharine's training camp of the Black Hawks in the fall of 1957. An hour before a preseason game with the Rangers, the blond, hulking Hull was told to suit up for the game.

The high-school senior rapped in two goals and the Hawks signed him to a big-league contract; he was the youngest player ever signed by the team. When the 1957–58 season began, he was on a line for the first game. In 1959–60, his third season, he led the league in goals with 39 and in scoring points (goals plus assists) with 81. A season later the Hawks won the Stanley Cup.

Twice during the 1960s and early 1970s he led the league in scoring. His long-striding speed, and the momentum he built up with his quickness and bulk, plus the speed of his slap shots, made him the league's most feared scorer. Opposing teams retaliated with "shadows" who tried to stop Hull with body checks. They swung sticks that hooked, held, and slashed him. One stick tore out six of his teeth. Another splattered his nose, smashing the orbital bones near the bridge. Twice in one season he was tripped and tore knee ligaments.

One afternoon as we watched TV in his hotel room in Detroit, I talked to him about how he had been harassed illegally. "The shadow men," he snarled, his lips curling in contempt. "The less said about them the better."

Damage had been done to him off the ice. He had invested in a cattle ranch in Ontario and in Bobby Hull Enterprises, a public-relations firm in Toronto. Neither had been profitable. He talked to me of people who had not been helpful to him as a businessman. "There are always people," he said, staring at the floor, "who want to ride on your coattails because they can't do it themselves." He laughed icily.

The phone rang. Calling was a business associate from Chicago. In a mild, disinterested voice, Hull asked a few questions, listened for a while, and then said softly, "How are my kids. Are my kids all right?" He listened for a few minutes, said goodbye, and hung up. He stretched out on the bed. "I like hockey but I hate the traveling. I hate all the time I am away from my children. But hell, nothing is ideal . . . nothing is perfect. Anything worth doing has its drawbacks."

His five children, his fans, the goals he had scored, they were what he treasured most after fifteen years of pro hockey. That night, after the Hawks had defeated the Red Wings, I saw Detroit fans clamor for his autograph as he tried to leave the dressing room. He was pushed against the wall by children and adults who shouted, "Bobby . . . Bobby . . . Bobby . . . please . . . Bobby . . ."

For a half-hour he patiently signed autographs while the team bus waited for him. Later, in a plane flying from Detroit to Chicago, I said, "You sure had a big crowd of fans back there in Detroit."

He turned toward me, surprise on his face. "Oh, no, that crowd wasn't really big,"

he said. He talked, his face shining with pride, about really big crowds that had mobbed him for his autograph. "Didn't you see that crowd in Montreal?" he said. "Didn't you see *that*? Now *that* was a crowd, they went wild . . ."

His teammates told me of seeing him limp, aching, into an airport lobby after a bruising game, the time near midnight. As dozens of people swarmed around him, he patiently sat down at a table and signed autographs for more than an hour, asking only that his fans form an orderly line so they wouldn't disturb anyone.

The jet plane was sliding down toward Chicago when I decided to bring up a sensitive subject: a hair transplant that had given the once-Golden Jet a new, albeit sparse, crop of blond hair. "It was painful, wasn't it," I said. "Why did you decide to do it?"

He shrugged, face flushing. "Ah, it was nothing," he said, looking away. "Anyway, who the hell would want to be bald?"

A few nights later I watched him smack in a goal to help the Hawks win, 3–1. In the dressing room I told him I was going back to New York. Our first unpleasantness, the business of his being paid for an interview, had been forgotten. "Did you get everything you wanted?" he asked. "Want anything more about my kids?"

That was one of his last games in the NHL and for the Hawks. That fall of 1972, for a sum said to be $2.75 million over ten years, the thirty-four-year-old Golden Jet jumped from the NHL to the Winnipeg Jets of the new World Hockey Association. The team was named for him—and he was its first coach. It went to the 1973 finals for the league's Stanley Cup, the Avco World Cup, but lost to New England. During the next five years he played often in pain, bothered by injuries and gout, but he stayed among the new league's high scorers. As the team's coach he fined players who refused autographs to fans. In a protest against the near-murderous violence of professional hockey, he sat out a game during the 1978–79 season. The WHA collapsed in 1979. In 1980 he attempted a comeback by joining the New York Rangers, but left the team before the season started. In recent years he has made several appearances in the Masters of Hockey games sponsored by the Phil Esposito Foundation. In 1984 he and his high-school buddy, Stan Mikita, who was also a high scorer for the Hawks in the 1960s and 1970s, were elected to the Hockey Hall of Fame. Characteristically, he was critical of the Hall of Fame for not being nicer to his beloved fans. The Hall of Fame in Toronto, he said, should not charge admission. "After twenty-three years of having to pay to see me play," he said, "I don't think people should have to pay to see my broken hockey sticks and dirty underwear."

Bobby waves to a Chicago Stadium crowd after receiving the Milestone Award in 1983.

Charley shows he is a passer and a scholar in 1966.

Charley Johnson

"NO ROOTING IN THE PRESS BOX" IS AN old rule of sports journalism. But if you believe that sports reporters have no favorites among the players they interview, you are a likely purchaser of a bridge during your next visit to the Big Apple. As I paced the sideline of Yankee Stadium on an October day in 1965, I rooted for the St. Louis Cardinals to beat the New York Giants. My only reason for hoping the Cardinals would win was their quarterback, Charley Johnson, whom I had come to admire.

The Giants led, 14–10, late in the fourth period, but the Cardinals were charging for the go-ahead touchdown. They rolled to the Cardinal 24, but on fourth and two the Giants held. As I stood behind the Cardinal bench, I saw the moon-faced Charley Johnson jog off the field. Blood poured from a gash on his chin. A trainer patched the gash, but the blood trickled through the bandage, spattering red dots on Charley's white jersey. A teammate glanced at the spots of blood and asked, "Are you all right?" Charley, staring intently at the action on the field, did not reply—or even seem to hear.

A minute later the Cardinals forced the Giants to punt, the ball rolling dead on the Cardinal 5. Charley buckled on the chin

112

strap of his helmet as he spoke to coach Charley Lemm. The huge crowd's noise washed against the concrete walls of the stadium and I could not hear what Charley said, but I did hear Lemm say, "Okay, do that."

There were fewer than two minutes left to score the touchdown the Cardinals needed to win. And there were 95 yards guarded by unfriendlies between the Cardinals and that touchdown. But within a minute, after mixing darting passes with bolts up the middle by his fullback, Charley steered the Cardinals to the Giant 14. The Cardinals were standing at their bench along the sideline. I ran down to near the end zone as the Cardinals came out of their huddle. It was fourth down, 10 yards to go. I sensed—and so did the New York crowd as it let out a hungry roar—that on this play the game would be both won and lost.

The Cardinals lined up. Johnson took the ball from the center, stepping back into the protective pocket. I saw his five-foot-nine wide receiver, Billy Gambrell, a pygmy among all the towering linemen, weave through the jumble of white and blue jerseys. He streaked toward the end zone, straight toward me. I could see his face under the white helmet as he turned to look over his shoulder. No Giant was within 5 yards of him. The ball flew out of Charley Johnson's right hand and arrowed on a low line toward Gambrell's outstretched hands. And then I saw Gambrell go down as though he had been shot.

Gambrell had tripped on a stubble of torn turf. The ball flew high over his sprawled body. It hit the grass, skipping crazily end over end toward me. As it came by, I gave it a kick that sent it bounding back toward a pair of grinning Giant defenders.

A few minutes later I sat in the dressing room with Charley as a doctor staunched the bleeding from the rip in his chin and stitched up the wound, Charley wincing every once in a while. When the doctor had gone, Charley stared impassively at the floor. He was watching a scene forming on the floor, coming into focus, dissolving, then coming into focus again—the scene of Gambrell dashing out for the pass, breaking into the open, and falling down as the pass flew over him.

Charley turned to me and said in his rounded Texas drawl, "I get that little pass to Billy, he's all alone, and this would be a different day." He stared again at the floor. "A *mighty* different day."

He absent-mindedly rubbed the bandaged chin. "On Tuesday I'll look at the game films and I'll look at the plays and I'll see how we could have scored. But anyone can see the right plays to call on a film. My job is to see them in a game."

He ran his hand through his wet, straw-yellow hair, the smile now rueful. "You know," he said, glancing at my pad on which I had been scribbling, "it's going to be kind of hard for you to find something to write about me."

I didn't think it would be so hard—and it wasn't. For one thing, Charley was the only pro quarterback I'd ever met who was also a chemical engineer. He was studying for his master's degree at Washington University in St. Louis while playing for the Cardinals. One day, a week before the game against the Giants, I visited him in his laboratory at the university where he and other graduate students were overseeing the construction of a machine called an extruder. "We designed it," he said, showing me the machine, which looked like a jumble of glass and metal snakes coiled together. "It will be used to test new plastic resins."

St. Louis friends had urged him to give up engineering and do public-relations work. Doors would swing open for him, they said, because he was a St. Louis hero. "I get a lot of job offers to do publicity work for people," he said, "and I'm the type who has trouble saying no to people. What I do, I use my schoolwork as an excuse to turn down job offers. Even if I could make more money in public relations, I'm not going to junk engineering until I find out whether I like it or not."

What also made Charley Johnson easy to write about was his good-natured, casual humility. I was driving with him one afternoon to his suburban home. He was returning from a shopping mall where he had handed out trophies to boys who had competed in a punt, pass, and kick competition. He was smoking one of the small cigars that he favored. "You signed a lot of autographs there today," I said. "It can get tiring after a while, can't it?"

"I don't mind," he said. "You know, when I was a kid back in Texas, we never saw any famous athletes. I know how much it would have meant to me to meet—or even just see—a sports star."

A sports star! He had called himself a sports star. Immediately he tried to pull the words back into his mouth. "Oh, look," he said, glancing at what I had scribbled in my note pad, "I mean it's not *me* they get a kick out of seeing. It's the position I hold—a pro quarterback—that's what they look up to."

As a high-school student in Big Spring, Texas, where he was born on November 22, 1938, Charley had talked to his parents about becoming a doctor, but alone he dreamed of being a football hero like John David Crow, then a Texas A & M running back. His chances seemed dim: of eight high-school quarterbacks in the Big Spring area during his senior year, Charley was the only one who didn't get at least one vote for the area's All-Star team.

No college wanted him as its quarterback. He went to a junior college that didn't have a football team. Charley played basketball, and played it so well that a New Mexico State scout offered the six-foot-one, one-hundred-ninety-pound freshman a basket-

ball scholarship and said he could also try out for the New Mexico State football team.

At State were a stable of racehorse receivers, notably Pervis Atkins and Bobby Gaiters, both later NFL receivers. Charley threw long arching passes, as many as 30 a game, that Gaiters and Atkins ran under to catch over their shoulders. Charley finished second in the nation in total offense in 1959, third in 1960. Twice the team went to the Sun Bowl and both years Charley was on the winning team and voted the game's Most Valuable Player. Away from football he won A grades as an engineering major.

By now he was married to a high-school sweetheart and both he and Barbara thought they might settle down in New Mexico, perhaps Las Cruces, while Charley began a career in engineering. They were surprised when Charley was chosen by the Cardinals in the 1961 draft. "I'd seen only one pro game live," Charley told me one day in St. Louis after a practice, lighting a cigar. "I decided to go to the camp just to see what pro football players were really like. I wanted to get a close look at all the famous names I'd read about—Unitas, John David Crow, Tittle. I figured that even if I was cut the second day, the thrill of getting to see some of those guys close up would be worth it all."

At the 1961 Cardinal camp he started as fifth of five quarterbacks. "I had a good day at one scrimmage and I told myself, 'This isn't so hard,' Then I started to read about defenses and I thought, 'Oh, no, I'll never learn all this.'"

He learned so well that by 1962 he was the Cardinal's number-one quarterback. In 1964, when I joined him for a week, the Cardinals were flying close to first in the NFL's East. The Cardinals had hired Bobby Layne, the old Detroit and Pittsburgh quarterback, to tutor him. "I still have a lot to learn," he told me in his humble-pie way one day as we walked across the campus at Washington University. "When my receivers would be covered a few years ago, I'd run around back there, hoping somebody would get clear. I just hated to see a play, one that we'd worked hard on during the week, go down the drain. But I would have thrown fewer interceptions and lost less yards if I'd thrown the ball away.

"I also had to learn to have faith in our game plan. If a play didn't work, I scrapped it. I had to learn that when a play doesn't work, the reason may be any one of three things. One, the play may be no good against this team's personnel, and in that case it should be scrapped. Two, the defense may have used a stunt that busted the play this time, but the play is still good if I use it when they're not stunting. Or three, someone on our side busted an assignment. The good quarterback finds out why a play didn't work. It's easy to get disillusioned about a play. It's hard to find out why it didn't work."

That loss to the Giants, when Gambrell slipped, probably cost the Cardinals the 1964 eastern division championship. They finished second in the East to Cleveland, which posted a 10–3–1 record to St. Louis' 9–3–2. Cleveland went on to beat the West's best, Baltimore, for the NFL championship, a game the Cardinals might have won if they had beaten the Giants.

They never came closer to an NFL title during the years Charley was their quarterback. Twice during the 1960s Charley threw six touchdown passes in a game. But too often the Cardinals gave up points more frequently than they scored them. In 1970 Charley went to the Houston Oilers, played two years for them, and finished his career from 1972 to 1975 as the quarterback of the Denver Broncos.

Texas always in his heart, Charley bought a home in Houston when he was traded to the Oilers. By 1976 he had a doctorate in chemical engineering and for several years

he worked in Houston for oil companies. In 1981 he switched to the natural-gas field and now is the owner of his own company, Johnson Compression, which is involved in equipment to pump natural gas. He and Barbara, with their son and daughter, still live in Houston.

In 1985 Charley calls signals as head of his Johnson Compression.

Eddie Johnston

EDWARD JOSEPH JOHNSTON—EVERYONE on the Bruins called him E.J.—was the first hockey goaltender I ever talked with for any length of time. When I left E.J. after a week of hanging out with him and the Boston Bruins in 1972, I had reinforced my long-held opinion that of all the sports available to the youth of North America, the one that takes the most courage to play is professional hockey. The swinging sticks that can cut open a face or spear the belly seemed reason enough to stay clear of a rink. But until my week with E.J., I had not realized that the little rubber puck could be just as perilous.

E.J. and I were standing together one night at the bar of E.J.'s, a nightclub he had opened in Rowley, a Boston suburb about a half-hour's drive from Boston Garden on the North Shore. Young people twitched on the dance floor as a rock band thumped and wailed. At the bar, customers in jeans and short skirts clamored for steak sandwiches and beers. E.J., swilling from a bottle of Bud, waved to peple who shouted his name. That night the Bruins had beaten the Rangers, 4–1, to win the National Hockey League's Eastern Division. But E.J. had been on the bench. The Bruins had two goalkeepers; against the Rangers, Gerry Cheevers had stood in the cage.

I asked E.J. if he had wished he had been on the ice. "The name of the game is win," he said with a voice that was part-Boston and part the Ireland of his parents. "Right?" He often punctuated a long burst of words with a "right?" It was not really a question but a way of affirming what he had just said. "We don't feel any rivalry, Chessy and me, never have. It's not like the two of us were trying to win one job. Today there are two goaltenders on every team, so there is no

E.J. in the cage for the Bruins in 1964.

reason for any animosity. It's good to have another goaltender watching you. He knows what you should and should not be doing. Right?"

What he said next, as we talked about his past, made me wonder why anyone would want the job. He was then thirty-five, but he looked younger, his figure rangy (six feet and one-hundred-ninety pounds), his narrow face fat-layered under the chin. He had been playing hockey for money for more than a dozen seasons, and people called him a veteran, but he looked a member of the Age of Aquarius, wearing tan boots, a blue-and-white beret, his long black hair a helmet that half-covered his ears. His face, I once wrote, "was the last one you saw on the Irish tenor singing 'Mother Machree.'"

In telling of his past, he told me of the puck that had almost killed or crippled him, and I got my new perception of just how dangerous hockey was. "That puck," he said, "was almost enough to leave me nothing but a vegetable."

The puck was hit by a man who had become the most important hockey player for the Bruins—Bobby Orr. During a practice session in Detroit in 1967, Orr hit a rising shot that E.J. lost for a moment. E.J. was wearing a mask, but the puck struck a tad above the mask, hitting him in the left side of the head. He dropped to the ice, conscious but dazed. An ambulance took him to a hospital where he stayed four days. Doctors told him he could fly home to Boston.

"The Detroit doctors didn't know it," he told me and two of his pals, one a hulking longshoreman, the other a graying Boston lawyer, as we stood at the bar, "but a clot had formed near the brain. If the clot had moved an inch during that flight, the doctors told me later, I would have been dead. As it was, I was sick on the plane all the way to Boston. I don't remember much at all of the flight. [Teammate] Teddy Green met me when I got off the plane and he hardly recognized me, the side of my head was so puffed out. Right? Anyway, he took me directly to Massachusetts General Hospital, which was the nearest one he could find.

"I was in the hospital eight and a half weeks. Priests came, my brothers came. I'd talk to them and an hour later I wouldn't remember that I'd talked to them. I'd have a blank on the conversation. My weight dropped from around one-ninety to one-hundred-fifty-five pounds. Every morning for the first ten days they took me to the operating room. Most of the doctors wanted to put a hole in the brain. It would probably have ended my career as an athlete. Right? They wanted to get at the clot before it moved and killed me. One neurosurgeon kept saying to the others, 'Wait, it might go away.' They didn't operate and finally it did go away.

"I came back to play in the middle of the season. I wore a heavy helmet-type mask. I remember the first time I practiced. I was thinking, I hope I'm not gun-shy. I thought, This is my business, right? If I'm going to be gun-shy, this is the time and place, at practice, to find out. Now. Right? So I took off the mask and I told them to shoot the puck right at me.

"Milt Schmidt [then the Bruin general manager] saw me taking off the mask. He came running down to the ice yelling, 'You put that mask on, you put that mask on.'"

E.J. was laughing. The lawyer, longshoreman, and I stared, silent. I left E.J.'s that night and drove back to Boston. On the way I wondered to myself what impels a man to go out on the ice and brave those flailing sticks and whizzing pucks. It couldn't have been the money; in those days hockey players were among the lowest-paid performers in sport—$25,000 a year a high salary.

Later, talking about his career, E.J. tried to explain why a man would take off a mask after a near-fatal injury and face those

pucks. He was born on November 25, 1935, in an Irish working-class section of Montreal. He was one of seven brothers. His parents were happy to see him and his brothers do their battling on playing fields instead of back alleys. "We played hurling, hockey, baseball," he told me one afternoon as we drove from his Bruin practice sessions at Boston Garden to his suburban home. "I was a Golden Gloves boxer. I fought at one-hundred-forty-seven pounds. I lost only one fight. I played all the positions in hockey. But because I was tall and had done some fighting—it takes guts to be a goaltender, right? —they made me a goaltender. I got an offer of a hockey scholarship from the University of Michigan, but I decided to take a shot at pro hockey." He began with the Montreal minor-league system in 1957 but then was drafted by the Bruins, whom he joined in 1962.

"When I first came up to Boston," he told me in the Cadillac, "I'd see forty to fifty shots a game. It was a losing team, but with a losing team I got the chance to play. We kept improving. And when Bobby Orr and then Phil Esposito came along, instead of beer we were drinking champagne."

In 1970 the Bruins won the Stanley Cup, their first in twenty-nine years, and they won it again in 1972, E.J. and Cheevers their goalkeepers. The Bruins called him E.J. and Downtown Eddie because he was the well-dressed bachelor who knew where all the good places were no matter what city the Bruins visited. In 1970, however, he met Diane, the friend of a friend, married, and settled down. But Downtown Eddie still liked his evenings out. "I think we spend a thousand dollars a year on babysitters," he said in the Cadillac.

Later that afternoon I talked with Gerry Cheevers, an apple-cheeked, cherubic thirty-one-year-old goaltender whose off-the-ice hobby was training thoroughbred horses. (He later became coach of the

Bruins.) I talked to Cheevers about E.J. "He is the classic old-time goaltender," Cheevers said. "He stays in the cage, he keeps his feet, he tries to force the shooter to take a shot from an impossible angle. E.J. is a legitimate goaltender. I fall, stand, skate a lot. I'll skate out and try to blitz the shooters."

That night, at E.J.'s nightclub, E.J. talked to me about goaltending. "The style of a goaltender is less important than being experienced," he said as he signed his approval on bills to be paid. "As you get older and have more experience, you learn to accept the pressure. If you have a bad game, you got to forget it. You've got to be able to say after a game,————it. Right? A goaltender doesn't come into his own until he's thirty and has the mental maturity to accept the pressure. That's why Gerry, who's just about thirty, is just now becoming a super goaltender."

E.J. later played with Toronto, St. Louis, and Chicago before retiring in 1977 after sixteen seasons in the National Hockey League. He left as a player holding the distinction of being the last goalie to play every minute of a season, standing in the cage for all 70 games of the 1963–64 season with the Bruins. In 592 games, he had 32 shutouts and a per-game average of 3.25 goals scored against him. He became a coach during the 1978–79 season with the New Brunswick Hawks of the American Hockey League. Later he coached the Chicago Black Hawks. In 1980 he took over as coach of the Pittsburgh Penguins and twice stood behind the bench as the team went to the

In 1984 E.J. was the general manager of the Pittsburgh Penguins.

playoffs in 1981 and 1982, losing both times in opening rounds. In 1983 he left the bench to become the team's general manager. He lives in Pittsburgh.

Sandy as a Dodger in 1962.

Sandy Koufax

I WAS SITTING IN THE VISITORS' CLUB-house at Los Angeles' Dodger Stadium in September of 1966, talking with Roberto Clemente, then the right fielder of the Pittsburgh Pirates. We were discussing Sandy Koufax, who had stopped Clemente's Pirates the night before by a score of 5–1. Koufax had struck out a half-dozen Pirates and given up only six hits. "I talked to the Dodger catcher after the game," I said to Clemente. "He said Koufax's arm is aching."

Clemente jumped up from the stool on which he had been seated. He stared down at me with a look of disbelief on his handsome cocoa-brown face. "Sore arm?" he said sharply. "Sore arm? That catcher must be crazy. Koufax may have a sore arm after he pitches, but no one can throw fastballs like he does with a sore arm."

But the catcher, who was Jeff Torborg, had not been crazy. I had asked him after the game: "Did Sandy's arm hurt tonight when he was pitching?"

"A couple of times it did. You can see his face tighten up."

"How often do you see that?"

"Maybe, if he throws a hundred pitches, five or six times a game. But, gee, I shouldn't be telling you this. Sandy doesn't like to talk about it."

That 1966 season Koufax won 27 games, the most he had won in his career. It was also his last big-league season. A few weeks after the season ended, he announced he was quitting baseball because of that aching arm that Clemente could not believe had pained him when he pitched. "I've had a few too many shots and taken too many pills because of arm trouble," he said. "I don't want to take the chance of disabling myself."

I have never forgotten that conversation with Clemente about Koufax—a great hitter's disbelief that anyone could throw so fast with an aching arm. But I had already learned from Koufax and from one of his Dodger teammates that he was something different.

I had met him for the first time the afternoon before my conversation with Clemente. I had come to Los Angeles late in the 1966 baseball season to watch the Dodgers and Pirates in a three-game series that might decide the winner of the National League pennant. The Dodgers won the first game, stretching their lead over the Pirates and the Giants. Koufax was pitching the second game. I was standing in the Dodger clubhouse talking to Maury Wills, the Dodg-

ers' chatty shortstop. He was telling me how the pressures of a tight pennant race had strained his nerves. "I've got butterflies in my stomach for the first time this season," Wills said. "Everybody here"—he waved a hand around the clubhouse—"they tense up before these games in September. But I don't know about Sandy. He's different. The game starts and he shuts himself in a closet, he concentrates so hard. What he's really feeling I can't tell you."

A few minutes later I was trying to find out what Koufax was feeling as we spoke in front of his dressing stall. He had just arrived. As my Irish mother said of beautiful people, "Your eyes wouldn't get tired looking at him for a year and a day." He was wearing a sky-blue cardigan, white turtleneck, and coal-black slacks. His face was bronzed with that glow that people of Semitic heritage acquire after a few hours in the sun. The dark eyes were set deeply under thick black eyebrows. I asked him if he had prepared himself differently for this important game.

The eyebrows arched. "Why?" he asked in a deep baritone. A slight smile, a cousin to a sneer, crossed the handsome face. He threw wide his hands. "Look, you do things no differently whether you're in first place or in fifth place. You have a responsibility to your team. You are paid to win so many games, and you're supposed to go out and do your job, win those games, no matter whether you're in first place or in sixth place."

I remembered what Clemente had told me just before the first game of this series. In these big games, he had said, hands trembled before a game in which one error could waste six months of striving by twenty-four teammates. "Isn't there pressure during a September run for the pennant?" I asked Koufax.

"I don't think so. To me the pressure is game to game, inning to inning, batter to batter, pitch to pitch. And it's that way in May, June, September—any month."

He lit a cigarette. "In September there is more fan interest. There's more press coverage of the games. But to the ballplayer he doesn't feel any more pressure on the field in September than he does in May. Hell, you win a game in May, it's as important as a game you win in September. Suppose you start the season and you're, say, one and two. You win a game and now you're an even five hundred. That game could be a real big one for you, because it puts you even. Now you can get started on winning a string of games and building a base for a real good year. That game in April could mean more to you than any game all year."

He was pulling off the turtleneck, baring a thick chest and muscled shoulders. In his uniform the six-foot-one, two-hundred-pound Koufax looked gangling, even skinny, but up close you saw the pectorals of a weightlifter and you knew whence came the velocity of his fastball. "I will say this," he went on. "You lose in September, when there isn't so much time to make up that game, and you may be losing for twenty-four other guys. Naturally, you feel bad but that's not pressure. There's also one big difference between a game in May and a game in September. You lose in September, there's less time to get it back."

"But isn't that a big difference?"

"Well, maybe," he said, hesitantly. "That may be true."

From the doubtful look on his face and the tone of his voice, I guessed that he was saying that it wasn't true for him.

Years later, though, I decided he had not been telling me the whole truth about his feelings during a September stretch run for the pennant. After his retirement he was asked what he missed about baseball. "I miss above all," he said, "playing late in the season when there is a pennant at stake." September games, it seemed, had been—at

least as Koufax looked back—more memorable than games in the merrier time of May.

Indeed, more than most people in the public spotlight, Koufax seemed to hide much of his inner emotions. Writer Bill Libby once said that Koufax's handsome face was "a mask behind which he seemed to conceal secrets." As Wills had told me, Koufax was not an easy person to know or understand. He was unwilling, as Torborg had disclosed, to let people know of the pain he was enduring during the last few months of his pitching career.

That career was divided sharply into two parts that were just about equal in time—six mediocre years and six great years.

Sanford Braun was born in Brooklyn on December 30, 1935, the son of Jack and Evelyn Braun. He was three when his parents divorced. Evelyn married Irving Koufax, a lawyer, and Sandy took the name of his stepfather. As a teenager he was fascinated by electronic gadgetry, once wiring the family home for sound. He also was popping basketballs through the hoop for the Lafayette High School basketball team and pitching fastballs for the baseball team. In 1953 he accepted a basketball scholarship from the University of Cincinnati, intending to be an architect. Brooklyn Dodger scouts had seen him pitch on sandlots, however, and told him he could be a big leaguer. Late in 1954 he signed with Brooklyn for a $14,000 bonus that would guarantee his college education.

Since the nineteen-year-old left-hander was a so-called bonus baby, big-league rules of the time did not allow the Dodgers to send him to the minor leagues. He needed experience to erase his nervousness. And he was nervous. The nervousness made him so wild during his first week of spring training in 1955 that Dodger coaches asked him to throw behind a building. They didn't want other Dodgers to see how wild he was and by their needling make him even more tense.

During his first six seasons as a Dodger, in Brooklyn and Los Angeles, he lost more games than he won. In 1957 Roy Campanella, the former Dodger catcher, told me that Koufax was the fastest pitcher he had ever seen. "He can throw a grape through a battleship," Gil Hodges, then the Dodger first baseman, told me in 1958. "Trouble is, he can't always hit the battleship."

Dodger coaches knew that Koufax was trying too hard, disturbing the flow of his pitching motion. "We kept telling him what he was doing wrong," coach Joe Becker once said. "But it is easier to tell yourself to slow down than to do it."

After an unhappy 8 and 13 season in 1960, Koufax talked about returning to college to study architecture. At spring training in 1961, he was riding to a game on the team bus with catcher Norm Sherry. "Why not have fun out there today, Sandy?" Sherry said. "Don't try so hard and use more curveballs and changeups."

A more relaxed Koufax had fun in the game and his fastball went where it was supposed to go. His curves broke sharply. That 1961 season he won 18 games. During the next five seasons, baseball historian Bob Broeg has written, "Koufax was probably as overpowering as any pitcher who ever lived." He won 129, lost only 47 with records like 25–5 in 1963, 26–8 in 1965, and 27–9 in 1966, his last. In each of the four seasons from 1962 to 1965 he pitched a no-hitter. One, against the Cubs on September 1, 1965, was a perfect game. The 4 no-hitters was a record later broken by Nolan Ryan's 5. He won the Cy Young Award as baseball's best pitcher in 1963, 1965, and 1966. In each of those three seasons the Dodgers won the pennant, winning the Series in 1963 and in 1965. (Koufax won 2 series games in 1963 and 2 in 1965.)

The Dodgers had lost the first 2 games of that 1965 Series. "What sticks in my mind about that Series," Koufax once told me, "was one writer in Minnesota who went through the stands after the first or second game, I don't remember which, and belittled and belabored the Dodger wives sitting there. He told them what the Twins were going to do to the Dodgers. And he put a few things in the paper that were a little bit out of line and possibly in bad taste. It sort of lifted up the team. There is a good chance that you are going to be down after losing the first two, and I think this writer may have lifted us up."

The Dodgers won 3 of the next 4 games to tie that 1965 Series at 3 games apiece. The seventh and final game was played at Minnesota. Dodger manager Walter Alston had the choice of pitching a rested Drysdale or a worn Koufax, who had pitched two days earlier. He chose Koufax. Sandy limited the hard-hitting Twins to only 3 hits and shut them out, 2–0.

In 1966 the cause of his sore arm was discovered: traumatic arthritis. In previous seasons the arm had seldom hurt when he pitched, the tissue lubricated by a fluid that was being pumped by the arthritic elbow. After a game, he disclosed after his retirement, "for an elbow I had a knee, that's how thick it was with fluid." And he was alarmed to discover that the arm, painful now during a game, was shrinking in length. Shortly after the 1966 Series, won by the Orioles in 4 straight games (Sandy lost 1 of the games), he told the world that the outstanding pitcher of the decade was quitting. "The arthritis would only get worse if I continued to pitch," he said. "I've got a lot of years to live after baseball, and I would like to live them with the complete use of my body." His career record was 165 victories and 87 defeats.

NBC-TV signed him as a $100,000 commentator on baseball telecasts. But Sandy was too shy and reserved to be critical of players. He left NBC in the early 1970s. A bachelor during his playing days, he married Ann Widmark, daughter of actor Richard Widmark. They lived in Maine and later in Los Angeles. In 1971 Koufax was elected to the Hall of Fame, the youngest, at thirty-six, ever to be honored at Cooperstown. An investor in motels and FM radio stations, and an avid golfer, he finds time each spring to go back to the Dodgers in Florida as a pitching coach. In 1983 the former Pirate slugger, Willie Stargell, told me this about Koufax. "Trying to hit Sandy Koufax," Willie said, "was like trying to drink coffee with a fork."

Sandy (*right*) as a Dodger pitching coach in 1983 with ex-teammates Larry Sherry (*left*) and Ron Perranoski.

Clyde as a Hawk in 1957.

Clyde Lovellette

WE WERE SEATED IN A RESTAURANT IN downtown Terre Haute, Indiana, big Clyde and I. During a long afternoon chatting with him in the fall of 1965, I learned more about the dirty tricks of basketball than anyone could expect to learn in a lifetime.

While on my way to the 1965 World Series in Minneapolis, I had stopped off in Terre Haute to talk to the thirty-six-year-old Clyde Lovellette, who had retired in 1964 after eleven years in the National Basketball Association. I wanted to know about the bloody goings-on in the NBA. During the previous two seasons, players had been carted off courts and carried to emergency rooms at a rate that alarmed coaches. The Knicks' Willis Reed went with a broken nose, Boston's Willie Naulls with a concussion, Cin-

cinnati's Jerry Lucas with a broken rib, Baltimore's Gus Johnson with a snapped wrist. The St. Louis owner, Ben Kerner, had called the violence as savage as the hitting in pro football. Jack McMahon, coach at Cincinnati, had said that pro basketball had become an "alley fight."

"Pro basketball has always been an alley fight," Clyde told me, tipping back the restaurant chair and smiling as he rubbed a hand through close-cropped brown hair. He was a mountain of a man even for a basketball player—six-foot-nine and some two hundred sixty pounds of packed beef. His voice and his laugh were as large as his body. "Pro basketball is bloody and violent because that's what the customers pay to see. Knock out the rough stuff and what have you got? College basketball. Sure, the pros shoot better and jump higher, but if you've seen one jump shot, you've seen them all. After you've seen a seven-footer stuff a ball through the hoop for a dunk shot, you can bet your life he isn't going to do it differently the second time around. What makes the pro game so appealing is that it offers people the speed of basketball and the violence of football."

As we talked, however, Clyde conceded that some players, including himself, were at fault for the blood-letting, using muscle to inhibit the high scorers and employing imaginative stunts to go up higher for rebounds.

"You have to muscle the scorer out of their favorite spots," he said. "You shove Elgin Baylor out of the corners, you stand in Jerry Lucas's spot at the side of the key, you make life miserable for Wilt Chamberlain or Bill Russell underneath. When I guarded Wilt or Bill and they turned their backs to the basket, I pulled the hair on their legs. I sneaked punches to their kidneys, tugged at the elastic of their pants, tried to step on the backs of their low-cut shoes. Get him out of his shoes and not even Wilt can score in his socks.

"You do that to someone for three periods and he's going to start to steam. He may throw a punch at you. Or sneak one to *your* kidney. Or aim an elbow into your mouth.

"That's good. Not necessarily for you, but for your team. You've taken his mind off what he should be thinking of: how to score points. In taking time to bloody your mouth, he may have wasted two baskets and that could mean the game. So you're even. Of course, if he cuts you up badly enough, it's a long season and you'll pay him back.

"A second reason for all the violence in the NBA is the crushing pressure to get rebounds, especially if you're a forward or a center. 'You can't win,' Red Auerbach used to tell us in Boston, 'if you don't get the ball. You can only score when you have it and the other team can't score without it.'

"You use all the dirty tricks you know to get those rebounds. I had some tricks that got me hundreds of rebounds I had no right to get. For example, if I was behind a man, he had the better position for taking the ball off the boards. But sometimes I beat him to the ball with this dodge: Just as he flexed his knees to jump, I'd stick my knee in the cup made in the back of his knee. My knee would stop him from flexing his knee all the way. He'd straighten his legs to get free of my knee. When he did, up I went over him for the ball while the poor sucker was still on the ground.

"Not one ref in a thousand would catch me doing that. Not one in two thousand caught me messing up rebounders who jumped higher than I did. We'd be standing side by side, both of us flexing our knees to jump. As he was midway through his flex, I'd nudge the side of his knee. It would be the slightest of nudges. But it messed up the sequence of his jump and he wouldn't go three quarters as high as he would normally leap.

"Of course, the man next to you can always nudge *your* knee. That's why, in the NBA, you'll often see two good jumpers form a pyramid under the backboards—backs flat against each other, legs far apart. That way neither can hit the other's knee."

Clyde had his own strategies for defending against the high scorers. "I tried to keep Wilt away from the basket," he said of Chamberlain, who routinely poured in 50 points a game. "Both he and Bill Russell are close to one hundred percent accurate within seven feet of the basket, but Wilt won't hurt you much from seven feet on out, and Russell is pathetic from even halfway out to the foul line.

"When Russell or Chamberlain moved close to the basket, I'd place my hand in the small of their backs. Every time they moved a foot to the left or right, looking for a pass into the pivot, I pushed them a half foot away from the basket.

"Muscle. That's what defense is all about in the NBA. Sure, against the smaller men— Oscar Robertson, Jerry West—you also have to be quick. But when they beat you by a half step with quickness, then you lean on them with muscle to keep them from running you out of the league.

"In the NBA right now there are Tom Meschery, Rudy LaRusso, Tom Sanders, Bob Boozer, Wayne Embry—tough, hard-headed types who have the strength to punish the scorers with muscle for period after period. They go face to face with the shooter and put thumbprints on him, meaning they hammer at his arms when he doesn't have the ball. When he has the ball and tries to go around them, they stick out a stiff arm to hold him. If he barges past the stiff arm, maybe they trip him, even tackle him. Of course the whistle will blow. That's okay. You're better off having Robertson shoot one-pointers than two-pointers. And sometimes the whistle won't blow when it should. I fouled jump shooters like Robertson all the time and seldom was caught. As Oscar went up, I'd reach high with my right hand as if to block the shot. Nineteen out of twenty referees will fix their eyes on that hand, looking to see if I touch the shooter. With my left hand I'd poke a finger into Oscar's chest. It would be just a tiny poke, but because he was up in the air, it'd knock him back a foot or so, enough to make his jumper fall short."

Clyde had learned from masters like Harry (The Horse) Gallatin, a brawny Knick center when Clyde came into the league in 1953. "When The Horse was guarding me in the pivot," Clyde told me, "he waited until I tried to move left or right. Then he stuck his knee under the seat of my pants and lifted me a couple of inches. Now that took strength because I was the original Baby Bull. What amazed me was this: When Harry lifted me, not only did the referee fail to see it, I didn't realize I was being lifted myself. That's how delicate Harry could be with that big knee of his. I'd get a pass, wheel for a hook shot, and—ooops!—my jaw would drop open because somebody had moved the basket five feet back."

Clyde Lovellette was born in Terre Haute on September 7, 1929. Tall and overweight in high school, he was too ungainly and awkward to be a good basketball player. His height, however, got him an invitation in 1949 to attend the University of Kansas. Coach Phog Allen put him through a strict regimen of diet and exercise. In his junior year he wheeled out of the pivot to drop in 44 points against St. Louis in an NCAA tournament game, at the time a record. In 1952, his senior year, he was the tournament's Most Valuable Player as Kansas won the NCAA championship. He scored 1,888 points at Kansas, up to then the most ever scored by a college player. He joined the Olympic team that won the gold medal at the 1952 Games in Helsinki. He signed with the Minneapolis (now Los Angeles) Lakers and helped that team win the 1953–54 NBA championship. He was the first of only four men to play on a NCAA champion, an Olympic champion, and a NBA champion. (The others are Bill

Russell, K. C. Jones, and Jerry Lucas.) He played for the Lakers until 1957 when he went to Cincinnati. He played for St. Louis from 1958 to 1961 and for Boston from 1962 to 1964, winning two more NBA championships as a Celtic. During his eleven-year career he averaged 17 points a game.

After leaving basketball he was a sheriff in his hometown of Terre Haute. He now lives in Wabash where he is a vocational coordinator for teenagers who have had trouble with the law. His proudest moment, he says, was winning the Olympic gold medal. "When you win the gold medal and stand on the box and they play the national anthem, you get a big lump in your throat and tears in your eyes."

He is embarrassed, he says, by what he sees of today's pro basketball. "Defenses just stand there and watch those people slam-dunk," he told me in 1984. "In my day we wouldn't let them dunk. If they tried, they'd pay for it—physically."

Clyde as a juvenile aid officer in 1984.

Mickey Mantle

Mickey as a Yankee in 1957.

I HAD BEEN WARNED BY OTHER WRITERS that Mickey Mantle was very shy and, as a result, difficult to interview. I had heard stories of how he had stared, mouth agape, at a questioner, his face turning red with embarrassment, and then had walked away without saying a word. I also knew he had been close to his father, who had died in 1952. During one of our first conversations, outside a batting cage during the spring of 1956 in St. Petersburg, I brought the talk around to his father. "When you think about him," I asked, "is there something special you will always remember about him?"

"Let's go on over there," he said in his cowpoke-ish Oklahoma drawl. He pointed with his bat toward a grassy area behind third base. There, as we talked, he knelt with one knee on the ground, gripping the propped-up bat with huge hands clasped around its knob. He was twenty-four, his face sunburned, his canary-yellow hair poking out from the sides of his blue Yankee cap. We talked for about ten minutes and during that time I had to ask him only a few questions because he seemed eager to talk about his father. Without his father's advice, he said, he would never have been a big leaguer. He told me about an incident in Kansas City in 1951. That spring he had come north from Florida with the Yankees, a nineteen-year-old outfielder acclaimed "the new Joe DiMaggio." But he had hit poorly in April and May; Casey Stengel, the Yankee manager, sent him to Kansas City, then a Yankee minor-league club. "I was a bigger bust there than I'd been with the Yankees," Mantle told me, never smiling during the entire time we talked. "I was feeling real low, having gone nothing for five in one night game, when I met my dad outside the park. He used to drive up from our home in Oklahoma to watch me play.

"After we talked a while, he got into his car. 'Dad,' I said to him, 'I might as well go home with you. I'll never be able to hit major-league pitching.'

"He turned and stared at me. 'All right,' he said, 'get in. If you've got no more guts than that, you don't belong in the big leagues.'"

This was his dad talking, the father who had named him Mickey after Mickey Cochrane, the Detroit Tiger catcher and the idol of the elder Mantle. Elvin Mantle had dreamed of being a big leaguer himself and had been, Mickey told me, "the proudest man in Oklahoma" when Mickey had come north with the Yankees that spring of 1951.

"My face turned red," Mickey said. "I stepped back from the car. Dad drove home alone that night. I went back to my hotel and thought about what he had said. He'd embarrassed me but he'd made me realize something. If I could hit, I'd make the Yankees. If I couldn't—well, I'd find that out too."

Mickey began to hit; within a few weeks he was back in New York with the Yankees. "I don't think I would've made it without the help of my dad," Mickey told me, rising from his kneeling position. "You can write that up any way you want, but try to get across what he was telling me that night."

I nodded. We shook hands and he trotted back toward the batting cage, grinning, his ears reddening, when some of the players taunted him about his "press conference." I wrote the article, which appeared under his byline, with this title: "The Night I Didn't Go Home." And I ended it this way: "I haven't forgotten what he taught me that night: to succeed—in baseball or in anything else—takes a lot more than ability. It also takes courage."

The next spring, 1957, I was still congratulating myself on my ability to interview a Mantle I had not found shy at all. I walked up to him in the Yankee clubhouse. He showed no sign of recognition, staring at me blankly as I asked whether his tremendous power came from his back or his arms. He flushed, scratched his head, then saw that two of his teammates were listening for the answer. "Aw, I don't know," he blurted, and hurried away.

I talked to the other Yankees about him. "To understand Mick," infielder Jerry Coleman, the most articulate of the Yankees, told me, "you've got to remember two things. One, he's a fiercely proud man. And two, he's still very shy."

How shy was he? Pitcher Whitey Ford, one of his closest buddies, said, "When he came up north with us six years ago, he was a real country boy, all shy and embarrassed when he arrived with a straw suitcase, two pairs of slacks, and one blue sports jacket that probably cost about eight dollars in a store in Commerce, Oklahoma. I'd say hello and he'd put down his head and grunt something."

In talking about Mantle's pride, Coleman mentioned how often Mantle kicked water coolers in dugouts after striking out. "When he strikes out, he feels he's been made to look like a fool. Nobody likes to be made the fool while thousands look on—and Mantle never forgets that people are looking at him. With his tremendous pride, is it any wonder that he has to kick something as an outlet for his anger?"

He would strike out more often than any player in history—1,710 times, or about once every five times at bat. But only four other players drew more walks. And when he retired in 1968, he had batted .298 and hit 536 home runs, more homers than anyone before him except Babe Ruth.

Other ballplayers, all strong men themselves, talked with awe of the six-foot, one-hundred-ninety-five-pound Mantle's strength. "You gotta print it, you gotta," Tito Francona, a strapping six-foot one-hundred-ninety-pound Cleveland outfielder shouted at me one day in 1963 after telling me a story about Mantle's strength.

"I heard that story," I said. "Mantle told me it's a story that one of your pitchers made up."

"Nah," Francona said. He was standing at the batting cage at Yankee Stadium. He turned, looked into the Yankee dugout, and saw Mantle. "You gotta print it!" he shouted even more loudly so Mantle could hear, jabbing a finger at my notebook. Mantle obviously knew what Francona was telling me; an embarrassed aw-shucks grin was spreading across his face. "It's true, I was an eyewitness," Francona said to me, and then he shouted toward the dugout, "I saw it, Mick, you can't deny it.

"It happened last year," Francona had told me, "right here in Yankee Stadium. Somebody knocked down Joe Pepitone [then a Yankee first baseman] and suddenly ballplayers are charging out toward the mound. But when they get there, nobody's doing much of anything except making noise. Then Mickey shoves one of our guys. Bang! The guy flies back like he's shot, ricochets into someone else, and knocks him down. That guy bangs into someone behind him and pow!—like a row of ten-pins—a dozen guys go down. The crowd's yelling, thinking they're all fighting on the ground. Hell, they just wanted to get up before Mickey shoved someone else and knocked another dozen ballplayers on top of them.

"There was this game here in Yankee Stadium," Twins' pitcher Jim (Mudcat) Grant said to me later. "We're ahead one to nothing in the bottom of the fourth when the wind and the rain start blowing in from the outfield. I mean, it's a real gale. The Yankees get two men on base off me, but there are two out when Mantle comes up. I get the count to three and two against him, and now it's really blowing, the wind and rain smacking him right in the face. I can see he's having trouble seeing against the lights. I figure I'll throw him my best pitch, the fast-

ball, and he'll never see it with all that water in his eyes. I put that ball exactly where I wanted it, low and outside, and I don't know how he ever touched it. But he drove it right into that gale, knocking it into the bullpen out there for a home run. The next inning they call the game and we lose, two to one."

His strength. The ballplayers talked about his strength with awe in their voices. When they talked about how he played in pain, there was also awe in the voices of these men who themselves played, as they said, "with the small hurts." "Those legs of his," Cleveland pitcher Jack Kralick told me, "I'd heard how they were all bandaged up. But before the 1962 All-Star game, I happened to walk by the trainer's room and I saw him being taped up. I was amazed—all those bandages, they ran from his ankles all the way up."

"I see him swing sometimes," Boston's Carl Yastrzemski told me in 1963, "and even from the outfield you can see the leg buckle under him and the way he winces in pain. I wince, too. It's like your kid is in pain, and you can feel the pain yourself. That's the way the ballplayers feel about Mantle.

"When he runs he's in pain all right," Cleveland shortstop Dick Howser said to me. "But what amazes me, he runs so hard, even though he must know that one bad step and his career is all over, shot, finished. I'll tell you something: When Mickey wants to steal a base, he steals it. I've been on two ballclubs so far in the big leagues, but I've never been on one so far that's caught Mickey stealing.

"What first made me respect Mickey," Yankee third baseman Clete Boyer said, "was the 1961 Series against the Reds. He had a hole the size of a golf ball in his thigh [the result of an abscess]. Ninety percent of the ballplayers wouldn't even be at the ball park. But he got two hits and didn't want to leave until the blood began to run down his leg and you could see it splotching his pants."

The bandages, the pain, the recurring injuries, they all probably traced back to a childhood injury. Mickey was born on October 20, 1931, in Spavinaw, Oklahoma, but grew up in Commerce, where his father, Elvin, worked as a zinc miner. Mutt, as people called Elvin, taught his son how to be a switch hitter. When Mickey was sixteen, his left knee pained after a football game. A doctor told him he had osteomyelitis, a bone disease that could not be cured. He was told to give up football and to "take it easy" in baseball. Of course, he never would.

Yankee scout Tom Greenwade signed him in 1949. The eighteen-year-old, fleet Mantle, then a shortstop, hit .383 in the minors in 1950 and made the Yankees as Joe DiMaggio's heir-apparent in center field the following season. In the 1951 World Series, the rookie played right field. He drifted over to catch a towering fly hit by another rookie, the New York Giants' Willie Mays, and suddenly fell down as though shot. DiMaggio caught the ball, looked down at the fallen Mantle, and asked, "What's the matter, kid?"

Mantle's right knee had given way, a ligament torn. That was his "good" knee; the left knee had been damaged by osteomyelitis. Those knees, his arm, his shoulders, all would pain him during the rest of his career. In 1952 his father died, a victim of Hodgkin's disease, which had also killed Mickey's paternal grandfather. For years Mantle wondered whether he would die before forty as had his father and grandfather.

In 1952 he took over for the retired DiMaggio in center field. During the seventeen years from 1952 to 1968, when he retired, the Yankees won eleven pennants and seven world championships. In four of those seasons he led the American League in homers, his best a total of 54 in 1961 when he

finished second to Roger Maris's 61. In 1956 he led the league in hitting (.353), homers (52) and runs batted in (130) to win the Triple Crown. He was named the Most Valuable Player in 1956, 1957, and 1962.

In recent years Mantle has said publicly that he might have been a greater player—and lasted longer—if he had taken better care of his fragile body. On road trips, Mickey was renowned among the Yankees for lurching into hotel lobbies at four or five in the morning, and then playing the next day with a headache. As the Yankee manager, Casey Stengel knew about Mickey's late-hour roamings. Years later, when Casey was the manager of the Mets, he told me and my wife, Barbara, one night in the bar of a St. Petersburg Beach motel, "What could I do? I couldn't fine him. He was the best ballplayer I ever had."

A believer in even-handed justice, Barbara disagreed. "You should have fined him just as you would have fined any other player," she said.

Stengel, growing angrier by the minute, insisted he could not treat a star the way he would treat a utility player. He became so angry, shouting louder, arms waving, and dancing around Barbara as he raged, that later I wondered whether he had some guilt feelings about not having been tougher on Mantle.

"What could I do, lady?" he was shouting at the end (before one of his coaches, Wes Westrum, led him away). "He was the best ballplayer I ever had." Then, on his way out the door, he threw back a final reason that sounded as though he thought this clinched his case: "And do you know how many games that man won for me?"

Early in his career Mantle married a Commerce sweetheart, Merlyn Louise Johnson. "I don't know how Merlyn and Mickey ever got acquainted," Merlyn's mother once said. "Neither of them ever says a word." The

Mantles had four children (including a Mickey, Jr.). One of the boys, Billy (named for Billy Martin) was being treated in 1984 for the Hodgkin's disease that had spared Mickey.

Mickey always seemed more at ease with children than he did with adults. He was especially close with the sons of other Yankees, particularly those who frequently visited the Stadium clubhouse. I once asked Mickey what his favorite story was about himself and he told me of the time he had struck out three or four times in a game. One of Yogi Berra's sons approached him after the game. "I thought he was going to tell me to cheer up or something like that," Mickey said with that typical embarrassed grin of his. "He comes up next to me, and he says, 'Hey, Mickey Mantle, you stink.'"

In 1982 Mickey went to work as a greeter for the Claridge Hotel and Casino in Atlantic City. Mantle was no longer a springtime batting coach for the Yankees, as he had been after his retirement. Baseball Commissioner Bowie Kuhn ruled in 1983 that baseball and gambling-casino employment "are inconsistent." While missing baseball, Mantle liked the casino's hours and the pay—$100,000 a year for appearances several days a month. "They're paying me to play golf," he said, "and that's what I'd be doing anyway."

Mickey as a greeter in Atlantic City in 1984.

Willie throws for the Giants in 1961.

Willie Mays

I WAS ONE OF 50,000 FORTUNATES WHO stood in the Polo Grounds on a cool October afternoon in 1954 and watched what I believe was the greatest catch in postwar Series history. (I saw Al Gionfriddo's catch of Joe DiMaggio's towering drive in the 1947 Series, and on a scale of 1 to 10 I would rate Gionfriddo's catch a 5 or a 6 to Mays's 10.) What made Mays's catch memorable, to me, was that he turned his back on the ball and ran for the wall, looking like a sprinter dashing for the finish line. It seemed for several seconds that he had given himself no chance to catch the ball and only wanted to get close to the center-field wall and capture the ball as it rebounded off the wall. (Gionfriddo, by contrast, never had to take his eyes off the ball that DiMaggio hit.) As Mays sprinted toward that wall some 500 feet from home plate, I remember standing in the press box and shouting like the Giant fan I was: "Look up . . . look up!"

Finally he did, glancing over his left shoulder at the ball slammed by Cleveland's broad-backed slugger, Vic Wertz. Mays stretched out both hands like a supplicant asking for alms. I had my eyes on his distant brown glove and suddenly I saw a white oval in the pocket for just an instant before Mays's body blocked my view.

He was already whirling even as I shouted amid the oceanlike roaring, "He's got it!" Two Cleveland runners were on base, scurrying now back to their bases as Mays threw the ball toward the faraway infield, the force of his whirl spinning off his cap. I remember looking down at Vic Wertz, who was standing near first base. He was turning toward the third-base dugout and I have often wondered since what went through his mind. An almost-certain 3-run homer had just become another long out. The Indians lost the game on that catch, the Giants winning it, 5–2, in the tenth when Dusty Rhodes conked a 250-foot home run into the nearby right-field seats.

Some fifteen years later I sat with Willie Mays in the clubhouse of the San Francisco Giants during the closing days of the 1966 pennant race. They had called him the Say Hey Kid back in New York in 1951 when he laughingly played stickball with ten-year-olds on the streets of Harlem. Now he was thirty-five and he looked closer to forty-five, wrinkled smudges under his eyes. "The seasons," he said, "they seem to get longer and longer," and I sensed he was not talking of 154-game seasons versus 162-game seasons. Gone, he was saying, was something that had made yesterday's seasons seem short.

Only a few people were in the San Francisco clubhouse, the game several hours away. Willie was the kind who liked to come to clubhouses earlier, joshing with the other players, dealing out cards, the hub around which the younger players revolved; Willie was the center of attention and, being human, he liked that. He'd been screeching in his high, scratchy voice to outfielder Len Gabrielson, teasing Gabrielson about something. I could see the awe in Gabrielson's eyes. He had been in high school when Willie Mays made Vic Wertz just another Series player.

I had come here to talk about the 1966 pennant race, but first I wanted to know about the catch. "Oh, I think I made a lot better catches than the one I made against Cleveland," he said, the piercing voice still boyish even if the face was not. "I couldn't name them others for you, but I knew I had that ball all the way from the time it left Wertz's bat. I could see the ball as soon as it left the bat. I got a good jump on it. But what a lot of people forget about that catch was that I had to make the throw on it because there were two men on base who could have moved up after I caught it. It was hit a long way, I'll say that, and I don't think I ever caught any ball deeper than I caught that one."

He asked me where I had been.

"I was in Los Angeles yesterday," I said. "I watched the Pirates beat the Dodgers." While that was happening, the Giants had won, moving up to 3 games behind the Dodgers. "That big Los Angeles crowd yesterday," I told Willie, "they were standing watching that scoreboard in Dodger Stadium flashing the play-by-play of your game here. They were cheering each Giant out, and when the lights flashed, 'Hart up,' they were ready to yell at the final out. Then out blinked the words, 'Hart homers, Giants win,' and you could hear that crowd go dead."

His face was bunched up with the effort of holding in his amusement. When I finished he exploded with peals of laughter that reminded me, on this Sunday morning in September, of church bells. "Is that right?" he shrieked. "Is that right?"

"I guess you were pretty excited yourself on the bench when Jim Ray hit that homer," I said.

"No." He frowned as he turned back to his dressing stall to pick up a pair of baseball shoes and examine the cleats. "There is nothing in baseball that can get me excited anymore."

"Not even a big ninth-running home run during a September stretch run for the pennant?"

"No. I *got* to stay calm. We have so many kids on this ballclub, it's my job to stay calm."

"Is this the toughest pennant race you've ever been in?"

"Shoot, no. The first one is the toughest. After that you get used to them."

"Your first one was 1951."

"Yeah, I didn't know what it was all about then." He laughed. "I didn't get a hit I think the last two weeks."

I remembered seeing him kneeling in the on-deck circle at the Polo Grounds on the last day of that extended 1951 season when Bobby Thomson hit the home run that won the playoff and the pennant. "A lot of people," I said, "have thought that the Dodgers should have walked Thomson and pitched to you, just a rookie."

Again his face screwed up as laughter built inside him and came out as a screech. "Yeah, I guess they should have, because I was scared to death. No way I wanted to go up there."

He had come to the Giants early in that 1951 season, a nervous nineteen-year-old alone in a scary big city. Willie Howard Mays was born May 6, 1931, in Westfield, Alabama, near Birmingham. His father played for semipro black teams. I once talked to Kitty Kat, as his father was called. He was seated in a dugout at Shea Stadium when Willie was with the Mets. Kitty Kat stared at his hands and said, "I never made it to the good Negro teams of the time because I didn't have the hands. Willie's got the big hands. He got them from his mother. I remember as a little kid, he had this big ball and he'd go running after it, and if he couldn't get to that ball, he'd sit down and start to cry."

The fifteen-year-old Willie was playing for the Birmingham Black Barons, who criss-crossed the country playing local black teams. Willie played his first game in New York when he was sixteen, arriving in Manhattan with the Barons on their creaky bus. The bus broke down in a tunnel and Willie was ordered out to push. "I had the last laugh," he once said. "The bus caught fire and they all had to race out."

The Giants signed him when he was eighteen. After a year in the minors with Trenton and Minneapolis, where Mays was hitting .477 in the spring of 1951, the Giants' manager, Leo Durocher, demanded that the nineteen-year-old be brought up to help a team that had lost 11 games in a row. Mays failed to get a hit in his first dozen at-bats. In the clubhouse he broke down and cried, pleading that Durocher send him back to Minneapolis. "I don't care if you ever get a hit," Durocher said, impressed by his speed, throwing arm, and potential as a hitter. "You are my center fielder."

He hit his first homer off Warren Spahn, a mighty smash that I watched fly over the left-field roof at the Polo Grounds. Others began to realize that Durocher's instincts about the greatness of Mays were right. In 1951 he hit .274 and 20 homers for the Giants and lifted them up with his vivacious spirit (he called everyone "Say Hey" and got a nickname). The Giants came from 13½ games behind in midsummer to win the pennant. The Giants and Durocher soon discovered how much the Say Hey Kid had meant: He went into the Army in 1952 and stayed until after the 1953 season. The Giants finished second in 1952 and fifth in 1953. When Mays returned in 1954, he hit .345 to lead the league, smacked 41 home runs, drove in 110 runs, and was named the league's Most Valuable Player. The Giants won the pennant and swept the Indians in the Series to win the team's first world championship since 1933.

He hit 51 homers the following season. During the next eleven years he never hit fewer than 29, his best a league-leading 52 in 1965. He and the Giants moved west to San Francisco in 1958. In 1962 he was again the league's MVP, hitting 49 homers, tops in the league, and the Giants won another pennant. They met their former across-the-Harlem-River foe, the New York Yankees, in the Series. The Yankees won in 7 games, their seventh-game victory one that Mays still believes should have gone to the Giants.

The Yanks led 1–0 as the Giants came to bat in Candlestick Park for the last of the ninth.

With two men out and Matty Alou on first base, Mays came to bat against starter Ralph Terry. He hit a low line drive over first base. The ball skidded on the grass toward the right-field corner. If the ball had reached that corner, Alou would have scored from first to tie the game. But right fielder Roger Maris cut off the ball, scooping it up cleanly —the slightest bobble would have allowed Alou to score—and threw to the infield. Alou was held at third, Mays going into second with a double. The next hitter, Willie Mc-

Covey, slammed a line drive that second baseman Bobby Richardson, playing deep, caught at eye level for the final out.

"That was a base hit that McCovey hit," Mays screeched at me years later. "Richardson never would have caught that ball except he was playing out of position. He was playing on the outfield grass in short right field. If he'd been where a second baseman should have been, it would have gone through for a hit. Alou would have scored, I would have scored, and we would have won the Series. I was thinking of going all the way around the bases to score on that ball I hit to Maris, except he stopped it and I had to stop with a double . . . I was running toward third [on the ball McCovey hit] when I turned and saw Richardson catching that ball and I thought, Oh, geez, there goes three/four thousand dollars."

In the late 1950s he had married. He and his wife adopted a child. The marriage ended in divorce, but the child spent his childhood living with Willie in San Francisco and, later, New York. The Giants traded him back to New York in 1972 and as a Met he helped the team win a pennant in 1973. In the World Series against Oakland, won in 7 games by Oakland, he hit well but looked very much like a forty-two-year-old man playing a younger man's game when he stumbled under a fly ball. After the season he retired to become a Met batting coach and good-will ambassador. His career batting average was .302 and his 660 homers have been topped only by Babe Ruth and Hank Aaron.

In his last years with San Francisco and New York, the Say Hey Kid had lost all of his youthful exuberance. Often somber and sometimes surly in the clubhouse, he once said, "I know a lot of people and a lot of people know me. But friends? I have only a few friends." He guarded his privacy carefully. Once I was talking to him in the Met clubhouse when a friend of his came by and asked when he might retire. "Hell," he

Willie smiles a greeting in Atlantic City in 1984.

growled, pointing a thumb at me, "you know I can't say anything important when there is a reporter around." In 1979, elected to the Hall of Fame, he was asked who was the greatest player he had ever seen. "I am," he said, screeching with his old-time laughter. In 1983 he was asked to play in an old-timers game in Washington, D.C. Willie showed up but strode out of the stadium when he was asked to come into the game as a pinch runner. "They were nice people," Willie later said. "But me a pinch runner? They didn't know very much about baseball."

In 1981 he had to sever his coaching and public-relations work with the Mets after taking a job as a greeter at Bally's Park Place Casino Hotel in Atlantic City, a gaming resort. Plumper around the middle but much more jolly than during his last years as a ballplayer, he told one Atlantic City visitor: "I got to lose ten pounds, but it's hard to stay in shape when all I'm doing is eating."

Bobby as a Redskin pass catcher in 1963.

Bobby Mitchell

I WAS RIDING WITH BOBBY MITCHELL—
he preferred to be called Bob but fans called
him Bobby—in his cloud-gray Sting Ray
sportscar. The time was near dusk on a
warm August evening in 1963 in Washington, D.C. Mitchell swung the Sting Ray into
Pennsylvania Avenue, the sidewalks deserted, this being a Sunday. He was driving
me to my motel and on the way he was giving me an example of why his friends called
him Confidence Personified.

Some years earlier, he told me, Confidence Personified had been playing for the

Cleveland Browns, and he had decided that he could do a selling job for a meat-and-produce firm in Cleveland. He did not know any of the officials of the firm, but he looked up the phone number of the company's president and called him at home one night. "I'm Bob Mitchell of the Cleveland Browns," he told the president, "and I think I can be a great salesman for you."

"I don't need any more salesmen," the president replied.

"Just let me talk to you tomorrow at your office."

The next day he went to the president's office. They talked for an hour. When Mitchell came home, his wife, Gwen, asked if he had gotten the job.

"Yep."

"Did he say so?"

"No, but I'm sure I've convinced him."

"You're crazy," Gwen said.

That night the phone rang in Mitchell's living room. Calling was the company's president. He wanted to hire Mitchell.

"Now I ask you," Mitchell said to me as we rode in the Sting Ray, "was that Confidence Personified or was it not?"

Earlier that evening, sprawled on a couch in the living room of his rambling house, he talked more about Confidence Personified. During his first four years in the National Football League, he was a speedy, shifty ball carrier but he was always running in the shadow of Cleveland's other running back, Jim Brown, whom many still consider the greatest running back ever. After the 1961 season Bobby was traded to the Redskins, who asked him to switch from running back to wide receiver. Early in the 1962 season the Redskins went to Cleveland for a game. Much of the pregame speculation focused on how well Mitchell would do against his old team. Mitchell was eager to prove that Cleveland coach Paul Brown had made a grievous error in trading him. "I went into that game," Mitchell told me, "really determined that Jim Brown and all

my friends on the Browns would still think of me as a great football player."

The Browns knew how eager Mitchell would be to catch a pass and score a winning touchdown. They put an inside-outside zone on him, which meant that he was covered by two and sometimes three defenders.

"You realize I went most of four periods without touching the ball," Mitchell said in his dramatic way of speaking, his right eye squinting as he stared at me. "I wanted that ball real bad. But the more a receiver goes without the ball, the more he tightens up."

Cleveland led, 16–10, and there were only two minutes left in the game. Washington had the ball on the 50-yard line. In the huddle Washington quarterback Norm Snead called a pass play. Mitchell was supposed to run straight downfield. But he was bumped at the line of scrimmage. He couldn't go deep. As he turned, he saw Snead scrambling for his life, pursued by blitzing Brown linebackers. The desperate Snead saw Mitchell and hurled the ball in his direction. Mitchell was still spinning from the bump that had knocked him out of his route as the ball arrowed toward him. He lunged for the pass, snared it, and bolted toward the sideline, chased by a small gang of Browns. He ran away from them, then sped between two converging safetymen and crossed into the end zone with the game-winning touchdown.

"It was an impossible run," Mitchell told me in his living room. His face radiated the joy he had felt that day in Cleveland a year earlier. "I had nowhere to go but I found somewhere. I don't think that many individuals could have done that. It was the greatest run I've ever made, and I've made many a run, caught many a pass. And with all that pressure on me. *That* was Confidence Personified."

He wasn't always Confidence Personified. Robert Cornelius Mitchell grew up in Hot Springs, Arkansas, where he was born. "When I was a kid," he told me, "I guess I spent about three quarters of my time by myself. I'd take long walks and if I saw someone I knew, I'd cross the street. I never understood it, except sometimes I needed to be alone."

He was still the shy, diffident loner at the University of Illinois, which he attended on both track and football scholarships (he once set a world record in the 70-yard low hurdles). He came to Cleveland in 1958, playing alongside Jim Brown, whom he tried to emulate. He saw how Brown talked easily and with confidence to reporters and business executives. He decided that he had to be more like Jim Brown. "I've worked hard to build an image," he told me one afternoon as we rode in a bus to a Redskin preseason game in Norfolk, Virginia. "Suppose Bob Mitchell is thought of only as an athlete. I walk off the field and what have I got? If I've got nothing, that means I didn't build an image."

He called on Cleveland executives, even ones he didn't know, like the president of the meat-and-produce firm, and began to do sales, promotion, and public-relations work. He had come out of his shell not by creeping but by leaping. Soon he was known around Cleveland as the flashy one of the two Cleveland running backs. Jim Brown was the conservative, solemn one; Bobby Mitchell was his snappy, red-vested, always-on-the-go kid brother. But around the league, Mitchell knew, he could go on doing all the things he was doing—running back kicks, scoring on sudden dashes up the middle or around the end, catching passes—and he would still be the "other" Cleveland running back.

"I gained at least a thousand yards each of the four seasons I was with Cleveland," he told me in the bus, "but I never made the All-Pro team because they never pick two backs from the same team and I was on a team with someone you had to pick—Jim Brown."

Forces were at work, however, that would move Mitchell out of Cleveland—"the greatest thing that ever happened to me," he would say twenty years later. Late in the 1961 season Paul Brown, the Cleveland coach, had watched with awe the running of a Syracuse University halfback, Ernie Davis, whom scouts rated better than Jim Brown in his Syracuse days. That same season the Washington owner, George Preston Marshall, was being nudged by John F. Kennedy's U.S. Department of the Interior, which owned the team's stadium, to sign a black player or be thrown out of the stadium. Up to then Marshall had refused to sign black players, one reason being the popularity of the Redskins in the South, the games broadcast on a chain of radio stations across Dixie. "We will start signing Negroes," Marshall once said, "when the Harlem Globetrotters start signing whites." But if he had to hire a black, he decided, it would be a proven star like Mitchell. Having won only one game in 1961, the Redskins owned the number-one draft choice. Marshall traded his number-one choice to Cleveland, which picked Davis, in return for Mitchell. (Tragically, Davis died of leukemia before ever playing in an NFL game.)

Mitchell became the first black to put on the burgundy-and-gold uniform of the Redskins. He strode into Washington with his salesman's smile and was shocked to discover that some restaurants wouldn't let him in because of his color. He kept his confidence that bordered on cockiness. "I'm not cocky," he told me. "You're cocky if you say you can do things and you don't do them. It's confidence when you say you can do things and you do them. I have the power of confidence."

In Washington he won the same job with the Pepsi-Cola company that Brown had in Cleveland, making speeches in black neighborhoods. He adopted Brown's pin-striped boardroom manner as he talked about "the pressing dropout situation" in the schools and the need for Pepsi to make itself known among blacks "image-wise."

He was almost religious in his loyalty to Pepsi. Whenever he talked about Pepsi's rival, Coca-Cola, he referred to the drink as "Brand X." Once he and I were chatting in his hotel room before a Redskin game. Also in the room was Mitchell's roommate, a tall young running back whose name I have since forgotten. The roommate left the room and returned carrying a can of Coca-Cola.

Mitchell jumped up from the chair on which he had been sitting. "Roomie," he shouted, "what are you doing drinking that Brand X?"

"I don't work for Pepsi, you do," the roommate said, laughing. Mitchell shook his head in dismay.

The roommate finished drinking the Coca-Cola and tossed the empty can into a wastepaper basket. A few minutes later a Pepsi executive arrived to confer with Mitchell about his speaking dates. As the executive shook hands with Mitchell, he spotted the can of Coca-Cola.

"What's *that* doing here?" he shouted, drawing back as though it were a rattler uncoiling to strike.

Mitchell put both hands to his face. "I don't drink that Brand X," he said loudly. He pointed a finger at the roommate. "I told you, roomie, you got to stop drinking that Brand X!"

He told me proudly of the speeches he made for Pepsi. "During the last year or so I figure I spoke to more than a hundred thousand people. When you realize I spoke to no more than a hundred or so at a time, that's a lot of speaking engagements. I talk about different things. I don't believe in making what I call a football speech, telling them how I ran eighty yards down the field. I concentrate especially on the dropout situation. But I don't limit myself. I go into the physical-fitness sphere, the delinquency sphere, everything."

He also made more than his share of 80-yard runs during his years as a Redskin re-ceiver from 1962 to 1968, when he retired. Twice he led the NFL in pass-catching yardage. He played on three Pro Bowl teams. His total of ninety-one career touchdowns ranked him fifth in 1983, when he was elected to the Pro Football Hall of Fame, behind fellow Hall members Jim Brown, Lenny Moore, Don Hutson, and Jim Taylor. He never left football, continuing to make public appearances and after-dinner speeches for the Redskins. He decided to live in Washington which now welcomed him and other blacks into its poshest restaurants. In 1984 he was the team's assistant general manager. Of Mitchell, Jim Brown said in 1983, "I don't think anybody in the history of professional football has left one team as a star, gone to another team and integrated it, was switched to another position, and then led the league in receptions. Bobby Mitchell was the most unsung hero I've ever known."

Bobby as a Redskin executive in 1984.

Vinegar Bend Mizell

"I DON'T THINK I SAY ANYTHING FUNNY," Vinegar Bend Mizell told me as we sat in the lobby of a small hotel in St. Petersburg in early March of 1956. I winced.

I winced because I had come to Florida to write about Vinegar Bend and prove to the world that he was the "new Dizzy Dean." Like Vinegar Bend, Dizzy had pitched for the Cardinals. Like Vinegar Bend, Dizzy had come from the rural south. True, Dizzy had been righthanded, Vinegar Bend was left-handed, but we of the sporting press were not stymied by that anatomical difference: We simply called Vinegar Bend "the left-handed Dizzy Dean."

Vinegar Bend would never be a lefty or a righty Dizzy, certainly not as a pitcher. Nor did he become the Dizzy who made a nation laugh during the 1950s by telling people on radio and television that a player "slud" home and by singing at almost any time the Wabash Cannon Ball.

But Vinegar Bend had what would later be called charisma—in his case that meant you looked at him and you wanted him to make you laugh. His strong and handsome face nearly always wore an impish look, his mouth curving into an upside-down smile. Tall and rawboned (six-foot-three and two-hundred pounds), he had the rangy frame and sharply-hewn handsomeness of Li'l Abner, the comic-strip character. He wore a cap that seemed at least a size too small, giving the top of his head a pointy look. He donned the cap by grasping the top and, as he said, "kind of screwin' it on." He talked in a slow drawl, the I's coming out as ah's, the my's as mah's.

"He looks and talks like a good old country boy on his way to ploughing a field behind a mule," Cardinal general manager Frank Lane told me. "You don't have to say anything to make me laugh," I heard pitcher

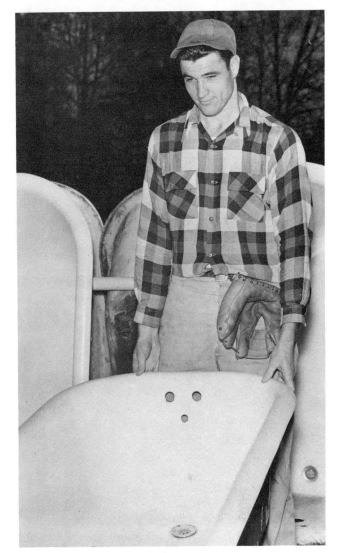

Vinegar Bend between seasons in 1953.

Ellis Kinder tell Vinegar one day. "All I've got to do is look at you."

Not that Vinegar didn't say funny things; occasionally he did. The St. Louis reporters were convulsed by a conversation reported by J. Roy Stockton, then the sports editor of the *St. Louis Post Dispatch*. Vinegar Bend's mother had named him Wilmer, but he liked Vinegar Bend much better, perhaps sensing even then that the name would make him stand out in sports or any other crowded field, including politics. "What does your mother call you?" Stockton asked him. "Wilmer," Vinegar said, despairingly.

He liked the name so much, he told Stockton, that when he wrote back home to relatives, he sometimes absent-mindedly wrote out their address as Vinegar Bend, Mizell. But all the letters, he said, were delivered.

He was born, on August 13, 1930, in Leakesville, Mississippi, which wasn't far from Vinegar Bend, Alabama. But he was still Wilmer when he pitched for the Long Branch Rebels: "My team was all relatives," he once said. "I was the pitcher and my brother Curtis, he was the catcher. A first cousin played first base, a first cousin played second base. . . . My uncle Irvin Turner—he raised me 'cause my daddy died when I was a year and a half—he played third base. . . . My other uncle was our eleventh man. He umpired. I didn't walk many on that club."

Cardinal scouts saw him at a tryout camp in Biloxi. A few weeks later a Cardinal scout, Buddy Lewis, came looking for him at his home near Leakesville. Wilmer was swimming in a creek. Seeing the scout, Wilmer dashed out of the creek and pulled on his trousers. "I threw four fast balls," he told me, "and the scout signed me on the spot." Pitching for Albany, Georgia, he told people he came from near Vinegar Bend. "They thought Wilmer was no name for a baseball player," he told me, "and they got to calling me Vinegar Bend."

In 1951, only twenty-one, he came up to the Cardinals and won 10 while losing 8. The next year he won 13 and lost 11. He went into military service during the 1954 and 1955 seasons and when he came back he was greeted by me and other reporters anxious to crown him the new lefthanded Dizzy Dean.

At 1956 spring training in St. Petersburg, I asked him to pose for a magazine's cover. "Smile," I said as the photographer focused his camera on his face, "just like you would

smile after winning your 20th game of the season."

He stared at me, mouth hanging ajar. "Smile like I just won my 20th?" he drawled. "Why, I tell you, mister. If I won 20 games in this league, no photographer would have to tell Vinegar how to smile. I'd be doin' it day and night."

He never did win 20. In 1956 he had a 14–14 season. His only winning season as a Cardinal ws 13–10 in 1959. But he gave the Cardinals a fair share of laughs. In 1959 he was pitching against the Braves. In five innings he gave up nine hits, seven walks and ten runs. Finally, his patience exhausted, manager Solly Hemus came to the mound and told Vinegar, "I think I'm going to take you out."

Vinegar stared at Hemus and said, "Why?"

In a game against the Dodgers, St. Louis led, 4–0. The Dodgers put runners on second and third and lefthanded-hitting Duke Snider came to the plate. Fred Hutchinson, then the manager of the Cardinals, waved in Vinegar Bend from the bullpen. At the mound he told Mizell:

"Mizell, I just want you to get this one hitter out. That's all I want you to do."

Vinegar Bend got Snider out. The next hitter was Gino Cimoli, a righty hitter. Hutchinson decided to let Vinegar pitch to him. Vinegar walked Cimoli, filling the bases.

"Well," Hutchinson said later, "he hadn't given a hit yet and we were ahead. I let him pitch to Hodges."

Gil Hodges, the Dodger first baseman, smacked a bases-loaded home run to tie the score and the Dodgers went on to win. "It was Hutch's fault we lost," Vinegar said, not unreasonably, in the clubhouse. "He said he wanted to get Snider out, but he didn't say nothin' about Hodges."

In 1960 the Cardinals gave up on their hopes for Mizell and traded him to the Pirates. There, for a brief time, he seemed close to being "the lefthanded Dizzy Dean" kind of pitcher that people had predicted he would be in 1956. He won 13 games and lost only 5 for the Pirates, who won the National League pennant. He started the third game of the Series against the Yankees and was less then Dean-ish, the Yankees scoring six runs in the first inning to drive him from the box. The Pirates won that Series in seven games but Vinegar left it with an ERA of 15.43.

That 1960 season was a high-water mark for Vinegar. His arm sore, he slipped to 7–10 the next season, and by 1962 was laboring for a pathetic New York Met team, his labors being not fruitful (no victories, two losses) and concluding with his retirement. In nine National League years he won 90 while losing 88, his career ERA 3.85. In 1,528 innings of pitching he struck out 918 batters. In some 400 more innings of pitching (1,966), Dizzy struck out only 237 more (1,155), so in the area of strikeouts, at least, Vinegar Bend indeed became a reasonably close facsimile of a lefthanded Dizzy Dean.

While pitching at Winston-Salem, North Carolina, during his minor league career, Vinegar Bend had met his wife, Nancy, and they went back to Winston-Salem after he left baseball. He joined a Pepsi-Cola bottling firm in a sales and public relations job. He also became County Chairman of the Republican Party and his charisma—you *had* to like Vinegar Bend no matter what your party affiliation—began to do more for Mizell than it had ever done for him in baseball. In a county that had three times more Democrats than Republicans, the Republican Mizell was elected to Congress in 1968, 1970, and by a huge margin in 1972. In 1974, though, "that Watergate issue," he says, "was too much to overcome and I was defeated." But people in Washington, especially Republicans, hated to see good old Vinegar leave. In 1975, with Gerry Ford now in the White House, Vinegar was appointed

an assistant secretary of commerce. In 1976 Jimmy Carter and the Democrats came to town and charisma if you were Republican counted for nothing.

Vinegar went back to Winston-Salem to work as a public relations representative for a tool manufacturer. By 1982, with a Republican back in the White House, the impish charm of Vinegar Bend was again being seen in the corridors of the Congress. Vinegar Bend was appointed an assistant secretary of agriculture for governmental and public affairs. He and Nancy and their two sons commute between a home in Virginia and their home in Winston-Salem. As I talked to Vinegar Bend and he told me about his manifold responsibilities in Washington, I thought to myself: Well, back in 1956 I tried to make out that you were dizzy, but never did I say, thank God, that you were dumb.

Vinegar goes to Washington every day in 1984.

Stan the Man (*right*) in 1958 with the author and ex-teammate Red Schoendienst.

Stan Musial

I HAD JUST ARRIVED IN ST. PETERSBURG, Florida, from New York to interview players at the 1957 spring training camps. I walked into the Cardinal clubhouse, pale after a winter in New York, and saw the rangy, pointy-faced Stan Musial. He stared at me for several moments, then began a high-pitched laugh that was close to being a giggle. "Hey," he said, "where did you spend the winter—in a flour sack?"

I said something to the effect that only millionaire ballplayers could afford to look as tanned as he did in early March. But he was still laughing, enjoying his own joke because he was first of all a baseball player and second of all a would-be entertainer.

He was a ballplayer who had a boyish enthusiasm for playing baseball, even when he was forty-two and approaching grand-fatherhood. In 1956 he said to me, "When I was only making about fifty dollars in the

minors I thought that being a big-league ballplayer was the happiest job I could find. I still feel that way, and it's not just the money and the crowd yelling. It's the game itself. When I do quit and sit in the stands, I'll look at the ballplayers and think, 'Hey, they are the luckiest guys alive.'"

Stan had been fascinated by baseball since he was a boy, his blond-haired wife, Lillian, once told me, "The first time I saw him," she said, "he was a gangling four-teen-year-old standing on the pitcher's mound at Palmer Park in Donora, Pennsylvania [where Musial was born on November 21, 1920]. My father had taken me, only four-teen myself, to see a local team play. As we walked to our seats, someone said, 'Look at that Polish kid pitch.' I looked, saw Stanley Musial on a baseball field with men in their twenties and thirties, and I thought he was such an amazing boy.

"I didn't know his name—he was still 'that Polish kid'—but I saw him play basketball for the high-school team and I thought to

144

myself how nice he looked in his uniform. After the game my sister Ann, her date, and I went to a skating rink. Stan was there. I asked Ann's date who the handsome fellow was—and he teased us both into making a date. The following year we began going steady.

"My father owned a grocery store and Stan would come down there to meet me and occasionally help my dad. When he did, he'd gulp down a quart of milk and pack away slices of luncheon meat. Watching him I'd laugh and say, 'You know why you go out with me? Because my father owns a grocery store.'"

Musial was offered a basketball scholarship at a Pittsburgh college, but in the spring of 1938 he chose the $50 a month the Cardinals offered him to play baseball. He came back to Donora during the off-seasons to finish high school. On November 21, 1939, Stan's nineteenth birthday, he and Lillian were married.

In 1940 Stan played for a Cardinal farm club in Daytona Beach. The manager was Dickie Kerr, a former White Sox pitcher. During the season Lillian became pregnant. The Kerrs insisted that the near-penniless couple move in with them. When the baby was born, Stan and Lillian named their first son Dick. Some sixteen years later, when the Kerrs were out of baseball and looking for a home in Texas, they found that they suddenly owned a $20,000 home in Houston, bought for them free and clear by Stan and Lillian Musial.

Musial played the outfield when he wasn't pitching, the Cardinals and Kerr aware that this six-foot, skinny one-hundred-seventy-pound left-handed hitter could spray long drives with consistency. He hurt his left shoulder diving for a ball, and his pitching career was ended (after that he never had a strong arm as an outfielder and played part of his career at first base). The Cardinals sent him to Springfield, Missouri, for the 1941 season and in midseason promoted him to

Rochester, New York, their triple A team. "On the train we were so excited," Lillian told me. "I remember Stan saying to me, 'It looks now like all our baseball ambitions are coming true.' Stan finished the 1941 season with Rochester, hitting a fine .326. He arrived home in Donora on a Sunday, went to Mass, then flopped into bed. While he was sleeping a telegram came. I woke him up and gave it to him. Knowing the National League race was still on, I said, 'I bet the Cardinals want you to report.' And they did."

On September 17, 1941, two months shy of his twenty-first birthday, Musial joined a Cardinal team nipping at the heels of the front-running Brooklyn Dodgers. In his first at-bat, he popped up a knuckleball. He had never before seen a knuckleball. In his second at-bat he rammed a knuckleball against the wall for a double to score a couple of runs. Playing in the last 10 games of the season he batted .426 but the Cardinals' dash for the pennant fell 2½ games short. A year later, however, they nipped Brooklyn to win by 2 games. They took on the lordly Yankees, winners of five World Series in the past six years. A scrappy, young, and hungry bunch of Cardinals—Musial, Country Slaughter, Marty Marion, and Mort and Walker Cooper—roared by the surprised Yankees to win in 5 games, winning the last 4 after dropping the first. "What helped us," Musial later told me one evening in St. Petersburg, "was we had gone through a tough race with the Dodgers—we caught them late in September in a doubleheader at Brooklyn—and winning a pennant in a close race, I think, might have made us more aggressive. We might have been more up than the Yankees were. For me, it was the greatest Series I ever played in, being it was my first and then beating the Yankees four games in a row."

In 1943 he topped the league with a .357 average as the Cardinals won another pennant, losing in the Series to the avenging

Yankees. In 1944 he hit .347 as the Cardinals won a third straight pennant and a second world championship in three years as they beat the St. Louis Browns. In the navy in 1945, he returned in 1946 to hit .365, best in the league. The Cardinals won another pennant and a world championship as they beat Ted Williams and his Red Sox in a 7-game Series. In five big-league seasons, Musial had helped to win four pennants and three World Series. They would be his last.

By June of 1947 he was hitting only .200. His appendix was inflamed, causing him such pain that ice packs had to be placed on his abdomen after each game. Doctors told him he could struggle through the season, wincing with pain, or have the appendix removed, but he would be through for the rest of the season. "I decided to stick," he told me in 1957. "Maybe it's just pride, but I've always wanted to hit three hundred or better each season. My chances, though, looked pretty slim. But I kept swinging and slowly my average started to climb. I'd finish a game near exhaustion. But one thing made me come back the next day. No matter how badly I did, no matter how many times I struck out with a winning run on base, the fans in St. Louis kept encouraging me. Sometimes, in fact, I think they cheered louder after I'd struck out than after I'd made a hit . . . I kept on playing—and in the season's closing days I put together a string of base hits to end the year at three twelve. I've often thought back to 1947. I learned how much good you can do by giving the other fellow a pat on the back when he needs it most."

The next season he hit .376 to top the league for the third time. In the thirteen years from 1946 to 1958 he led the league's hitters six times. Brooklyn fans gave him a name that stuck: Stan the Man. In 1948 he began to hit home runs with more consistency, banging 39, more than double what he had hit the previous two seasons, and

from then to 1956 he hit at least 21 a season and as many as 35.

He liked to hit against Warren Spahn, the left-hander for the Boston and Milwaukee Braves who was one of the most successful pitchers of the 1950s except when he faced Musial. "I'll bet Stan has hit five hundred against me during his career," Spahn told me late in the 1950s. "At least it *feels* like five hundred."

I asked Stan about Warren, and he told me about an incident that had happened in 1954 or 1955. "Warren, of course, throws overhand, and I had never seen him throw any other way," Musial said. "But one day he came whipping around sidearm. He blew the pitch right by me. I was so surprised I almost dropped the bat. He threw sidearm again—and got me out. I think Warren figured he had my number. The next four times I faced him, he wheeled in sidearm pitches and I looked helpless against them. The fifth time I hit a long, long home run." Musial began to let loose his distinctively shrill giggle as he said, "It's a funny thing but, do you know, Warren hasn't thrown me a sidearm pitch since."

Away from baseball, Stan lived quietly with Lillian and their children, Dick, Geraldine, Janet, and Jean, in suburban Ladue, Missouri. "He has always got to be busy," Lillian once told me. "He takes a great deal of interest in the house, making sure that everything is just right, from the shrubbery in the garden to the paneling in the recreation room.

"He likes to try his hand at photography, both still and motion pictures. At parties he enjoys telling jokes and he often does magic and card tricks. When Geraldine and Janet were younger, he taught them magic tricks. If you ever shake hands with Stan, be careful. He's a practical joker and he may have a buzzer in his palm."

In 1959 Musial slumped to .255 and hit only 14 homers. He was then thirty-nine and thought by more than one observer to be a has-been. Early in the 1960 season he was hitting so poorly that manager Solly Hemus had consigned him to the bench. I talked with Musial one wet night in Philadelphia. He had come out to the ball park early to take batting practice for almost an hour. In the cold drizzle I watched him swing at perhaps a half-hundred pitches and I wondered why this man, now almost forty, didn't retire to his successful St. Louis restaurant and his lucrative investments. I asked him why when he came out of the cage. He had heard the question before and he answered it quickly: "I want to win one more pennant." And, almost to himself, he added, "You've got to keep on swinging, you know?"

I watched his tall figure walk toward the dugout, uniform drenched with rain and sweat, and I thought: Even the good ones hate to admit when they're through. I wrote a sympathetic article about Musial: "Last Days of a Hero." I was premature. That season he boosted his average to .275. The next year he hit .288. And the following year, 1962, now almost forty-two, he hit .330.

Midway through the 1963 season he announced it would be his last. In September the Cardinals went on a tear to win 19 of 20 games and come within a game of the league-leading Dodgers, the team they had chased when Musial first joined them twenty-two years earlier. Musial stood within touching distance of the pennant he yearned for. The Dodgers came to St. Louis for a 3-game series that would decide the pennant winner. In the first game, the Cardinals trailed 1–0 as Musial came to bat in the seventh. Baseball's oldest player cracked a home run, his 475th and last, to tie the score. But the Dodgers won the game and the pennant.

When he retired he had played longer for one team than any player ever. He had played more games (3,026) than any National Leaguer. He also held league records for most at bats, most runs scored, most base hits, and most runs batted in. His career batting average was .331.

In 1969 he entered baseball's Hall of Fame. Today a statue stands outside Busch Stadium in St. Louis that shows Musial in his distinctive coiled batting stance, "looking," someone once said, "like a kid peeking around a corner to see if a cop is coming." He is prominent in St. Louis charity and business affairs and is seen frequently chatting with the customers of his restaurant. Today he is making much more than $50 a month but whenever I have seen him at a baseball game, those eyes twinkling, he seemed indeed like someone who thought the luckiest people alive were those players down on the ball field.

Stan the Man as a restaurant owner in 1984.

Joe as a Jet leader in 1967. No. 13 is Don Maynard, a favorite Namath receiver.

Joe Namath

IN THE SPRING OF 1965 I SAT IN THE lounge of a Viscount jet with Joe Namath as we flew from Chicago to Birmingham, Alabama. We were talking about whether Joe Namath, the much publicized quarterback from the University of Alabama, recently signed by the New York Jets for the astounding sum (in those days) of $400,000 for four years, would be a flop as a pro.

"Just write this down," he said, jabbing one of his long fingers at my notebook. "Take everything into account—my injury, all the publicity, all the pressure, and just throw them away because I am going to make it."

What struck me, as I scribbled, was how much Joe Namath's drawl made him sound like a good old country boy from the Alabama hill country. I knew well he was about as Dixie as a Philadelphia lawyer; he had grown up in a steel-mill town in Pennsylvania. It would be two years before I would find out, almost by accident, how and why he adopted that southern drawl.

I had met the twenty-one-year-old Namath in Chicago. He and his lawyer from Birmingham, Mike Bite, had come to Chicago to talk to insurance executives about creating a Joe Namath insurance agency. As we dined one evening in a restaurant near the Loop, I told him that he had a reputation for being cocky.

"Everyone is cocky to a certain degree," he drawled. He smiled and held my attention with his sapphire eyes, which always reminded me of blue marble. "If you talk only about yourself, that's cockiness gone too far. I don't think that has happened to me, or ever will." It was a politician's answer, delivered by a twenty-one-year-old college senior who had been a frightened freshman, I later discovered, only four years

earlier. No one I have ever met in sport, I believe, grew in sophistication as fast as Joe Willie Namath.

The next day, his business done in Chicago and after charming Chicago reporters at a packed press conference, he and I flew back to Birmingham. He planned to drive from there to the Alabama campus at Tuscaloosa, where he was finishing his senior year. In Birmingham we went to a restaurant, the Bun 'n' Bun, which was owned by a friend of his. He told them he had just come from Chicago. A young man shouted from a table, "Get any more of that New York money today, Joe?" "No," Joe shouted back, eyes glinting, "but they did make me the president of an insurance company."

He had loaned a friend his luxurious green Lincoln convertible, part of the $400,000 deal with the Jets. He and I slid into the car to drive to Tuscaloosa. I soon discovered that he had learned, among other Dixie skills, the southern young man's fine touch with fast cars, and I wondered how much late-night drag racing had been part of his education at Alabama. With his long fingers, he steered the big car masterfully through the night, a firm foot on the accelerator, seeking out dark side roads as we whisked toward Tuscaloosa and the Alabama campus. He let down the convertible's top. The radio blared rock. The wind blowing his black hair, he thumped one hand on the steering wheel and sang snatches of lyrics ("I'm a reelin' and a-rockin'"). "I like driving at night," he told me. "The air's so cool and sweet. And it's quiet out here in the country. I can't stand all that city noise. I love Alabama. I like the attitude down here about taking it slow. Why worry? People work too hard back home. I'd like to settle down here."

We arrived in Tuscaloosa about nine that night. He led me to several student hangouts. Namath entertained with card tricks, those long fingers wrapped like snakes around the deck. He invited me to stay over with him in what he called "Namath's Mansion," a one-story, ramshackle frame house he rented near the campus. He shared the house with Jimmy Walsh, a law student, and Ray Abruzzese, a former Alabama football player who was then a safety man with the Buffalo Bills. Namath entered, yelling, "Ray! Jimmy! Anybody home?"

The time was near midnight but he woke up Ray and Jimmy and challenged them and me to a game of darts. I said I'd watch, not wishing to compete against a $400,000 quarterback in any game of throwing for accuracy.

A target board hung askew on a smudged, cracked wall peppered with dart holes. Soda bottles were strewn on the floor. Dirty dishes were stacked high in the sink. Caved-in beds lined the other walls. "This wasn't a bad place when we moved in," he said. "But we sure have wrecked the place. The other night"—his voice was breaking into raucous laughter—"Ray and me were chasing cockroaches on the wall, trying to spear them with these darts. We didn't catch a-one."

The next morning I attended an English literature class with Namath. Just before the class a student approached him and said in a low voice, "I'll pay back that money I borrowed, Joe, by—"

"Don't worry about it," Namath said.

Joe listened more attentively than could be expected from the potential president of an insurance company to a lecture on "The Love Song of J. Alfred Prufrock." Later, as we strolled the campus, he told me he had a C average. "I still have about ten hours to complete before I graduate. I'm coming back here next spring to get those credits. I love this place." (And, indeed, he did return to get those credits.)

I didn't see much of Namath for two years. When I traveled with him again, in the late summer of 1967, he had, as he had predicted, made it as a pro quarterback. In 1965 he had been named the American Football League's rookie of the year and in 1966 he was the league's second team All-League quarterback. Fans had poured into New York's Shea Stadium, populated by empty seats before his arrival, to watch a quarterback considered by rivals as the strongest and most accurate passer in the game. Reporters called him Broadway Joe, although the places where he drank and danced his nights with mini-skirted blonds were nearly always on Manhattan's East Side, a generation gap from Broadway.

In that late summer of 1967 I stayed with Joe and the Jets at their training camp, then in Peekskill, New York, and traveled with them to preseason games in Bridgeport, Connecticut; Birmingham; and Cincinnati. In Birmingham I saw the splendor of Joe—and learned about the birth of that drawl—amid a social setting. We were at a party given for the visiting Jet players at the home of Dick Bite, his lawyer's brother. Later I wrote:

"As he always does among people he knows well, Joe dominated the room, talking loudly in a voice that ripped like a saw through the conversational hum. Joe caught the eye as well as the ear: white slacks, lemon sports shirt, a heavy gold bracelet dangling from his wrist. In his hunch-shouldered, slouching manner he moved from one group to another, his blond girlfriend clasping his arm, his long black hair falling over his collar, the hawkish face gleaming under the lights of the pool-side terrace. Joe had just finished telling of some wild experience and now he was laughing about it, the long body jackknifing with mirth."

As I approached him, Joe left the blonde, took me by the arm, and guided me to a couple standing in a corner. The man was tall, round-faced and husky, she was dark-haired and petite. "These two people," Joe said to me, "they've done more for me than I can ever thank them for. Bubba, you tell this writer what you did."

The man was Bubba Church, then an insurance executive in Birmingham but formerly a big-league pitcher for the 1950s Philadelphia Phils. Later, after Namath left the party, Bubba and his wife, Peggy, drove me to my motel and on the way they talked about the young manhood of Joe Willie Namath.

He was born on May 31, 1943, in Beaver Falls, Pennsylvania, the fourth son of a Hungarian-born steel worker. Once, when Joe was twelve, his father took him through the steel mill. "It was hot and dirty and all that noise," Joe once told me. "It scared me half to death. I never went back, never wanted to, never."

His parents were divorced. The boy ran the streets of one of the toughest sections of town, his best friends both white and black. "Joe had nothing," Bubba Church told me. "Think of the toughest times a kid could have growing up, he grew up that way."

Wearing number 19, the number of his idol, Baltimore Colt Johnny Unitas, "Joey U," as his teammates called Namath, led the Beaver Falls high-school football team to a western Pennsylvania championship. He was also the school's best pitcher and its highest-scoring basketball player. "He played against guys six-foot-eight and blocked their shots," Bubba told me. "He could dunk a ball two-handed with his back to the basket."

Big-league baseball scouts wanted him, college basketball coaches wanted him, football coaches wanted him. His mother pleaded with him to go to college. He chose the University of Alabama. But after his freshman year a homesick Joe was close to walking out of school and accepting a $50,000 bonus to pitch for the Baltimore Orioles.

A desperate assistant football coach

asked Bubba Church to talk Joe into staying. "I know what the big leagues are like," Bubba told him. "Suppose your arm goes bad. Then what have you got? No college degree, nothing."

The Churches befriended Namath. "Do you know what it can be like," Bubba told me, "to be a Hungarian Catholic kid in the South, missing his mother, not knowing anybody?" Joe was swarthy and he was from Yankee land and constantly he was ridiculed and laughed at for the way he looked and the way he talked.

Finding a home and friendly faces with the Churches, Namath began to fit himself into the campus society. He adopted the slow and easy Alabama drawl that he would still use as a movie actor some twenty years later. When he became the number-one Alabama quarterback, the students and the state adopted him as one of their own. During the next three years he became a state idol as the Crimson Tide went to 3 bowl games and lost only 3 regular-season games. Only one man of football was more revered in the state—Tide deity and coach Paul (Bear) Bryant. But when the Bear shocked the state by suspending Namath briefly for a training violation, he had to go on statewide television to explain why.

In 1965 the five-year-old American Football League was battling the National Football League for fan and television-network recognition. New York Jet owner David (Sonny) Werblin, a veteran of show-business wars, knew that stars sell tickets and boost television ratings. He sensed that Namath could be the star the AFL needed to prove it the equal of the NFL. By 1967, the AFL now meeting the NFL in the Super Bowl and a merger of the two leagues only three years away, I thought Werblin's $400,000 quarterback had more than paid back the investment in him. "After only two years as a pro," I wrote, "Joe Namath, only twenty-four, is a name more famous than anyone, apart from John Unitas and Bart Starr, in pro football today."

He had become famous for the accuracy and length of his passes and the quick way he released them before tacklers could knock him down. He had become famous for playing on two aching knees, braced and padded to hold them together. And he had become famous for being the playboy quarterback, the one who once explained a Jet defeat by saying, "Booze and broads."

He had been putting on a reporter when he'd said that, but forever he would be the booze-and-broads quarterback. At times the reputation angered him. Once, in Peekskill, he and I were racing to catch a taxi. Namath tripped over a pothole in the road. Inside the cab he said, "I could've broken my leg back there. And do you know what people would've said? They would've said, 'Joe Namath broke his leg falling down drunk.'"

One of his uncles, he once told me, had died suddenly at an early age, and sudden death seemed often on his mind. At Dooley's, a bar in Peekskill, he told me and several Jet players of a place in Texas where, he said, a scorpion had almost killed him with its bite.

"A scorpion can't kill you," a player said.

"A bumblebee can kill you," Namath retorted. A little later he asked me when an article I was writing would come out. I said in two months. He wondered how anyone could plan that far ahead when, he said, "this could be your last day, your last hour." I said he was only twenty-four and had no reason to think he'd be dead tomorrow. He turned and walked away. A few days later I mentioned how much had happened to him during his first two years as a pro. "You never know what will happen," he said somberly. "You can be dead tomorrow."

In 1968 the Jets won the AFL championship. Before the third Super Bowl game, against the Baltimore Colts, he said publicly that he "guaranteed" a Jet victory. The Jets did win, 16–7, the first AFL victory over an NFL team. That was the high-water mark for Namath's Jet teams. During his next eight seasons his Jets had only one winning season. His overall record as a Jet quarterback wes 60 wins, 63 losses, and 4 ties. But he will always be remembered in New York for that one championship and Super Bowl victory, New York's first.

In 1977 the Jets traded him to the Los Angeles Rams. He sat most of the season on the bench, and at season's end announced his retirement. He had appeared in a movie before his retirement, starring with Ann-Margret. Broadway Joe now turned full time to the world of entertainment. He made TV commercials for a maker of pantyhose and a men's fragrance. In 1980 he appeared on stage in a New York City summer production of Damn Yankees, playing Joe Hardy, the baseball hero. "I can't sing or dance," he told people, "but I'm just happy people like to come and see me. Maybe that's what being a good performer is all about."

By 1983 Broadway Joe had made it from the East Side to Broadway. He appeared in a Broadway revival of The Caine Mutiny Court Martial as Lieutenant Maryk, the officer on trial for instigating the mutiny against Captain Queeg. In Atlantic City he played the Jack Lemmon role in Sugar, a musical version of Some Like It Hot, the onetime football hero now in blond wig and skirts. In 1984, now 41, he ended his days of bachelorhood, marrying actress Deborah Lynn Mays, 22, in one of his favorite cities, Fort Lauderdale, the place where he had "guaranteed" the Super Bowl. He may have explained his longtime unwillingness to be tied down by marriage when he told me, as we rode free through that night in that open convertible toward Tuscaloosa, "Being able to get up and go wherever you want to go, isn't that what life is all about?" In 1985 he was elected to pro football's Hall of Fame.

Joe impersonates a female musician in Sugar, a 1984 musical in Atlantic City.

Floyd is congratulated after knocking out Archie Moore in 1956 for the heavyweight title.

Floyd Patterson

THAT PERCEPTIVE SPORTSWRITER, W. C. Heinz, once said of Floyd Patterson that "he has the instincts of a fighter and the compassion of a priest." In two meetings with Floyd, one shortly after he became the heavyweight champion of the world and the other more than twenty years later when he was a boxing commissioner, I saw the truth of that observation.

We met for the first time in 1957 in a lawyer's office in downtown Manhattan. His manager, the bouncy and excitable Cus d'Amato, was conferring with the lawyer about some contracts that the new champion had to sign. The twenty-one-year-old

Floyd had a dreamy look about him as he sat in a high-backed chair, his thoughts seemingly far away. He was the first heavyweight champion I had ever seen up close, and I was surprised at how slight he seemed in a gray sharkskin suit that looked to be off a chain-store rack. (Later I saw the five-foot-eleven, one-hundred-eighty-five-pound Patterson in boxing trunks, broad-chested, thick-legged, muscles bulging his arms, and he looked very much the heavyweight champ; Floyd was the kind who got bigger as he took off his clothes.) His nut-brown face was impassive during the half-hour we talked, seldom showing a smile, even though there was some humor in what he told me. The voice was soft, almost whispery at times, but the dreamy look gradually went away, replaced by the look of someone who thought deeply and intently about the things he told other people.

He said that he had been asked a number of times after he had knocked out Archie Moore in November of 1956 to win the title: "What inspired you to become a fighter?" He had thought a lot about that question, he told me, and had decided the answer went back to a place called Wiltwyck.

"I grew up in a pretty tough section of Brooklyn," he said, "and some of the boys I knew then are now in jail. I never did anything bad, but I skipped school a lot because it never interested me. My mother was busy raising my ten brothers and sisters and she didn't realize how much I was playing hooky. Then the truant officer caught up with me [when he was 11] and sent me to the Wiltwyck School [for truant children, it was in rural Esopus, New York]. I arrived expecting high concrete walls and the tough guards you see in movies. Instead I found a regular school without even a wire fence around it. Our classes would have only eight or nine kids, instead of thirty or forty, as we were back in Brooklyn. Each teacher, as a result, got to spend a lot more time with each boy.

"Being in the country, it also helped me to study more. I'd never been out of the streets of Brooklyn in my life, and the fresh country air was like heaven to me. After classes, we could leave the school and go for long tramps through the Catskill Mountains, and I did that every chance I got.

"On one of those walks I got to thinking what a difference it was for people—living in the country instead of the city. There was healthier air, better schools, sports like horseback riding and a lot less chance to get in trouble. Right then I decided that someday I'd make enough money to come back and build a home in the country for my mother, brothers, and sisters.

"When I was released from Wiltwyck after eighteen months, I went back to Brooklyn [where he had been born on January 4, 1935]. I was determined not to be a truant anymore, because I figured I'd have to get an education to make the money I needed to build that home for my family in the country. I finished two years of high school, but then I had to leave to take a job to support my family.

"I did well at several jobs before taking up amateur boxing. After winning some Golden Gloves tournaments, I went to the 1952 Olympics and I won a gold medal. I knew I was good enough to fight professionally, but I was positive I would never, never be a champ because I didn't think I had a chance. I felt, though, that I was working toward as good a goal as a championship—winning enough to buy that house for my mother and my family in the country.

"I won a lot of money and then I knocked out Archie Moore to win the heavyweight championship. However, I found out I had forgotten one thing—to ask my mother if she *wanted* to live in the country. When I told her she could have a house anywhere she wished, she said she wouldn't live in the country if you gave it to her. She said she preferred to live in a small city like Mt. Vernon, New York, and she then picked a house in that city that I guess isn't much more than ten miles from Brooklyn."

He smiled for what I recall was the first time since he had begun to tell the story, a rueful can-you-believe-that smile. I thought to myself that the story certainly had an ironic O. Henry twist, and I asked him the obvious questions. If he had known ten years ago that his mother would never live in the country, would he have made himself work so hard to make the money in boxing that would build a country house? Or would he have lacked the drive to steer away from trouble and have ended up in jail like so many of his friends?

That rueful, amused smile hung across his mouth and he said to me, as he stood up, "Frankly, I don't know."

We would not have another extended conversation for twenty years. In 1959 I saw him knocked out by Sweden's Ingemar Johansson in Yankee Stadium, and a year later I watched him regain the title by knocking out Johansson, becoming the first to lose the title and win it back. Floyd, never more than one hundred ninety pounds, was not big and strong enough to be a great heavyweight champion. After knocking out Johansson in their third fight, he was knocked unconscious in the first round by Sonny Liston, bigger, stronger, and meaner, and then humiliated in the ring by Muhammad Ali, who taunted him about being a white man's lackey and a fearful "rabbit" while punishing his face and body. He fought his last ring battle in 1972. He won 64 fights, 40 by knockouts, and lost 15.

When I met him again in a lobby of a hotel across the street from Madison Square Garden in the spring of 1977, he was a New York State boxing commissioner. Slightly thicker around the middle at forty-two, he looked otherwise much like the twenty-one-year-old champion I had met in the lawyer's office two decades earlier. He walked through the crowd in the lobby unrecognized, the brown face still as somber as I remembered it, but during the next three hours that we were together, a knowing smile often creased the side of his mouth, the shy boy from Brooklyn now a man of a world that he knew only too well.

He was wearing a chocolate-brown leisure suit. He was friendly and yet there was also that remote look I had seen when I first met him in the lawyer's office, the look of someone telling you not to get too close. At the invitation of a mutual acquaintance, we would be attending a fight that night at Madison Square Garden between heavyweights Ken Norton and Duane Bobick. He told me he was living in New Paltz, New York, near the Catskill Mountains, and not far from the Wiltwyck School of his youth. It was about a two-hour drive from the city. His marriage to a childhood sweetheart had broken up, and he had married again.

At the Garden we settled into our seats near ringside as the preliminary bouts began. People in the crowd recognized him and Willie Pep, the former featherweight champion, who was seated with us. They shouted Floyd's name. He waved with that good-humored smile on his lips. I asked him about the effect of television on boxing. "TV hurt boxing in the fifties and sixties because people got accustomed to watching boxing at home on TV," he said in his even-toned, sleepy voice. "When TV moved out of boxing in the seventies, people didn't come out to see live boxing. We got to find fighters that people will come out to see the way they came out to see a fighter like Cassius."

"Why do you still call him Cassius?"

"Why not? Cassius is a beautiful name." He was smiling. "He called me the Rabbit. Why can't I call him Cassius?"

"Cassius Clay was good for boxing," Pep said. "His beliefs are his own, but he saved the fight game."

"I agree," Patterson said. "I disagree with

the manner in which he kept boxing alive, but he did keep it alive. That much credit I will give him."

I asked if he had any regrets about his career.

"None. I had every kind of experience. I wouldn't change any of the defeats because it was the defeats that helped me to know myself. After I lost the title the first time to Ingemar, I got this idea to disguise myself with a mustache and beard. I was ashamed. Then when I lost the title to Liston, I actually wore the disguise. I had let millions of people down. I wouldn't do that again. I learned never to be ashamed of being shamed. Today I would have the same feelings of shame, but I would be able to face it."

"You obviously miss being a fighter."

"I never wanted to think about leaving boxing. I hung on as long as I could. It wasn't the money. If there had been no money, I still would have been a boxer. Many people see only the brutality and the chicanery of boxing, but to me it's a beautiful sport. Once it gets in your blood, it's with you forever.

"During the 1950s the Mafia was very strong in boxing. But while there was chicanery, the fighter got paid. After the businessmen and the lawyers took over in the 1970s, there was one fight which I didn't get paid for. I went before a committee investigating boxing and I told them, 'Bring back the Mafia. There may be all kinds of underhanded stuff, but at least the fighter will get paid.'"

A little later we watched a semifinal bout between light heavyweights Mike Rossman and Mike Quarry. Rossman sliced open Quarry's right eye and the fight was stopped after six rounds.

Floyd watched the bleeding Quarry walk, head down, from the ring. He glanced at me, shook his head, and said, "You do the training, throw all those punches for

months, and now it's all over. Plus the fact that he let down his friends. After I lost the title to Ingemar, I stood in the ring and thought I'd pay a million dollars if they would cut a trapdoor in the ring so I could crawl underground to the dressing room [in Yankee Stadium]. The walk back to the dressing room through the crowd . . . that's the worst part. I like to go to a loser's dressing room. That's when he needs friends, not when he's won."

He and I went to Quarry's dressing room. He watched as a doctor sewed the gash over Quarry's eyes, the beaten fighter sitting on a low bench, his body shaken by sobs. Patterson told me how boxing had ended his marriage. "My wife wanted me to stay home more. I stayed in training camp so much. That's why she divorced me. I couldn't help it. Boxing was my first love. When I married my wife, that was adultery because I was already married to boxing. I would quit boxing for the woman I'm married to now, if she asked me, but it had to be a special kind of woman for me to let go of boxing."

He talked to a still sobbing Quarry, who stood before him as erect as a soldier being inspected. "You are a better boxer than Rossman," Patterson said. "You were ahead but then your eyes closed. That happened to me in my fight with Clay. I had to fight with one eye and it messed up my whole style. You have nothing to be ashamed of. You heard the people applaud you because they knew what you went through."

Quarry mumbled his thanks through swollen lips. As Floyd and I walked back to our seats, I said, "You told him what he wanted to hear."

"Yes, because that was what I wanted to hear when I lost." And, almost to himself, he added, "But I didn't hear it."

In the main event Ken Norton knocked out young Duane Bobick in the first round. After the fight Patterson and I went to a nearby nightclub where friends of Bobick were throwing a party. As the gangling Bobick came into the place, women kissed him and men pounded him on the back. I remarked to Patterson that someone might think Bobick had won instead of losing.

"What he's receiving here," he said smiling at the scene, "is worth more than he made tonight. After I lost my title the first time, I sat in the cellar of our home for a week. My wife said, 'You might as well be up in camp.' I thought, 'Even she doesn't want me anymore.' Tonight Bobick knows he's still wanted."

Patterson still lives in New Paltz near the Catskills he had fallen in love with as a truant teenager. He operates a boxing club for youngsters. In 1984 he appeared in a TV movie, *Terrible Joe Moran*, and became friendly with Jimmy Cagney, who played the title character, a former boxer. For a while they talked about opening a New York City restaurant. In 1983 he showed he was still in prime condition by running the 26-mile New York City Marathon in three and a half hours—his fourth marathon and his best time ever.

Floyd with a fellow actor in 1984.

Willie drives a punch at Sandy Saddler in 1947.

Willie Pep

THE THREE OF US—WILLIE PEP, FLOYD Patterson, and I—were strolling through the dusk of a warm spring evening in 1977 toward Madison Square Garden, crowds of fight fans eddying around us. On West 33rd Street a bunch of black boys recognized Patterson and engulfed him, beseeching his autograph. Willie Pep, the greatest feather-weight of his time and perhaps of all time, pushed his way by the kids with the chesty way he had of walking, unrecognized, barely coming to the shoulders of some of the teenagers clustered around Patterson. Countless punches had twisted the nose, hammered lumps onto the face, and pounded the eyes into slits. During World War II he won 28 fights in a row, lost 1, then won another 44 in a row. But heavyweights are remembered, featherweights not as well. The burly Patterson was being mobbed by kids as the jockey-sized Willie and I marched unattended toward the Garden.

He told me how highly he thought of today's fighters. "I was lucky to have come along when I did instead of today," he said. "I don't know what I would have done against today's kids."

"You were so quick. You would have murdered what there is around today."

"Nice of you to to say that, John. True, there's not that many good fighters. But the good ones are stronger and quicker than in my day. And they're smarter. They got to be. In my day you fought four-rounders, worked yourself up to six rounds, then eight-rounders before you got main bouts. Today a kid wins a dozen in a row and he is in the main event at the Garden on national television. They're pushed up so fast they got to be smart. They have to learn everything quick."

As Patterson, who had rejoined us, and Pep and I waited for the main event between heavyweights Duane Bobick and Ken Norton, I reminded Pep that we had met before. He nodded when I reminded him of the time and the circumstances: 1966 when he was attempting, at the age of forty-three, to make a comeback. "Yeah," he said, "I remember you coming up to Hartford and we talked," he said good-naturedly. But I knew he had no reason to remember either me or that ill-fated comeback.

He was born in Hartford on September 19, 1922, his name Guiglermo Papaleo, the son of an immigrant factory worker. Like so many fighters of his time, he grew up in the Dead End section of town, ducking and slipping punches in dozens of street brawls; he and his father finally decided he should be paid for what he had been doing for free. And the ring was safe territory compared to the back alleys where kids like Guiglermo lurked. His father introduced him to Lou Viscusi, a fight manager, who shortened the pint-sized, one-hundred-twenty-pound kid's name to Willie Pep, then turned him over to trainer Bill Gore.

"I started him off in the gym," Gore once recalled. "Show him something and—bingo!—there you are, he learns it for life. I remember I once showed him how to spin a man. What you do is spin him and take the step past him and come out behind him. 'I don't know,' he said, 'I just can't get it.' That was the first day. He went to work on it all afternoon. The next day he worked on it. After that he could do it like it was second nature. He learns a move that nobody in the business can do—and he learns it in a day or two."

On July 2, 1940, he fought the first time for money. By 1942 he had defeated Chalky Wright to win the featherweight championship. He was only twenty years old. After the fight Chalky said, "I'd like for Mr. Willie Pep to stand still for just one second and leave me get a shot at him. I'd just like to see what it feels like to nail that guy."

He swarmed in with a quickness that few opponents, if any, had ever seen, ducking and slipping, jabbing and hooking. He smashed Sal Bartolo's nose, made a mess of Allie Stolz, knocked out Jack Leslie, Humberto Sierra, and Eddie Campo, all in defense of the title. He had won 28 straight fights when he lost a close decision to Sammy Angott in a nontitle bout. He then stormed undefeated through his next 44 fights, only a draw with Jimmy McAllister a blemish on that streak—and Willie eradicated the blemish by flattening McAllister the next time they met. In 1948 the streak ended when the lanky, spindly legged Sandy Saddler shocked Willie's backers by taking out the heavily favored Willie Pep in four to win the title Willie had held a half dozen years. It was Willie's first loss by KO and only his second defeat in 136 fights.

They met again on February 11, 1949, at Madison Square Garden. A packed house roared as Pep stepped on Saddler's shoes, spun him, and hit him front, back, and on the sides. Saddler answered with looping jabs. By the twelfth Pep's face was a mask of blood. Then he rallied and by the end of the fifteenth they had to pull Pep off a dazed and bloodied Saddler to tell him he was once more the featherweight champion of the world.

They met twice more. In the next fight Willie dislocated a shoulder and was counted out. Their fourth and final bout was a wrestling, biting, gouging, backroom brawl. At one point Saddler, Pep, and the referee were a tangle of arms and legs pretzeled together on the canvas. Sandy Saddler won, on a technical knockout in the ninth round, and New York State asked the old champion not to come back into its rings.

He kept on fighting wherever there was money to be won. In 1958 he got a nontitle fight with Kid Bassey, then the featherweight champion. A victory would have given him a shot at the title he had won sixteen years earlier, but Bassey knocked him out and Willie retired. He had won 229 fights, 65 by knockouts, and lost 11, 6 by knockouts.

He had also made almost a half million dollars, but by 1966 that money was almost gone. He announced he was coming back to fight again at forty-two, weighing only a few pounds above his old fighting weight of one twenty-five. He won his first 2 fights, but they had been against what the trade calls ham 'n' eggers, part-time boxers looking for dinner money. Even so, his first opponent cut his face and the second, a Philadelphia bar-

tender, caught him several times on the chin. I went up to Hartford to talk to Willie before his third fight. We talked in the living room of his small frame house on McKinley Street. Nearby were framed photos of his daughter and son. He was dressed in gray gym pants and shirt, just having come back from 2 miles of road running. I asked him who his next opponent was. "I don't know what his name is," he told me quickly. "All I know is, it's in Norwalk next Friday."

I asked him about the half million dollars that had vanished. "It went like this," he said. "I'd be walking along the main street of Hartford and a friend would drive by and spot me. He'd slam on the brakes, jump out of the car with the motor still running, grab me by the lapels and ask, 'Willie, I need 50 dollars real bad. Case of life or death.' Thinking nothing of it, I'd peel off a fifty and say, 'Here, don't bother me.' The fellow would jump into the car, drive away, and I'd never see the 50 dollars again. I was young and I thought it would never stop rolling in.

"I am doing this, making this comeback, you know, because I'm a bug on physical fitness." Now he was striding across the room. "When some people today get to be forty, they lay down and play dead. I am not playing dead. I'm keeping in shape. I've always tried to keep in shape.

"Then another thing, I want people to see the real art of self-defense. Too many fighters today, they go into the ring and they try to knock each other's heads off. They don't know how to move in, jab, duck, slip, all that jazz. I'm not a strong guy, you know, and I've got to live on my wits."

He took some poundings in the ring, however, and retired for good, deciding he would live on his wits elsewhere. He got a job working with the Connecticut Boxing Commission and when we talked again, at Madison Square Garden in 1977, he seemed much more mature and realistic than the Pep I had met eleven years earlier. He

Willie works out as a jogger in 1983.

talked, without the illusions of an old fighter attempting a comeback, about how smart and strong today's fighters were. He said he thought Duane Bobick, only twenty-one at the time, might have a chance against the more experienced Ken Norton.

Patterson, sitting with us, disagreed. "If Bobick was my fighter," he said, "I would have waited a year or two before putting him in against Norton. But they need new faces."

"By 'they,'" I said, "I assume you mean television."

Patterson nodded. Pep tapped me on the sleeve. "Listen," he said with a grin on his crooked face, "television was good for the fighter. You got fifty thousand, a hundred thousand dollars from the television alone."

The fight began. Within the first few seconds Norton nailed Bobick with a right hand and Bobick sagged against the ropes.

Pep had jumped up from his seat, the old fighter pumping his fists, his body swaying with the shifting moves of his youth, "Get off the ropes," he yelled, "get off the ropes. Move . . . move . . ." But Bobick stood rigid and Norton dropped him with a right. Moments later the referee stopped the fight.

Pep, Patterson, and I left the Garden. I said goodbye to the old featherweight who said he had to hurry to catch a train back to Hartford. "Bobick must be disappointed," I said.

"Why?" Pep said with a shrug. "It was a good pay day for him." The next day's papers said that Bobick had earned $300,000. He had made more than half as much in a half a round as Pep had made in twenty years. In 1984 Pep was still living in Hartford, jogging three days a week—"just to keep fit," he said emphatically. I asked him if he had any regrets and he said, just as emphatically, "Any fighter who ends his career with regrets never should have been in the ring in the first place."

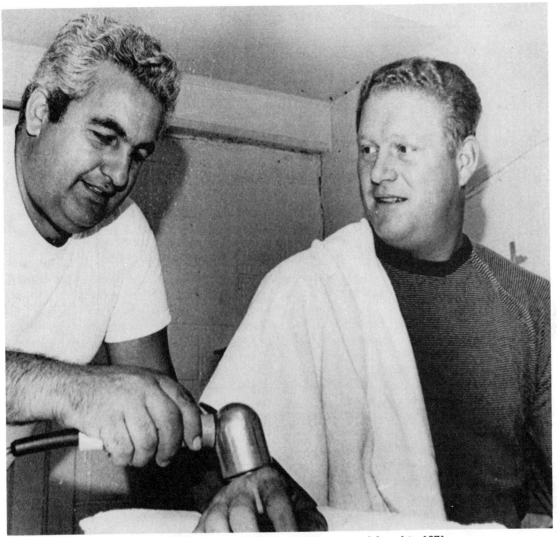

Boog gets ultrasonic heat treatment for injured hand in 1971.

Boog Powell

I AM NEVER SURPRISED WHEN I SWITCH on my television set and see Boog Powell being one of the funny people in those Miller beer commercials, which are heavily populated by newly minted comics like Mickey Spillane and Billy Martin. I will concede that as a mammoth slugger for the Baltimore Orioles, the six-foot-three, two-hundred-fifty-pound Boog did not have a public reputa-

tion for being a wit. In fact, I think most fans thought of him as big, solemn, and silent. He was big, of course, and sometimes solemn and silent, but he had a wit that drew blood both as a rapier and as a blunt instrument. I saw Oriole pitcher Eddie Watt and third baseman Brooks Robinson being bloodied by that wit one March morning in 1971. The crew-cut, double-chinned Boog and I were sitting on stools, chatting in the Oriole spring training clubhouse in Miami. Watt, a stumpy relief pitcher who stood no more than five-foot-eight, shouted across the room:

"Hey, Boog, how does it feel to be fat and red-headed?"

Boog never lifted his eyes, which were staring down at the shoes he was tying. "How does it feel," he said in a deadpan voice that carried across the room, "to be so squat that you get sand in your shoes when you sneeze?"

Oriole shortstop Mark Belanger, seated next to Powell, began to quiver with silent but uncontrollable laughter and finally collapsed, body still shaking, onto the floor.

Boog's tape deck was playing a country-and-western song, the drawling voice of Charlie Pride yodeling " . . . and that was before I met yewwwww . . ." Powell was tapping a foot to the music. Brooks Robinson touched me on the shoulder and said, "I'll tell you the truth about Boog. The booger is really a hillbilly."

Brooks scooted quickly toward the shower to escape the brick he knew would come as a reprisal, but he wasn't fast enough. "Well," said Boog, still tying his shoes, "at least I wasn't born in Little Rock, Arkansa*wwwwww*."

Boog did like country music. He had a collection of over six hundred country records, many by Roy Clark, his neighbor in south Miami where Boog lived during the off-season. One of his favorites was Clark's "Yesterday When I Was Young."

A few days later, sitting in the dugout at Miami Stadium, he cupped a cigarette in one huge hand to hide it from the sprinkling of tourists watching the Orioles work out while he told me of his interest in music and fishing. He liked both at least as much as baseball—and, in the case of fishing, perhaps more than baseball.

"My father was interested in music. My dad collected records of big-band jazz, Benny Goodman, people like that. He didn't play any instrument and neither do I. But I love most every type of music except classical and pop. Country music is progressing. It's getting away from someone sitting up there on a stool and picking on a guitar. You're hearing better backgrounds, a lot of strings, and you are getting more technical equipment for better sound."

The talk turned to fishing as Boog surreptitiously lit another cigarette. "I like the water," he said, "no phones ringing, no one bugging you. When you are fishing, you are alone, away from everything. It's peaceful and quiet out there."

Out there, off the Florida keys, he once caught a 274-pound jewfish. "That was the biggest edible fish I ever caught. The most challenging fish there is down here in the keys is bonefish. They run about ten or twelve pounds—the biggest ever caught was twenty-one—and they are real fighters. But they're not edible. We're big fish eaters at home, so I go out mostly for mackerel. I'll catch twenty or twenty-five, filet them myself, and put them in the freezer."

On request he briskly ticked off the Boog Powell gourmet recipe for cooking mackerel. "I prefer to use a batter. Fried fish can be heavy and you don't get that oily taste when you use a batter. The batter is half flour and half cornstarch, plus three eggs and some beer for consistency. You dip the fish in the batter, then fry it in a pan of peanut oil for about five minutes, maybe a little shorter, until it's brown."

I asked him if he had ever been frustrated when he sat in a boat for hours and felt not one tug on the line.

He stared at me, mouth open, as though he couldn't believe I would ask such a question. "Oh, no," he said quickly. "You have the peace and quiet even if you don't catch anything. Some days, when I go out with a friend of mine, we'll get tired of fishing after a few hours. We'll go to an island he owns, it's about seventeen miles from Miami. We'll sit on the beach, cook the fish we've caught, and then take a nap or just sit and enjoy the scenery." He smiled.

This talk about the peacefulness of fishing and the beauty of music was coming from a man whom Harry Dalton, then the Oriole general manager, had called "the most feared hitter in the American League today." After a few days with Boog I decided that he was fearsome to pitchers on two counts. One, he could cost a pitcher a ballgame with anything from a line-drive single to a long home run; in 1970, the previous season, he had hit 35 homers, batted .297, and driven in 114 runs to win the league's Most Valuable Player award. (In 1969 he had finished second in the MVP voting.) Second, at a gigantic six-foot-three and two hundred fifty pounds, he smashed line drives that had to make pitchers nervous when they faced him from only 60 feet away. "Look at him," Clete Boyer, a skinny one-hundred-seventy-pound Atlanta third baseman said to me one day before an Atlanta-Baltimore preseason game. "Wouldn't it be great to be that big? When you're as big as Powell, you intimidate a lot of pitchers. For example, Felix Millan (the Atlanta second baseman) is a good little hitter but he's small and as skinny as me. The pitcher isn't afraid to challenge Felix with a fastball down the middle. He knows Felix isn't going to hurt him with a long home run or take his head off with a line drive right back at him. But a pitcher looks down from only sixty feet away at big Boog, he isn't going to challenge him. He is going to pitch him very carefully."

One day in Miami Stadium, while Boog was taking extra hitting practice, I stood at the center-field wall, 450 feet from the plate. Boog swung at a pitch and a circle of white, growing larger by the second, shot straight at me. Instinctively, I ducked. The ball thudded into the grass no more than 20 feet in front of me, then ricocheted into the concrete wall behind me with a loud *thuck!* I walked

quickly toward safety while marveling how anyone could permit himself within 60 feet of Boog's swinging bat. Later I read that Detroit pitcher Denny McLain had said that he always pitched inside to Frank Howard, a batter as huge as Boog, so that big Frank wouldn't hit a ball toward the pitcher's mound. I understood what Denny was saying.

Boog had been frightening people since little black kids in Key West, where he grew up, stared at the six-foot-three, two-hundred-twenty-pound high-school senior and called him Boogerman. "My dad gave me the nickname Boog," Powell told me one morning as we rode in a chartered Greyhound bus from Miami to West Palm Beach for a game against Atlanta. "In the South they call little kids who are always getting into mischief 'buggers,' and my dad shortened it to Boog. I was christened John Wesley but now, when someone calls me John, I don't even think to turn around."

John Wesley Powell was born on August 17, 1941, in Lakeland, Florida. His father, a former middleweight boxer, owned a grocery store. His three sons played on the Lakeland team that went to the 1953 Little League World Series in Williamsport, Pennsylvania. Boog was the pitcher, his brothers Carl a catcher and Charlie an outfielder. The team lost its first game, 16–0, but Boog told the world what was coming by hitting a long double.

In 1955 the Powells moved to Key West. He played baseball and basketball and was the biggest lineman on a football team that had George Mira, later an All-American at the University of Miami, at quarterback. "What I liked," Boog told me, "was banging heads against bigger men. Once I played against a two-hundred-seventy-pound tackle and I moved him around like he was a toy."

Colleges offered him football and basketball scholarships and fourteen baseball teams dangled bonus checks. He chose baseball and the Orioles. "Baseball always had been my favorite sport since we went to the Little League world series. I remember when we lived in Lakeland, the Tigers trained there, and one day Johnny Groth and Virgil Trucks gave me a Tiger cap. It was the biggest thing that ever happened to me."

He came up to the Orioles in 1962 as an outfielder. A left-handed hitter, he had trouble hitting left-handers like Whitey Ford. "In my first big-league game," he told me on the bus, "Whitey Ford threw nine curveballs at me and struck me out three times. He was great—the greatest pitcher I ever faced."

Playing mostly against right-handed pitching, he hit .265 and 25 home runs in his second season, 1963, and in 1966, when the Orioles won their first pennant (and swept

Boog gets ready to perform during a Miller beer commercial in 1984.

the Dodgers in the Series) he hit .287 and 34 homers. In 1968 Earl Weaver replaced Hank Bauer as Oriole manager. "You bat third or fourth, depending who is pitching," Weaver told Boog, now the team's first baseman, "and you play every day no matter whether we face a lefty or a righty." His confidence boosted, Boog was one of the big sluggers on an Oriole team that won three straight pennants in 1969, 1970, and 1971.

Against the Reds in the 1970 World Series, Boog hit his first Series home run. That home run—he hit a pitch that he had no right to hit—was a testimonial to Boog's strength. "It was against Gary Nolan," Boog told me on the bus ride to West Palm. "He fooled me. I was expecting a breaking ball and he threw me a fastball. I caught it late, hit it to the opposite field, but it went over the left-field wall." He hit another homer in that Series, went 5 for 17, drove in 5 runs as the Orioles beat the Reds in 5 games. (They had lost to the Mets in the 1969 Series and they lost to the Pirates in the 1971 Series.)

By 1974 his bulkiness had aggravated knee problems that had hobbled him early in his career. The Orioles sent him to Cleveland where he had a comeback kind of year in 1975, hitting .297 and 27 homers. After an injury-marred season in 1976, he was sent to the National League and the Dodgers, where he played only occasionally in 1977, hitting .244, before retiring.

In his career Boog batted .266 and hit 339 home runs. Living now near Key West, and the fishing he loves, he has a son, John Wesley, whom most everyone calls J.W. The crew cut is gone, his reddish-blond hair now flowing around his ears. He is still big, an extra chin added to the two he had as a player, but I would not advise anyone to call him fat and red-headed. Remember what happened to Eddie Watt.

Oscar as a Buck in 1971.

Oscar Robertson

THERE ARE FIVE BASIC SKILLS IN BASKET-ball: scoring, passing, rebounding, dribbling, and playing defense. Until the coming of Larry Bird, I never saw anyone do all those things as well as The Big O, as Oscar Robertson was called. He did all of those things so well for the 1970–71 Milwaukee Bucks that the team won the National Basketball Association championship. That team's high scorer was Lew Alcindor, later to be known as Kareem Abdul-Jabbar, but I have always thought, having watched the team for much of its championship season, that its single most important player was The Big O.

I went to Milwaukee in the fall of 1970 to write a book about the team. I was wary about meeting Oscar. From what I had read about him, I sensed he was standoffish, even suspicious of people he didn't know, a proud black man with a chip on his shoulder. He often glared at a world that only smiled at him because he could put a ball through a hoop. "They want to talk to me because I'm a basketball player," he had told writer Dick Schaap. "Suppose I was a ditch digger. Would they want to talk to me then? Why don't they like me just because I'm Oscar Robertson . . . ?"

For ten years he played for the NBA's Cincinnati Royals. Shortly after the end of the 1969–70 season, Cincinnati traded Oscar to the Bucks where he joined the seven-foot-two Alcindor. The Bucks now had one of the two best big men in the game (the other was Wilt Chamberlain), and one of the two best little men (Jerry West was the other). At six-foot-five and two-hundred-twenty pounds, Oscar had the muscle and the size of most heavyweight boxers, but by basketball standards he was "a little man."

Oscar had never played on a championship team in college or the pros. He was openly delighted to be on a team that could win the title. "I have pride in what I do," he said shortly after the trade. "Naturally I don't like to hear things like what has Oscar Robertson ever won? Naturally I want to be on a championship team."

Alcindor, then twenty-four, and Oscar, then thirty-two, each was obviously well aware of what one could do for the other, which in basketball is simple but vital: feed the ball to the other guy. Lew could soar above people to pull down the rebounds and pass the ball to the fast-breaking Oscar. And Oscar, a clever strategist as well as a superb shooter, could do a dozen things for Alcindor. "Oscar can get the ball in to Lew in the pivot position more than we did last season," coach Larry Costello told me. "Our guards last season were not real good passers, and Oscar hasn't led the league in assists all these years by keeping the ball to himself. Oscar knows you win in this league because of your big man. But, of course, Oscar will also go one on one against his man to score his share of points. No one in this league can stop Oscar consistently one on one."

Indeed, few had over the years. I thought the unstoppability of Oscar was put best by New York Knick guard Dick Barnett, who once said: "If you give Oscar a twelve-foot shot, he'll work on you until he's got a ten-foot shot. Give him ten and he wants eight. Give him eight, and he wants six. Give him six, he wants four. Give him four, he wants two. Give him two, you know what he wants? That's right, baby, a lay-up."

So I was not surprised, considering how important each was to the point-scoring health of the other, that they were soon close. I was surprised to find that Oscar had a dry sense of humor. Once, riding with the Bucks on a bus to a game, I heard this exchange across an aisle:

Lew: "I couldn't sleep last night. I woke up at nine this morning and I couldn't go back to sleep."

Oscar: "My kids were up at eight o'clock banging doors."

Lew: "How many do you have—three girls?"

Oscar: "I'm trying to marry them off."

Lew (surprised): "How old is the oldest?"

Oscar (dryly): "Eight."

I also saw the standoffish, suspicious Oscar. One day in the Buck dressing room he asked me why I was spending so much time with the team, and I told him I was writing a book about the Bucks. "Well, I'm writing a book too," he said to me his voice loud. He was seated, water up to his chest, in a whirlpool tub. The other players overheard and suddenly became quiet. "There might be a conflict of interest. You'd better hold up on your book until I call and check my people."

"You do that, Oscar," I said, but I don't think I successfully hid my annoyance.

"Because when there's money involved," he said, staring at the other players, "I got to think of my creditors."

"It's always a good idea," I said, "to be careful when there's money involved."

"You see," he said, addressing the curious players, "I've become a real American. I think only of money."

The room was silent as he went on. "I wasn't always that way. When I was behind a mule in Tennessee and plowing the field, I never thought about money."

He had been born in Tennessee, but his family had moved to Indianapolis when he was small, so he was joshing about walking behind mules.

"You know, don't you," he was saying, well aware that the attention of every man in the room was riveted on his shining face and flashing oval eyes, "that a mule is smarter than a man. All animals are smarter than man." The last sentence was said with finality—there obviously could be no argument.

Still rankled by what he had said about holding up on my book, which I had no intention of doing, I decided to argue. "I would think," I said, "that it would be more likely that some animals are smarter than some men."

"No," he said, briskly, "all animals are smarter than men."

The players' eyes ping-ponged between us. "I don't know how you can say that," I replied, "when man is the only animal that is aware of his own mortality. Animals don't realize they are going to die."

I thought I heard an approving murmur coming from our audience. Had it said, I wondered, *he's got you there, Oscar!*

He glanced at me, the king of the jungle measuring this interloper. "Do you think that's a good thing, knowing you have to die?" he asked in a hushed voice.

I started to say something, but he cut me off: "A shark won't kill you unless you thrash about and he thinks you're a fish. Only man kills his own."

Flustered, I said, "Well, sharks have poor vision. They—"

"No, they don't," he said in a crowing voice. "Sharks have good vision."

"They need pilot fish, don't they?" I said, but I knew my rising voice bared my uncertainty.

"They're for different reasons altogether," he said firmly. "Sharks have very good smell. They smell other fish, then they hear other fish, then they see the fish."

"Ah," I said weakly, "but their vision ranks third."

He rose from the tub, water sloshing down the sides. "Well," he said impatiently, "who can see underwater anyway?"

I had found that in one-on-one debate with Oscar, The Big O was every bit as unstoppable as he was one on one on a basketball court.

Our relationship was cooler after that, but I think it warmed near the end of that season, his warmth coming from the winning of a championship he wanted very badly, mine coming from my growing awareness of all the things this man could do on a basketball court. He was born on November 26, 1938, in Dickson County, Tennessee, on his grandfather's small farm. When he was four, his mother moved her family to Indianapolis. "I've always told my boys three things," she once said. "I want them to believe in God. I want them to be gentlemen. And I want them to be honest."

Oscar attended Crispus Attucks High School. In 1955 it became the first all-black school to win the Indiana high school championship. The next year it won the title again with the team going unbeaten, making it the first unbeaten team in the Indiana High School Athletic Association's 46-year history. Oscar averaged 25 points a game during the season, and he scored 36 in the game that won the 1956 state championship.

I saw the Big O for the first time when his University of Cincinnati Bearcats came to Madison Square Garden in 1959. To me, Oscar seemed to be a grown man playing against little leaguers. The other team could not stop him from doing whatever he liked. He popped in one handers. Double teamed, he drove around his panting opponents. Under the basket he leaped higher than taller men as though his calves were coiled springs. He tapped in shots, dunked, jumped, and finished with 59 points—the most ever scored up to then at Madison Square Garden.

An All-American during each of his three seasons at Cincinnati, he led the nation in scoring all three of those seasons, a first in college basketball. In 1960–61, his first in the NBA, he led the league in assists, was third in scoring with 30 points a game, and was the Cincinnati Royals' second-best rebounder. He led the Royals in scoring during each of the next nine seasons, but the team lacked the Bill Russell and Wilt Chamberlain type of towering center who could get the ball off the boards, block shots, and score, the type that no NBA team ever has won a title without having.

Oscar was playing with that kind of center, the soon-to-be Kareem Abdul-Jabbar, in the 1970–71 season. On April 30, 1971, I watched from the press row in Baltimore as the Bucks beat the Bullets in the fourth and final game of the playoffs for the NBA championship. In that game Oscar led all the scorers with 30 points. He popped in one-handed jumpers from each side of the foul lane as though the ball had eyes only for the basket. On each shot he rose like a tail-heavy rocket (he had a big posterior), hanging for a moment as his defender came up a fraction of a second too late. He lofted the ball over the defender's fingers, seeming to use the fingers as gunsights, and another shot swished through the nets.

Later I wrote: "Good Lord, for one who loves this game, this is something to see, the pure artistry of the man. . . . He is all over the place tonight, this No. 1, and watching him you know how each Buck feels: With Oscar on our side, we cannot lose."

After the Bucks won that game and the championship, Alcindor was voted the team's Most Valuable Player. I voted for Oscar for all the things I had seen him do: score, rebound, and bring the ball to the other Bucks so they could score. I thought my judgment was proven correct by what happened during the next two years. Oscar's talent began to decline while Jabbar's ascended. Having an Oscar who was not as good as the Oscar of 1971, while having a Jabbar who was better than the Alcindor of 1971, the Bucks never again were champions.

Oscar retired after the 1974 season, his career average 25.7 points a game. He is now a member of basketball's Hall of Fame. He lives in Cincinnati where he has been active in the construction business and helping to promote Pepsi-Cola's youth basketball program. Only slightly thicker around the middle than he was as a Buck, he showed he could still do so many things when he played in a 1984 NBA oldtimers' game. He scored 12 points, pulled down eight rebounds, and handed off for six assists—among his contemporaries, in my mind, still inch-for-inch the best.

Oscar (left) shows his ball-handling skill in a 1983 old-timers game.

O.J. as a Bill in 1972.

O.J. Simpson

IN A FIGURATIVE SENSE, I CLUNG TO THE coattails of O.J. Simpson for much of a month in January of 1974 as we bounced from San Diego to Kansas City to Philadelphia to New York and to Florida. (I was writing a book about him.) What I remember best about that odyssey was my trying, without success, to teach the greatest football runner of his time how to run a half-mile race.

What I also recall, from all our conversations in planes, clubhouses, hotel lobbies, and airport terminals, was what he told me about his growing up in San Francisco. He first told me about that boyhood on a flight from Kansas City (where he had just played a postseason game with the American Football Conference All-Stars) to Philadelphia, where he was accepting an award as the 1973 Player of the Year. We were an hour out of Kansas City. He had just finished a couple of Bloody Marys and a steak. I mentioned Potrero Hill, the section of San Francisco where he had grown up. He settled back in his seat, his wife Marguerite next to him, and stared upward at the roof of the cabin, his large brown face showing both contentment and that warmth in the eyes that comes with recalling a story with a happy ending. "Everything I am," he said in his rich voice, "all that made me, it all came out of growing up on Potrero Hill."

He had been born in San Francisco on July 9, 1947, the fourth child of a bank janitor. His mother had a sister who liked to dream up exotic names for children. The aunt viewed the newborn baby and said, "You've got to call him Orenthal."

"What kind of name is that?" asked his mother.

"It's the name of a French or Italian actor. I forgot which. Orenthal."

"I want to call him after his father."

"Orenthal James," said his aunt. "That's a beautiful name."

When Orenthal James was six, the family moved into a public housing project in the Potrero Hill section of the city. There Orenthal James quickly became O.J. O.J. and his pals in this black ghetto learned from masters how to steal cars for what he called "joy rides," and a favorite pastime was stealing bottles of wine from a liquor store.

"Other kids on Potrero Hill would try what I tried and they would get caught," O.J. told me on the jet plane, smiling and shaking his head in mock horror at the little boy he had been. "But I never got caught. Well, once I did. And when I did get caught, when I got busted by the police, it was for something I didn't do. I was innocent. Now, understand, I was guilty of a lot of things they never caught me for, and then I was busted for something I didn't do."

By the age of sixteen he had found safer ways to make money. He went to nearby Kezar Stadium where the NFL's San Francisco 49ers played their games. He bought tickets for $6. On game day he stood on a corner near Kezar and sold the tickets for $30 or $40 each. On good days he netted $200.

But he had loftier ambitions than making money. "Many people," he told me in the plane, "they think that with a guy from the ghetto the driving force is money. With me, I don't think so. I've always wanted to be known, a somebody." Once in the early 1960s, he walked into a restaurant near Kezar after a game and saw Jimmy Brown of the Cleveland Browns, who was then football's best rusher. The teenager strolled over to Brown, stared up at him with that cocky look O.J. still has on television, and said, "Mr. Brown, one day I'm going to break all your records, wait and see." O.J. remembers that Brown only stared.

At the time O.J. was the best hitter on the Galileo High School baseball team, the fastest sprinter on the track team. He had joined a football team that hadn't won a game in three years. In his senior year the long-striding six-foot one-hundred-seventy-pound O.J. streaked by tacklers and the team came within a game of winning the city championship.

O.J.'s grades were not high enough for a major college. He decided to join the army, most of his Potrero Hill pals already fighting in the muck of Vietnam jungles. A few days before he was to sign up, he met a friend who said O.J. wasn't good enough to play on the football team at City College of San Francisco, a junior college. "Oh, yeah?" growled O.J. On the last day of registration, he signed up for City College. The army lost a grunt and football won a running back.

In 1970 he gained almost 10 yards a crack for the City College football team, slashing through the arms of tacklers, running away from even the speediest backs. "Nobody ever taught that boy how to run," his City College coach once said. "Tying to teach O.J. how to run would be like trying to teach Bing Crosby how to sing."

In two years at City College—1965 and 1966—he scored 54 touchdowns, breaking a record set a decade earlier by Ollie Matson, later an NFL star. During those two years City College won 17 of 20 games and O.J. had become the prey of dozens of college coaches thirsting for Juice. He chose the University of Southern California where he averaged 5 yards a try in the 1967 season to lead the nation in rushing. That season he finished second in the voting for the Heisman Trophy and then went to the Rose Bowl where the Trojans beat Indiana 14–3. In 1968, married now, he won the Heisman as U.S.C. swept through its season undefeated and went once more to the nearby Rose Bowl, this time losing to Ohio State, 27–16. By now O.J. was a nationally known fig-

ure, so well known that Bob Hope used him in a monologue on TV: "O.J." said Hope, "goes into the end zone more often than penicillin."

The Buffalo Bills, owning the first pick of the 1969 draft, chose O.J. He didn't come easy, he and his agent extracting a contract worth $250,000 over four years. It was the most paid up to then for a running back. And that was only the start. A publisher paid him to write a book about his rookie season with the Bills. General Motors agreed to pay him what was reported to be $250,000 over three years to be a salesman for its cars. Even then, before he ever went before a television camera for money, O.J. was recognized as having more than speed and strength. It was obvious that he had that magical quality called charisma. His agent told him he had a guaranteed income of at least $900,000 a year outside of football.

"All of a sudden," O.J. told me in the plane, "I was rich . . . rich . . . I was in the money." But he had always wanted more than money, as he had told me earlier, he had wanted to be known. But Buffalo seemed more likely a place where even a great runner could be forgotten, the Bills among the worst teams in the soon-to-be-dissolved American Football League, their record only 4–9–1 in 1968. O.J. finished sixth in the league in rushing, but his average was a tepid 3.9 and his longest run was for only 32 yards.

A month after that 1969 season I met O.J. at an automobile show in New York and I asked him if he thought he had been a flop. "I don't think I was a flop," he said with a pleasant smile. "Maybe the team was a flop, but I don't think I was."

He talked at length and with some anger in his voice about the Bills' coaches and the quarterback, who was Jack Kemp, now a Republican congressman. "Our big trouble last season was that we didn't run the ball enough. I believe you got to run to win. I'm used to carrying twenty to thirty times a game. In one game for Buffalo I ran only eight times and I got fifty yards. After the game I wasn't even puffing. It's frustrating to feel so fresh after a game. At USC I was used to being beat-up after a game. Let me run and we'll be a winner."

After the Bills suffered two more losing seasons, a new coach, Lou Saban, took over the team for the 1972 season. He inserted more running plays and began to fortify an offensive line with young head knockers like Reggie McKenzie who could blast people out of the way and give O.J. the room he needed beyond the line of scrimmage to take off. In 1972 O.J. gained 1,251 yards to lead the league and the Bills came back from a 1–13 record in 1971 to a more respectable 4–9–1.

"It was the next spring of 1973," O.J. told me as our plane swung into its approach to Philadelphia. "I met Reggie McKenzie and I said to him, 'Reggie, wouldn't it be nice if I could get up to seventeen hundred yards this season?' And Reggie said, 'Hey, let's get two grand and really set the world on fire.'"

The record was 1,803 for a season and it was owned by Jimmy Brown. O.J., as he had promised in that San Francisco restaurant, did break at least one of Brown's records, smashing right through it, and in his last game he went for the two grand and made it, ending the 1973 season with 2,003 yards, a record until 1984, when it was broken by L.A.'s Eric Dickerson. "Yeah," he told me early in 1974 after we had landed in Philadelphia and he was on his way to receive an award from a local touchdown club, "now I got what I'd really always wanted, now I'm really *known*, you know what I mean?" A few weeks earlier *Sporting News* had honored him as its Man of the Year.

A month after my cross-country flight with O.J., I met him in Florida. He and many of the nation's best athletes—Pete Rose, John Havlicek, Franco Harris among them—had come to Rotunda, a small west-coast resort, to compete before television cameras in the "Superstars" competition. The athletes competed against each other in seven events—baseball hitting, the 100-yard dash, bowling, swimming, bicycling, and the half-mile run among them.

He had entered the baseball-hitting contest. I drove him to the baseball field in my rented car. He told me how busy his life had become. He was making a movie (*The Klansman*) in Hollywood and he was commenting on sports for ABC-TV. "I was on a movie set yesterday in Hollywood," he said. "I flew to New York, taped some promos for ABC, and caught an 11 P.M. flight down here. I didn't get more than a couple of hours' sleep. I haven't had time to practice any of these events. I just hope I do well, that I don't embarrass myself."

Two days later he was among the top five in points scored. Coming up was one of his seven events, the half-mile run. "I had to enter the half mile for my seventh event," he told me, "but I'm dreading it. Last night I woke up in the middle of a nightmare that I was running the half mile with millions watching me on television and I had to quit because I was exhausted. It was a real bad nightmare."

I told him he wouldn't quit. I had run the half mile in college. I gave him perhaps an overly simplistic tip: to run a steady first quarter-mile lap and then gradually increase speed in running the second lap. "That way," I said, "You don't have to fear having to stop in the second lap because the first lap exhausted you." He listened, but a look of doubt lingered on his face. I suggested we jog through a quarter mile together, then go as fast as we could through the second lap. He ran the first lap but, instead of picking up speed for the second quarter mile, he slowed down and finally stopped. "None of us," he said, "are ever any good at these long runs." I think he was

referring to fellow blacks who, over the years, have distinguished themselves in track and field's sprints but not as often in longer races like the half mile and mile.

The next morning I tried to talk him into entering the half-mile race. "You could pick up a fifth place just by finishing if there are only five runners in the race," I said. "That would be worth a point that could make a difference of $10,000 in prize money."

He stared at me for several seconds. "You saw me die out there yesterday," he said. "There is no way I want to die out there in front of all these people."

He finished fourth in the overall standings despite skipping that one event and won $21,000. He flew back to Hollywood where $21,000, relatively speaking, was for tips. In 1975 he came back to win the "Superstars" competition. During the rest of his football career, he never had another year like 1973 but he led the American Football Conference in rushing in 1975 and 1976. He was the conference's scoring leader in 1975. In 1972, 1973, and 1975 he was the AFC's MVP. In 1978 he was traded to the team he used to watch at Kezar, the 49ers, and retired after the 1979 season. He joined NBC-TV as a commentator. He rejoined ABC-TV in 1983 as part of the Frank Gifford and Don Meredith Monday Night Football crew. In 1985 he was elected to pro football's Hall of Fame. He lives now in Beverly Hills and has been active in local campaigns to ban sightseeing buses filled with tourists from motoring by the homes of the stars. It was the kind of problem he never had on Potrero Hill. But becoming "a somebody" always has its costs.

O.J. as an ABC-TV sports commentator in 1984.

Bill Skowron

WHEN I THINK OF BILL SKOWRON, I THINK of the scowl. The scowl, fixed on his bulldog face, was framed by knitted eyebrows and a jaw clenched so tightly he seemed to be trying to crack a steel plate with his teeth. As you approached the burly Skowron and you saw that scowl aimed at you, there was an urge to spin on the heels and go the other way. But the scowl was as harmless as another man's stare, and both early and later in his career I found Skowron to be the gentlest of men, the kind who volunteers to canvass the neighborhood for a Red Cross drive or manage the kids' Little League team.

The scowl came from an intensity that traced back to worry. "I'm conscientious," he once said. "I'm not worrying about a bad day. But I'm wondering about it. I'm wondering what I'm doing wrong."

He called it wonder, I call it worry. The first time I met him, in the spring of 1956, the worry showed in his deep-set eyes as he sat on a bench in the Yankee spring training clubhouse at St. Petersburg, Florida. Around him a bunch of the Yankees, Yogi Berra and Phil Rizzuto among them, were arguing loudly about which one would room with Skowron. "Not me," someone shouted, "he snores." There was laughter, the Yankees having jest with the twenty-five-year-old first baseman. But Skowron, a Yankee only a couple of years, was obviously fretting about being accepted by these players whom he idolized. "Aw, come on, quit kidding," he was saying in a plaintive voice. "Who's going to room with me?"

Even after nine years riding planes, buses and trains as a Yankee star, Skowron never lost his fan's worship of people like Mickey Mantle. In the spring of 1964 I spent the best part of a week talking with Skowron at the

Bill as a Yankee in 1956.

Pompano Beach spring-training camp of the Washington Senators. The five-foot-eleven, two-hundred-pound Moose, as the Yankees called him, was a member of a tail-end team for the first time in his life. I mentioned to Skowron that I had just driven from the Yankee camp at Fort Lauderdale, "Yeah?" he said, eyes suddenly shining. "How's Mick?"

I had come to Pompano to write about a new role for Moose. Up to now he had been with winners all during his career. He broke into organized baseball in 1951 with Norfolk and Norfolk won the pennant. In 1952 and 1953 he hit homers for a Kansas City team, then in the minors, that won the American Association championship both seasons. Then came the eight Yankee years from 1954 to 1962—seven pennants, four world championships. In 1963 he went to the Dodgers and they won the pennant and beat the Yankees in four games in the World Series. Moose had won six world championships in both leagues, but now, in 1964, he was a Senator, a team that had finished last in the American League in 1963.

"What the hell, that's no story," he said to me as he sat on a stool in the humid, close Senator dressing room at Pompano, the temperature near 90 degrees outside. He was silent a moment, the scowl tracing tension lines across his broad forehead. He repeated my question: "What does it feel like to be with this team after being with contenders? It's no problem. This is my life, my bread and butter."

"You always want to have a good year," I suggested, "no matter what team you're with."

"That's right. Also, you could say my career is entering a new phase—that I'm more of a coach here than I was with the Yankees and Dodgers. That's because we have a lot more young ballplayers here than we had on the Yankees. I try to help to give the kids a hand. There are six rookies living at the motel I'm staying at. I'm alone. (Skowron was separated from his wife.) I tell them to come over, and I have room service send some things up. I'm making good money and I can afford it. Once, when I was a rookie with the Yankees, (pitcher) Allie Reynolds took me out to dinner. He picked up the check and I've never forgotten that."

His eyebrows had come closer as the scowl hardened. He had just thought of something else to worry about. "Sometimes I get on a kid. We had this squad game the other day and one of our young pitchers, you could see him let up after someone made an error behind him. Later on I took the kid aside and I told him, 'When they make a mistake behind you, that's the time to bust your butt even more. That's the way the Dodgers and Yankees play.'"

Later, after I'd observed Skowron pal around with other Senator rookies, I wrote: "Moose's world is bordered by a bat, a baseball, his two sons, and any rookie ballplayer who asks for help. It's a full enough world. As the song says, the luckiest people in the world are people who need people."

From his Yankee days he had learned the art of clubhouse needling, or "agitatin'," as southern-born ballplayers called their ceaseless off-the-field sport. Once, when the Senators came to Yankee Stadium, I saw him needle Marshall Bridges, a tall black pitcher who, like Skowron, had once been a Yankee. "I bet you just came from the Yankee clubhouse, I bet you even sat down right between Mick and Maris," Skowron said to Bridges, the other players laughing.

"I didn't," said Bridges, a pained look on his face. Skowron leaped to a wall phone and asked the Stadium switchboard to connect him to the Yankee clubhouse. "This is Moose," he shouted to someone at the other end. "Hey, did Bridges go into your clubhouse a few minutes ago?"

No, he was told. Skowron hung up, a foxy smile on his face. "All right," he said to

Bridges, "you didn't this time, but one day you will."

"No, I won't," said Bridges, still looking pained by guilt. The other Senators laughed.

A worrier in baseball, Skowron worried even more about things outside baseball, things that other players told him he had no reason to worry about. The previous winter, he told me in Pompano, he had agreed to appear in a Las Vegas night club show with fellow Dodgers Don Drysdale, Ron Perranoski, and Tommy Davis. After the trade was announced, he told the other Dodgers he would not appear. He told me why one afternoon as we sat by the side of his motel pool in Pompano. Skowron was dressed casually in corduroy slacks and a sports shirt, his blacksmith's muscles straining the silky fabric of the sleeves.

"I told the guys I didn't want to appear in the show. I was afraid somebody'd get plastered in the audience and holler, 'Hey, you're not a Dodger anymore,' or something else like that. It'd be embarrassing.

"Perranoski and Drysdale, they said to me, 'Are you nuts? Throwing away all that money?' But I didn't think it was right for me to go on stage with Dodgers when I wasn't one anymore. Later, though, a guy called me from the Morris Agency. He said I should go on, that I was a personality, and people wanted to see what I looked like. So I went.

"I was glad I did. I got to meet Sinatra and George Raft, Cyd Charisse and Tony Martin, people you only see on television. Once I was watching Cyd do those exercises the dancers do, you know? I said, 'Hey do you do those every day?' She said, 'Sure, don't you exercise every day?'

"I said, 'No, I don't,' and she said 'No wonder the Dodgers traded you to Washington.'"

Moose laughed. "She was kidding, of course," he said.

Indeed she was; no one could ever accuse Moose of not giving all of himself. Once that 1964 season I talked to him in the visitors' clubhouse at Yankee Stadium the day after Whitey Ford and the Yanks had stopped the Senators, 1–0. The Moose was scowling at a newspaper sports page and looking, I later wrote, "like those people in TV commercials who have headaches." I asked a dumb question: "Did he feel bad losing a close one to the Yankees?"

"Geez, of course you do," he said, putting aside the paper. "Whether you're with this club or with the Yankees, when you lose a game like that, sure you feel bad. You sit in front of your locker and you think how you, yourself, could have won it, you know? Sure I try hard against the Yankees, but I try hard against them all."

William Joseph Skowron was born in Chicago on December 18, 1930. His father was a noted semi-pro baseball player in a neighborhood of Polish families. As a boy Bill watched his father play as many as three games on a Sunday. In high school he starred as the husky one-hundred-seventy-pound quarterback and halfback on the football team. But when someone asked him in his senior year what he wanted to be, he wrote: "big league baseball player."

Dozens of colleges wanted him as a football player. He chose Purdue because one of the school's assistant coaches was Ray Schalk, a former big league baseball player. As a freshman on the baseball team in 1950, he hit .500, a Big Ten record that stood for a decade until it was broken by Bill Freehan, later a Tiger catcher. The Yanks offered him a $22,000 bonus and the newly married Skowron took the money. In the minors for only three years—1951, 1952, and 1953—he played both the outfield and infield. In 1954, when the Moose came up to the Yankees, he was made a first baseman, even though he threw righthanded (he also hit righty).

The Yankees were quickly impressed by

Bill, still crew-cut and still scowling, before an old-timers game in 1983.

his muscles. "He's got muscles on muscle," one Yankee said of him. "Johnny Mize once asked me where I got all those muscles," Skowron told me. "I was flattered because he was a big man himself." In that 1954 rookie season he hit .340, sharing first base with Joe Collins. In the next eight seasons, though stricken almost each season by one injury or another (his weightlifter's muscles may have been too compact for a stretching game like baseball), Moose helped win seven pennants and four world championships. His best season was 1960, when he batted .309 and hit 26 homers. In the 1960 World Series, won by the Pittsburgh Pirates in seven games, he hit .375 and had a pair of homers; the next year, in a five-game victory over the Reds, he batted .353 and hit a homer.

His best Series may have been as a Dodger in 1963. In that four-game sweep over the team that had traded him, the thirty-two-year-old Moose whacked New York pitchers at a .385 clip and he hit a home run in one of the two games at Yankee Stadium.

In 1964 he played only half a season with Washington, batting .271, before going to Chicago. He played until 1967 with the White Sox before finishing his career with the California Angels. In 14 seasons he batted .282 and hit 211 homers.

Bill and the scowl now reside in Schaumberg, Illinois, a Chicago suburb. He has been busy since his baseball days in various sales and promotion jobs, but the man who always wanted to be a big league baseball player has never forgotten his first love, and each year, when he gets an invitation to come to Washington, D.C., for the annual Crackerjack old-timers game, Bill Skowron scowls and says of course.

Charley as a Redskin pass catcher in 1966.

Charley Taylor

LIKE MOST YOUNG ATHLETES I HAVE met, Charley Taylor had a dream. As a running back at Arizona State and later for the Washington Redskins, Charley dreamed of one day breaking at least some of the rushing records set by that nonpareil of runners, Cleveland's Jim Brown. In 1966 a coach shot down the dream and Charley woke up one day to know he would never see it become a reality. "To lose a dream like that," he told me in 1967, "after you have gone out to do something and come so close, it's got to take something out of you."

The dream had been ripped away from him by Redskin coach Otto Graham, who told Charley in 1966 that he was being shifted from running back to wide receiver.

Charley was so distraught that his weight dropped from two hundred ten to one hundred ninety-five pounds and at six-foot-three a rangy football player suddenly looked skinny. "When I came home from practice," he told me, "I'd be so upset and worried I couldn't eat. There was a big ball of worry in my mind."

He had never been close to Graham, who had accused him of being lazy a few years earlier. Now he fretted about failing as a pass receiver and his career suddenly being at a dead end. Instead, in one of those quirky developments that abound in sports history, he rose to a lofty level that Jimmy Brown never scaled: Charley caught more passes than any pass catcher ever.

Bobby Mitchell, then a Redskin receiver, also had been shifted to pass receiver earlier in his career. He told me why Charley had been made so unhappy by the switch. "When you're a halfback," Bobby said in his emphatic way, "you *know* you will be involved in the game. The quarterback has to hand off to you. A receiver, he might be double-teamed and the quarterback may *never* throw the ball to him for an entire game. Before a game a halfback can say, 'I *know* I'm going to have a good game.' All a receiver can say is, 'I *hope* I'm going to have a good game.' A running back, you love that position. If you have the size, the speed, and the elusiveness, that is the premier position. A halfback can run with the ball, he can pass the ball, and he can catch the ball. All a flanker can do is catch."

Up to 1966 Charley seemed to have the size, speed, and elusiveness. He was born on September 28, 1941, in Grand Prairie, Texas, where he grew up running as fast as tumbling tumbleweeds caught on a prairie wind. He came to the Redskins from Arizona State in 1964. In his rookie season, 1964, he gained 3.8 yards a run and caught 53 passes, averaging 15 yards a catch. *The Sporting News* named him Rookie of the Year. But in 1965 he averaged only 2.8 yards a run. New coach Otto Graham began to doubt that Charley would ever be even a faint facsimile of Jimmy Brown. "Charley doesn't have the temperament to be a great running back," Graham told me in 1967 when I asked him why he had made the change. "He's too impatient. He wouldn't wait for the pattern of a play to develop. He'd run ahead of the interference on traps, for example, and the man who was supposed to be trapped would be there waiting for him. Charley never learned to glide, to run under control. He couldn't even force himself to do it. We noticed that his best runs were on the outside, where he just outran people."

After Charley was shifted to wide receiver midway through that 1966 season, people saw a change in him. Two years earlier Graham had been coach of the College All-Stars and Charley was one of his players. Graham told a reporter: "Charley is a great athlete, but he is very lazy. He comes late for practice and he is the first to leave." Charley didn't get mad—he got even by being voted the game's Most Valuable Player (although the All-Stars lost to the Bears, 28–17). And later that season when he was named rookie of the year, Charley asked a reporter, tongue firmly in cheek: "Is Otto Graham still in football?"

Charley could have bitten off that tongue a year later when Graham showed he was very much in football by becoming Charley's new boss. The two shook hands, but a Washington reporter told me early in the 1967 season: "Otto thought Charley was lazy in 1964 and he thought so in 1966. Charley used to clown around a lot in practice but he doesn't anymore. As a halfback, Charley could get by on his natural ability. As an end he has had to work hard to learn a new job. No one on this team works harder."

He worked so hard in 1966 that the reformed halfback led the NFL with 72 catches. I was talking to him just before the start of the 1967 season as we sat in a motel room in Cherry Hill, New Jersey, where the Redskins were staying overnight, before their first game of the season, the next day against the Philadelphia Eagles. I asked him about his change in attitude toward football.

"Being a running back," he said, "that was something I was just God-given. Being an end was something I had to learn myself. I was starting from the ground up. I had to do extra work. I couldn't afford not to. I know I clown around less. I'll only fool around now when I have everything down perfect.

"I know I don't have the great speed of most of the receivers in this league. I have to learn more complicated pass routes than most receivers use to get them [defensive backs] to react the wrong way and to get myself loose. I can't run with Bob Hayes or people like that. Once in college they timed me in the hundred-yard dash at ten-point-two seconds, and that was my best. It might be up to ten-point-five or even worse by now. Or even an eleven."

"But Otto Graham told me that as a running back you ran away from people. How could you do that and not be fast?"

"It puzzles me." He was laughing. "But I'll tell you. You get into certain situations, a big man on top of you, you may run that one hundred in nine-point-two when you feel people coming down on you. I'll tell you something—I try to keep people off me."

"Why don't you have yourself timed to see how fast you really are?"

"No, sir," he said, shaking his head. "I don't want to find out how fast or how slow I am. I might find out something that wasn't good for me."

"You were last season's leading pass catcher. You know that teams will double-team you and you may never see the ball. How do you get yourself up for a game in which you may be little more than a spectator?"

He told me that he fixed his mind on how he would beat the man who had the primary responsibility to cover him. In tomorrow's game that would be Philadelphia's Jimmy Nettles. It was then that I learned about Washington's secret play—one that would keep me on the edge of my seat the next day, waiting for the Redskins to spring it.

"Nettles will have seen in the game films all those Packers [short right-angle cuts to the sidelines] that I ran all last year to the outside," Charley said after pledging me to secrecy. "We know he's sometimes weak on passes to the outside. So we want to make him conscious of the short Packer to the outside and catch him coming up fast on me. When he does, *boom!* I go deep for a long pass."

At Franklin Field the next day I watched a free-scoring game, the Redskins losing 29–24 late in the fourth period. So far Washington quarterback Sonny Jurgensen had thrown those short Packers toward the sideline to Charley, and so far he had caught eight for a total gain of 144 yards. That was a well-above-average day for any pass catcher, even one who had led the league the previous season. But I knew how badly Charley wanted to go *boom!* for a long one that could win this game. With five minutes left in the game, Washington had the ball on its 27, first down, 10 yards to go. Jurgensen decided that Nettles had seen enough of those short Packers. In the huddle he told Charley that now was the time to go *boom!*

The Redskins lined up, Charley flanked only a few yards from the left sideline. Gripping my binoculars, I could see, even from the press box high above, a tense look on his mustached, coal-black face. Nettles, a slimly built back, watched him warily from the other side of the line, no more than 10 yards of grass between them.

The ball was snapped. Charley ran the same route, the Packer, that he had traced

Charley as a Redskin coach in 1984.

so often today, right-angling toward the left sideline. Nettles jumped for the lure, rushing forward. Charley burst by him, racing down the sideline, Nettles braked, reversed, and chased after him. I could see at least 5 yards of green between him and Charley as Jurgensen arched the pass. Charley had turned his head to the right. He was slowing down—the pass was a foot or so short. Nettles, closing the gap, also turned, leaped, and batted the ball away.

Charley slammed his hands together, unable to cork his anguish. A week of planning and effort had gone down a tube because a 40-yard pass had been perhaps 24 inches too short and, also as Charley conceded later to me, because Nettles had recovered after being fooled "and made a great second effort." Washington lost, 35–24.

In the dressing room I tried to console Charley by asking him about the passes he had caught in the game. He shook his head. "Don't want to talk about those now," he said. "You can understand, can't you, all that work . . . we made him think outside . . . and then . . ." He turned away.

The work hadn't been a waste, of course. That kind of work in eluding faster defenders would free Charley Taylor to catch 70 passes that 1967 season and again lead the league. By 1975 he had caught his 634th pass of his career to go ahead of Don Maynard as the leading pass catcher of all time. During his thirteen years as a pro, from 1964 to 1977, he caught 649, a record until 1984, when Charley Joiner broke it.

He stayed with the Redskins as their pass-receiver coach, teaching players all the things he learned when he had to give up on a dream. In 1984 he was living year-round with his wife, Pat, in Reston, Virginia, only a short distance from the Redskins' practice field.

Bobby waves during a parade in New York after his 1951 homer.

Bobby Thomson

THE SMILE DIMPLED HIS HIGH-CHEEK-
boned, long face as he recalled the place in
which he hit the most famous home run in
history. Bobby Thomson and I were seated
in Toots Shor's, a Manhattan restaurant, on
a hot July day in 1966, fifteen years after that
home run. He had hit it a few miles north
from where we sat, in the horseshoe-shaped
Polo Grounds, now torn down and replaced

by rows of high-rise apartment buildings. "It
would've been nice," Thomson was saying
in his understated, almost blushing way, "to
drive by the Polo Grounds with my little fellow and hear him say, 'Daddy, is that where
you used to play?' And I'd say, 'Yeah, son,
that's right, the old man got a hit there
once.'"

That hit was "the shot heard 'round the
world," a rising line drive that climbed from
Thomson's bat and vanished into the lower
left-field stands. With one swing of his bat,

the rangy, six-foot-three, one-hundred-ninety-pound Thomson had won a pennant.

It was a memorable ending to a memorable season. In mid-August Thomson and his New York Giants trailed the Brooklyn Dodgers by 13½ games. The Giants won 37 of 44 to catch the Dodgers on the last day of the season and force a playoff. The Giants won the first game, the Dodgers the second. In the third and deciding game, the Dodgers led, 4–1, as the Giants came to bat in the last of the ninth. "With four men up ahead of me," Thomson told me in the restaurant, "I didn't think I'd get a lick. I felt helpless. I was never more depressed in my life. I kept thinking, We've come so far and now to lose because we weren't good enough."

But two singles and a double brought in one run against the tiring Dodger starter, Don Newcombe. There was one out and runners on second and third, the score 4–2, as the Dodgers called in from the bullpen the tall, slouching Ralph Branca to replace Newcombe and pitch to Thomson.

"I wasn't nervous," Thomson told me. "Now I had a bat in my hand. I had a chance to do something. I kept reminding myself to sit back and wait and watch for my pitch. I'd always been overanxious, not sitting back and waiting."

Indeed, the lanky slugger had often been a disappointment to Giant fans like myself. As a rookie in 1947, he had been hailed as the next Joe DiMaggio. Both were tall center fielders who chased after drives with a long-striding, flowing grace. Both batted right-handed with a classic bat-held-high style. In 1947 Thomson walloped 29 homers and batted .283. But he slipped to 16 homers and a .248 average the following season. Even though Thomson hit .309 and 27 homers in 1949, sportswriter Jimmy Cannon wrote that Thomson "lacks the private furies that drove DiMaggio." From a fan's point of view, I thought of Thomson as one of those people who hit home runs when your team was ten runs behind or ten runs ahead, not nearly as often when a home run really mattered.

"I never lived up to my potential," Thomson told me as we lunched that afternoon in 1966. "I was never a .300 hitter lifetime. They said I'd be another DiMaggio. I never was."

He said that in a matter-of-fact tone, with no bitterness or disappointment in his voice. But when I mentioned that moment when he stared out at Ralph Branca from 60 feet away on the overcast afternoon of October 3, 1951, his blue eyes glittered, lit I am sure by an inner emotion that will always be his alone. "Yeah," he said. He put down the fork and knife that had been slicing his steak. He gripped an imaginary bat. "Yeah, I give myself credit for that. That was one time I was ready. That time I wasn't overanxious. That time I sat back and waited. That time I produced."

Branca threw a fastball that hummed by Thomson for a strike. Branca, a seven-year big-league veteran, knew that Thomson's anxiety often caused him to jump at bad pitches. He decided to throw a fastball inside, a wasted pitch. The ball streaked toward Thomson's fists. Thomson leaned back on his heels. He hammered down on the white blur like someone trying to drive a peg into the ground. The ball shot off the bat on a low but rising line—a "clothesliner" in the dugout's lexicon—and streaked toward the grandstand wall some 300 feet away. Dodger left fielder Andy Pafko stood at the base of the wall, watching helplessly as the ball cleared the top of the fence by no more than a couple of feet and vanished into the arms of jubilant Giant fans.

The Royal Scot Express, as Giant broadcasters had named Thomson, was born in Glasgow, Scotland, on October 25, 1923. His parents moved to the United States when he was a tot and he grew up on Staten Island, a New York City borough that is a ferryride across New York Harbor from Manhattan. A high-school star on Staten Island, he was signed by Giant scouts. In his first five full seasons with the Giants he hit a total of 129 home runs, an imposing total, but after that dramatic one off Branca, he was expected to hit even more. "Sure, that had to affect me," Thomson told me. "I know people expected me to hit a home run every time I came up. You're a pro and it's not supposed to affect you, but if you think at all, it has to affect you."

It certainly had to affect a batter who had always been overly anxious. Nonetheless, Thomson hit 24 and 26 home runs during the two seasons, 1952 and 1953, that followed his historic shot. Again he was the Giant center fielder. In 1951 he had moved to third base when the Giants brought up a young center fielder from the minors, Willie Mays. The sensational Mays was now in the army. At times Thomson seemed almost day-dreamy as an outfielder. "I was up to here in 1951," he told me in the restaurant, holding one hand over his head. "That high. I could never get that high again. After that it was all down."

When Willie Mays came back from the service in 1954, the Giants traded Thomson to the Milwaukee Braves, getting left-handed Johnny Antonelli, who would win 21 games for a Giants team that won the 1954 pennant. Early in that 1954 season Thomson broke an ankle and never again was the hitter he had been. He played two years with Milwaukee, went back to the Giants, now in San Francisco, then was with the Cubs in 1958 and 1959. He retired in 1960 after playing with Baltimore and Boston in the American League. In his fifteen-year career he hit 264 homers and had a .270 batting average.

Through with baseball—he had no interest in staying in the big leagues as a coach—he realized he knew nothing of the world outside a clubhouse. "I sized myself up," he told me in the restaurant. "I was helpless. I lived in a shell. Outside of a clubhouse I didn't know how to talk to people. I knew how to put on a baseball suit. I knew how to catch a baseball—sometimes. I didn't know what was going on in the world—in Washington, Wall Street, nowhere. If I wanted some thinking done, I went to my lawyer."

He watched me writing down what he was saying. "Oh, look," he said, "don't make me sound corny, like a Hollywood actress saying she wants to play Shakespeare. But I wanted to find out about myself, to see if there was something inside this noggin besides knowing how to hit fungoes."

He would live up to his potential away from baseball, he told himself, as he had not lived up to his potential in baseball. He took aptitude tests at a New Jersey school and decided he should be an industrial salesman. He had job offers. "I could have signed with a company interested in my name. But I wanted a company interested in my talents, interested in what I could produce."

He went to work for the West Virginia Pulp and Paper Company in New York City, selling paper bags to industrial giants like the Titanium Corporation of America. "Doesn't sound very glamorous, does it?" he asked me, eyes gleaming with good humor. "Paper bags. I get up at seven. I ride subways with all the working stiffs. No more breakfasts at noon in hotels, taxis to ball parks, and I love it. This is fun. I'm part of the real world. I'm producing.

"My idea is to be a successful businessman. Oh, I still got a long way to go. I got a lot of courses to take—in management, economics, I have a lot to learn—how to talk to people, how to get answers, how to make decisions, how to produce."

He learned well enough to become a national account representative for the West-vaco Corporation, as West Virginia Pulp and Paper is now called. He had accomplished as an industrial salesman what he had never accomplished, to his disappointment, as a ballplayer—he had lived up to his potential.

In 1984 I asked him if the home run, undoubtedly the most famous of all time, had helped him to sell paper bags. "Very little," he said. "I can't walk in there with my clippings. Sure, an occasional person I call on, they want to talk about the home run but then they say, 'It's been great talking to you about the old days, Bob, but now what have you got for me?'"

But the home run is what he will be forever remembered for, and he was reminded of that as recently as 1983. He was one of the former All-Stars who played in a special All-Star Game in Chicago, to commemorate the fiftieth anniversary of the first All-Star Game. The game was held before the 1983 All-Star Game and old-timers like Thomson used the same dressing room as the 1983 All-Stars. Thomson shared a locker with a 1983 Giant outfielder, Derrel Evans. "Here I am," an awed Evans told reporters, "sharing a locker with the guy who hit the most famous home run in history." Evans was not even born in 1951 when Thomson socked that home run, but like everyone else who saw it or who has been told about it, it is a homer that will never be forgotten. It is a link, I once wrote, "that will never free Thomson and Branca to be strangers and never permit them to be friends."

Bobby (*left*) and Ralph Branca together in 1983.

Bob as a young Yankee in 1956.

Bob Turley

BOB TURLEY ALWAYS SAID HE WAS THE first to make the trip. Thousands have followed him on a similar journey from dusty Little League diamonds to triple-tiered bit-league stadiums. Today more than half of all big-league players were once Little Leaguers.

Bob didn't play in one of today's Little Leagues, which are sanctioned and approved by Little League headquarters in Williamsport, Pennsylvania. In 1942 he pitched for a kids' team in East St. Louis, Illinois. The team was sponsored by the local chamber of commerce and had no ties to the Williamsport organization, which was then in its infancy and limited mostly to eastern states. But when I talked to Bob during the latter part of the 1957 season (he was on his way to winning 21 games for the pennant-bound Yankees), he claimed to have been the first little leaguer to become a big leaguer.

"We had the exact same rules as today's official Little League," he told me. "We had shortened baselines, no stealing, and six-inning games. For us kids, the most important things our little league had was equipment. Before little league we never had enough bats, balls, or gloves. We hardly knew what a catcher's mask looked like. Our bats were often nailed boards. It was only after the little league started that I saw, for the first time, a brand new baseball. Now we had brand-new bats and baseballs and what we found almost impossible to believe—uniforms. There were six teams in the league, each representing a zone of East St. Louis. Money for our team came from the Burke Funeral Parlors, and we soon became known as the Undertakers."

Bob and I were talking in the players' lounge of the Yankee clubhouse. Several players had been watching a TV screen showing a game show, but as Turley and I talked, the set was clicked off. Players began to listen as Turley talked about his little-league days. Several—I can recall Mickey Mantle and Elston Howard among them—occasionally tossed in a remark about how they had played baseball as kids. What they said I didn't note nor do I remember. But from the way they listened to Turley and said things like "Oh, yeah, that once happened to me," I got the impression that I was hearing what it was like to have played baseball as a kid during the 1940s in small-town America.

"There weren't many kids in our area, so we never could get enough to play a game

of baseball," Turley said. "What we played instead was what we called Indian ball. You needed only two or three players. One kid pitched underhanded to the batter. He tried to hit the ball over the pitcher's or the out-fielder's head. That was the only kind of baseball I knew. In fact, until the little league came to town—when I was twelve [he was born September 19, 1930]—I don't recall ever playing a real game of baseball.

"One day, I think it was in June, tryouts started for the Undertakers. Being kind of shy, I hugged the sideline as the other kids—there must have been over a hundred of them—warmed up. But our team's coach, a Mr. Ross Elkins, he saw me and he made me work out. If it hadn't been for him, I might have given up baseball then and there.

"In our first workout I almost got knocked off the team anyway. I was catching tosses at first base when I turned to say something to Mr. Elkins. A ball smacked me square in the eye and I learned—right off the bat—baseball's first rule: keep your eye on the ball.

"Black eye and all, though, I made the team along with fourteen other boys. Nearly a hundred kids, of course, were disappointed by being left off. We lucky ones got uniforms. We wore the caps to school every day. Some of the boys even put on the uniforms to walk the streets. And I am sure a few even wore those uniforms to bed.

"I pitched our first game and we won, two to one. I was big for my age—the kids called me 'Clunker'—and I was fast. But I was also very nervous. When I got that last out, I was close to tears.

"We played twenty games. I don't recall how many we won, but we did finish just a half game out of first place. Sometimes I look back and think we might have won if we hadn't practiced so hard. We were so tickled with our uniforms and equipment that we would show up for a six thirty twilight game at about noon. After six and a half hours of warming up' for a six-inning game, I sometimes think we were too bushed to play.

"My mother watched nearly every game in which I was pitching. My father was in the service. Like all kinds of Little League mothers today, she thought her son Bob was the best and she wasn't shy about letting this be known. The result was some pretty fierce bickering in the stands between her and the mothers of some of the other players.

"Those ladies could be tough. One day I threw a fastball that almost hit one of the hitters on the other team. The kid's mother dashed out of the stands after me. If people hadn't stopped her in time, I think she would have clubbed me with her son's bat.

"The next summer, 1944, I was thirteen. I played again for the Undertakers, but mostly I was an outfielder. It seemed that the other parents protested to the officials that I threw so fast I might hurt one of the other kids. So on account of me they passed a rule forbidding kids of thirteen to pitch."

A few days later, after I had typed up my notes on the interview with Bob about his little-league days, I asked him if his little-league experience had been his biggest stepping stone to the big leagues. "Absolutely," he said. "If it hadn't been for that East St. Louis kids' league and people like Mr. Elkins, I'm sure I wouldn't be a big leaguer. When I played on a uniformed team in real games, I saw what baseball was really like. I fell in love with it. I was enough in love to want to make it a career."

At sixteen he was being watched by scouts from the St. Louis Browns. He signed with the Browns and in 1951, only twenty, he was brought up for one game, which he started and lost. He was in military service during 1952 and half of 1953, coming back late that season to finish with a 2-won and 6-lost record.

The Browns moved to Baltimore in 1954 and became the Orioles. He won 14 games that season (while losing 15) for a team that won only 54 games. In 1955 he was with the Yankees, for whom he had a 17–13 record. In the World Series that year against Brooklyn, he started the third game and was gone by the second inning, the eventual loser in an 8–3 Brooklyn victory.

"Control had always been my biggest problem as a pitcher, even when I was in the little league," he told me in 1958. "As a little leaguer I began to throw without a windup, and I wasn't so wild. I hadn't been willing to gamble on a no-windup delivery in the minors or when I was in St. Louis or Baltimore, but in 1956 I went back to the no-windup delivery of my little-league days. As a result, I had much better control."

The 1958 season was his best. He won 21 games, the most in the league, and lost only 7. He also led the league in complete games, and while his control was better, he led the league in bases on balls. His most memorable pitching performances came in the 1958 World Series. In the 1957 Series the Braves had beaten the Yankees and in 1958 they led, 3 games to 1. Turley started the fifth game against Lew Burdette, who so far had beaten the Yankees four straight times over the two Series. Turley shut out the Braves, 7–0, and the Yankees were still alive as the two teams flew to Milwaukee for the sixth and seventh games. In the sixth game Turley was called in from the bullpen in the tenth inning, the winning run on base. He got the last out in a 4–3 Yankee victory. The next day he was called on by manager Casey Stengel in the third inning, the Yankees ahead 2–1 in this seventh and decisive game. Pitching for the third time in four days, he gave up only 1 run the rest of the way, the Yankees winning, 6–2, when Bill Skowron hit an eighth-inning homer. Turley was the Series' Most Valuable Player.

That was the high-tide mark of his career. His best year after that was 9–3 in 1960. Bothered off and on by a sore arm, he went from the Yankees to Boston in 1963 and fin-

Bob is today an Atlanta insurance executive.

ished his career with the Los Angeles Angels that season. In twelve years he won 101, lost 85, and had an ERA of 3.64.

He returned to Boston in 1964 as a pitching coach. "Then they fired [manager] Johnny Pesky and I went with him," he told me in 1984. "I went to the Atlanta Crackers as coach for the 1965 season."

There his life took a new turn. He and several men in Atlanta formed a group that sold term insurance. Today he has some 10,000 people working under him. His company is part of the nationwide A. L. Williams insurance group, the largest seller of individual term insurance in the country. "Last year we sold four billion dollars in term insurance," Bob told me. "That's four *billion*. Life," he adds, "has been good to me." He and his wife, Carolyn, have three daughters and three sons. Bob works and lives in Dunwoody, a suburb of Atlanta. "And whenever I can," he says, "I'll watch a Little League game."

Johnny Unitas

I WENT TO CLEVELAND LATE IN DEcember of 1964 to watch Johnny Unitas and his Baltimore Colts play Jimmy Brown and his Cleveland Browns for the championship of the National Football League. I walked into the lobby of a hotel in downtown Cleveland and saw Unitas standing in a corner, hunch-shouldered, a toothpick sticking from the corner of his thin mouth. He stood, grinning, amid a small knot of Colt players. People in the lobby were staring at the great Colt quarterback. He had that flushed, embarrassed look of a shy man wishing he could duck somewhere else and flee the spotlight.

A Colt running back, Tony Lorick, came by. "I just heard some fan say that Johnny Unitas stood six-foot-four and weighed two hundred fifty pounds," Lorick told Unitas.

The six-foot-one, one-hundred-ninety-pound Unitas laughed. With a buzz-saw voice that seemed surprisingly loud coming from so diffident a man, he said, "You tell him I *hit* like two hundred fifty pounds."

Unitas was thirty-one at the time. He looked younger; his bristly crew cut and boyish face could have belonged to a college senior. The only sign of age was crinkly lines around the slitted eyes and a quiltwork of tiny stitches across the bridge of his nose, the occupational scars of a quarterback savaged over nine NFL seasons by blitzing linemen. He wore a rumpled tan raincoat, a blue alpaca cardigan, red sport shirt, and gray slacks. I told him I had been assigned to follow him around before and after the big game. Would he mind?

"Nah," he said, shifting the toothpick in his mouth, "why should that bother me?"

I hadn't expected him to be bothered. Johnny Unitas never took himself or the way the world exalted him too seriously. "Quarterbacks," he once said, "get too much credit

Johnny as a Colt quarterback in 1959.

when a team wins and too much blame when it loses."

A Colt official, Harry Hulmes, had told me earlier: "If Unitas completes a pass or if he has one intercepted, he comes off the field looking the same. If you hadn't seen the play, you couldn't tell from his expression whether he'd thrown a touchdown pass or fumbled."

I rode on a bus with Unitas and the Colts to Cleveland Stadium, where they would trot through a light workout. At the stadium the Colt players walked up a ramp into the lower grandstand seats. They stared out at the deserted, tarpaulin-covered field. There was a silence of perhaps ten seconds, each player, I sensed, wondering what he would find on this field twenty-four hours hence—the joy of victory or the depression of defeat. Unitas, who had been among the last to leave the bus, came up the ramp. He stood on tiptoe and poked his burr-head over the line of players to see what they were looking at.

"Hey," he yelled, "haven't any of you ever seen a football field before?"

The stocky defensive captain of the Colts, Gino Marchetti, stood next to Unitas. He let out a barking, derisive laugh. The other Colts, uncertain at first and then in an abashed way, began to laugh at themselves and their fears. As the laughter grew louder, Unitas chanted in a singsong voice, "A football field is one hundred twenty yards long . . . it's about fifty yards wide . . . it's got goalposts . . ."

He was strolling down the ramp, away from them. The Colts followed, laughing loudly now, their worries left behind.

After the workout Unitas was walking back to the bus, head down, when a small boy swerved in front of him and asked for an autograph. "I don't want to," Unitas growled. The boy stared, too frightened to speak. "But I will," Unitas said with a little laugh. The boy grinned.

That afternoon I sat with Unitas in his hotel room as we watched an American Football League game on television. Between plays I tossed questions at him. Did he feel any differently before this 1964 championship game than he would before a regular-season game?

"Nah," he said, nibbling on the toothpick, eyes fixed on the screen.

Did he learn things watching games on television? "Nah."

I told him I had remembered watching him on television in a game against the Giants several years earlier. He'd been buried under tacklers. When he stood up, he had trotted to the sideline. As the camera closed in on him, I saw that a finger on his left hand was sticking out at a grotesque angle. At the sideline a trainer jerked the finger back into place while Unitas looked so cool you would have thought he was watching someone else's finger being yanked.

"Didn't you feel pain?" I asked him.

"Of course it hurt," he said, looking annoyed.

"You didn't look like it was hurting you."

He said nothing.

I asked him about an award he had just won—the Most Valuable Player of the 1964 season. Had he ever won that award before?"

"Someone asked me that the other day. I really don't know." (He had—in 1957.)

He told me he would stay in the room the rest of the day, have dinner sent up at seven, watch TV, read some plays, and be asleep by eleven. The next morning, game day, he attended mass at a nearby church. On the way back to the hotel, he saw coach Don Shula and Marchetti cross an intersection while the light was green. At that moment a police cruiser came by. Unitas ran up to it. "Hey, officers," he shouted, pointing at Shula and Marchetti. "Arrest those men! They crossed against the light!"

The cops were more interested in their fingerman. "Get some points today, John," one said. "Gonna need more than a few points," he said, suddenly somber.

He was right. He needed 28, the Browns winning 27–0. I flew with him and the Colts in their chartered plane back to Baltimore. The Colts had been quiet and subdued in the dressing room after the game. But as the DC-7 revved up before takeoff, beer cans were cracked open. Unitas had shucked the old raincoat and an even older-looking sports jacket and was dealing cards to three other Colts. It was the first hand in a poker game he would play all the way home, never once speaking of the game. (After the game he had told reporters, "It was their day, that's all you can say. They got the glory, we got the waterpot . . . Just one of those days.")

I talked with Bert Bell, Jr., a Colt official, who told me the shocking news that the most daring quarterback of his time was a fish at poker. "John is invited to every game we play," Bell told me. "I mean, if he isn't around for a poker game, we send a *messenger* to get him."

I stood behind him during the flight, watching the game. One hand told much of his poker luck. He dropped out after three cards. On the next deal he saw he would have been dealt an ace. He winced, and showed me the card he had been holding in the hole—an ace.

The plane landed in Baltimore. As he put on the old raincoat, he said to me with that rasping voice, a mock frown on his face, "Bad day all around, John. Bad day all around. I'm a *fail*-ure in poker, a *fail*-ure in football, a *fail*-ure with men, a *fail*-ure with women . . ." He was laughing now, softly, and even after he'd left the plane, I could hear the soft laughter coming from out of the darkness of the runway.

I later wrote of those two days with him: "This is a man who takes the world's criticism and praise with a wary eye, well aware that the world dispenses both with foolish extravagance. Thus Johnny Unitas didn't know how many MVP awards he had won simply because he doesn't place much value on such judgments. He is, very obviously, indifferent to the judgments of the world. Being indifferent to what others will say, he will be cool under pressure. On this December day he lost, and I have tried to tell you how he lost—laughing, kidding himself, detached. It also was the way he would have won."

The first time I met Unitas—at the Colt training camp in the summer of 1959—I was told about his insouciance by Gino Marchetti. "Nothing ever bothers him," the dark-haired Marchetti said. "That's because he never worries about what will happen if he fails."

Yet he knew of failure and its consequences. John Constantine Unitas was born May 7, 1933, in Pittsburgh. His father died when he was five and his mother raised her four children by working as a scrubwoman and later as a bookkeeper. He was a quarterback at St. Justin, a small Catholic school that lost so often no big college (he wanted to go to Notre Dame) would give him a scholarship. He went to the University of Louisville, where the team lost (23 times) more often than it won (12) from 1953 to 1955. The Pittsburgh Steelers drafted him, looked at him briefly in training camp, and sent him home with a $10 bus ticket. Johnny, married and the father of one child with a second on the way, pocketed the $10, hitchhiked back to Pittsburgh, and took a $3-an-hour job as a construction worker while playing semipro football for $6 a game. A year later the Colts asked him to try out. He won a job as the team's number-two quarterback. When the number-one quarterback, George Shaw, was hurt and lost for the season, Unitas took over. In his first game the Colts lost, 58–27. "Johnny wasn't the least bit shaken," Marchetti told me. "'If you just give me a chance,' he kept saying, 'I'll show you what I can do!'"

He showed them in the 1958 game for the NFL championship. With two minutes to play, the Giants led, 17–14, in a game that has been called "the greatest football game ever played." The Colts had the ball on their own 14-yard line. In the huddle the stony-faced Unitas told his teammates: "This is where we find out what we're made of."

He calmly flipped four passes that brought the Colts to the Giant 20. From there the Colts kicked a field goal that tied the score. In pro football's first sudden-death overtime, he called for passes and bolts up the middle by his fullback, Alan Ameche. The Colts moved to within distance of a field goal. Instead Unitas called for a pass and threw it to a receiver who caught the ball on the 1. From there Ameche scored the game-winning touchdown that gave the Colts their first championship.

After the game Unitas established his reputation for being icily poised. A reporter asked him if that last pass hadn't been risky. "A pass," he said briskly, "is never risky when you know what you're doing."

"John is so cool in victory or defeat that people misunderstand him sometimes," his favorite pass catcher, Raymond Berry, told me the following summer. "They think John doesn't care. He does. But a quarterback who has tremendous responsibilities must have a way to guard his own nerves." And Unitas later told me: "If you make mistakes, try not to make them again. But don't worry about them—they will drive you nuts."

He was the Colt quarterback from 1956 to 1972. During that time the Colts won the NFL title in 1958, 1959, and 1968 (they lost in Super Bowl III that season to the Jets). They won the AFC title in 1970 and then beat Dallas, 16–13, in Super Bowl V, Unitas's first and only Super Bowl championship. Unitas was the league's Most Valuable Player or the Player of the Year in 1957, 1959, 1964, and 1967. He played for the San Diego Chargers in 1973 and then retired. In eighteen seasons as a pro passer, he completed 54.6 percent of his 2,830 passes for 40,239 yards, more yardage than any passer up to then (Fran Tarkenton later topped him).

For several years Unitas was a television commentator at NFL games. In 1979 he was elected to the Football Hall of Fame. In 1984 he spoke out angrily when his old team, the Colts, moved from Baltimore to Indianapolis. Unitas does promotion work for International Harvester and other companies, and he appears at charity tournaments to play what has become his favorite sport—golf. He is seen frequently at his restaurant,

The Golden Arm, in Baltimore, where he lives. When he plays golf he is less icy than he was as a quarterback—he lets his emotions show.

Johnny as a golfer in 1978.

Roy as a Yankee player in 1968.

Roy White

ROY WHITE AND I WERE SITTING IN THE sun-flooded living room of his home atop a hill in New Jersey one January afternoon in 1971, talking about his job—playing left field for the New York Yankees. He had just finished telling me that at the age of twenty-seven, his childhood love for baseball had never been stronger. Growing up in Compton, California, he had read articles in *Sport* magazine about Stan Musial and Ted Williams and imagined his face on the cover of *Sport*. "I still hope I'll be on *Sport*'s cover one day," he told me. "I don't know what I'd be doing if I wasn't playing baseball," he said, smiling. His daughter Lorenna was playing with dolls on the floor. His wife, Linda, sat on a couch listening. "I majored in art when I was in junior college but I didn't have the concentration. I'd get started on a project and baseball would drift into my mind—how I could improve myself as a player—and I'd lose interest and forget the project.

"I remember my first season in the minor leagues. The Yankees sent me to Greensboro in North Carolina but I was hitting so bad, around .200, that they dropped me to a lower league, and I went to Fort Lauderdale. There I was only hitting around .210. I remember sitting up one night and saying to myself, 'If I can't play baseball, what am I going to do?' Then I started to hit and I thought, If I finish at .250 I'll be happy." Actually he finished at .284 and began a climb to the big leagues.

He was unusual, I thought, for a big leaguer: He was still very much the fan. "I really enjoyed being picked for the All-Star game in 1969. I'd been a spectator watching those guys play and now I was on the same field with players like Clemente and Mays and Aaron, players I had been reading about in magazines and on the sports pages all those years since I was a kid."

This fan and player was a sports historian, I discovered. We were talking about the difficulties of playing left field at Yankee Stadium, the sun glaring over the top rim of the stadium into the eyes of the left fielder. "I remember," I said, "seeing Norm Siebern miss a couple of fly balls in left field at the stadium during the 1956 Series."

He looked at the ceiling for several moments and then said in his rich baritone's voice (I always thought he would have been a great radio announcer): "That was the 1958 Series when Siebern missed those fly balls. The 1956 Series was the perfect-game Series, when Larsen pitched the no-hitter against the Dodgers."

"That's right," I said, impressed.

"Johnny Logan."

"Johnny Logan?"

"He hit one of those fly balls to Siebern."

I went away very impressed. I had known a number of clean-up hitters for the Yankees—Joe DiMaggio, Mickey Mantle, Yogi Berra among them—but I was sure that not one could tell me of the trivia of the 1958 World Series.

As the switch-hitting cleanup hitter for the Yankees in 1970 and 1971, Roy had created some amusement in press boxes. Unlike people like DiMaggio and Mantle who swung for the fences, Roy choked up on the bat and slashed line drives up the middle or to the opposite field for singles and doubles. But he could also hit the home run. During a 1970 game against Oakland, Roy made announcer Harry Caray eat his words even as Caray was getting them past his lips. As Roy stood at bat, Caray told his listeners: "It seems strange to see the Yankees with a cleanup hitter who chokes up on the bat . . . ooops, there it goes, folks!"

But Roy did not hit many home runs—the 22 he hit in 1970 was his most ever. "My style is to hit the ball up the middle and to the opposite side," he told me one afternoon at Yankee Stadium. "Not to pull. When I try to pull the ball, I overswing and I'm pulling my head away from the ball. I found that out the hard way in 1966."

In 1966, his rookie season, he hit a few home runs and began to imagine that he was something he wasn't—a slugger. He started to aim at the nearby fences down the foul lines at Yankee Stadium. His eyes off the ball, his average dropped a half-hundred points and he was soon back in the minor leagues. "I am not going to make that mistake again," he told me. "If I hit a home run I am not aiming for it. That's just where it happened to go."

While Roy knew he was not the big driver-in of runs that DiMaggio and Mantle were, he was a consistent RBI man. "The good RBI man won't bite at pitches outside the strike zone," he told me. "I think Harmon Killebrew and Frank Robinson, for example, are better hitters with men on base than when there is no one on. With men on base, they think more about base hits to drive in runners. Without men on base, they're more likely to swing at pitches outside the strike zone and strike out."

At five-foot-ten and one hundred sixty pounds, Roy was built along lithe and supple lines. "He is all muscle and bone, though," then-Yankee coach Dick Howser told me. The Yankees called him Sabu because he looked like one of those Indian boys who ride atop elephants in harem movies. He had Sabu's slanted eyes and a café-au-lait complexion. In his early Yankee years he wore goggle-type glasses (he was slightly nearsighted). The big goggles made his finely hewn, long, and bony face seem even smaller. Later he discarded the glasses and wore contact lenses.

He was born on December 27, 1943, in Los Angeles, but grew up in Compton. At ten he was a switch-hitting player of a game he and his pals called sockball. "We'd take an ankle-length sock and stuff it with rags," he told me. "We'd wrap it with tape or maybe sew it. The pitcher would stand about twenty-five feet away because the ball was so light. But you could curve it, even throw screwballs." After hitting those dipsy-doodling sockballs, he had less trouble connecting with baseballs and was a .400 hitter in

high school. There he played second base next to shortstop Reggie Smith, later a big leaguer with the Dodgers and Red Sox.

When Roy came up to the Yankees in 1966, there was no doubt that the switch hitter could hit. "The big question about him," manager Ralph Houk told me in 1971, "was the position he would play." The Yankees tried him at third and found him to be no Brooks Robinson. "My problem was on throws," he told me. "I tried to aim the ball and you can't do that, you'll throw it away." Moved to left field, he worked for hours at learning to judge and nab swerving line drives. "He made himself into a good outfielder by sheer determination," then-Yankee president Mike Burke told me. Ralph Houk said that "Roy covers more ground than any left fielder we've had in the twenty-four years I've been here. He goes into the gap in left center to make catches that have saved a lot of games for us." In 1971 he led the league's left fielders in fielding percentage with a perfect 1.000.

In 1970 he led the Yankees in runs, hits, doubles, RBIs, walks, and stolen bases. Only Bobby Murcer, with 23 homers, hit more than Roy, who hit 22. But Houk had no illusions that he had the perfect clean-up hitter. "If I had someone who could hit fifty home runs, I'd bat that man fourth and bat Roy second," he told me. "Roy would be a hell of a second hitter—he hits behind the runner, he's a good base stealer. But I don't have anyone who can hit fifty home runs so I go with the most consistent hitter I've got."

Roy liked to talk of baseball matters, but he and his wife were also deeply interested in modern jazz, the Broadway theater (especially musicals) and Post-Impressionist modern art. He talked to me with enthusiasm of an off-season job he had selling time for radio commercials for CBS, who then owned the Yankees.

By 1975, with the coming of sluggers like Thurman Munson and, later, Reggie Jackson, the Yankees had moved White to second in the batting order. Except for 1973, when his average dipped to .246, Roy hit so consistently from 1971 to 1978 that his average never fell below .268 nor was it ever above .292. He was on the pennant-winning Yankee teams of 1976, 1977, and 1978, those teams winning the world championships in 1977 and 1978.

By 1979 he was a designated hitter. Preferring to play in the field as well as hit, he de-cided to go to Japan, where he played in 1980, 1981, and 1982. He returned to the Yankees in 1983 as a first-base coach. In 1984 he was appointed an executive in the front office with the Yankees, a move he called "a great step forward for me." He and his wife still live in New Jersey, where he can look back on a career as a player in which he made youthful dreams come true—except one. He never made the cover of *Sport*.

Roy as a Yankee coach in 1984.

Ted as a Splinter in 1960.

Ted Williams

AS I PARKED THE RENTED CAR ON A curving road near the field, I heard a loud voice from the batting cage, a hundred yards from me. It boomed over the cracking sounds of batting practice. The voice came from the tall figure standing behind the cage, players clustered around him, most of them standing only to his shoulders. He wore a Boston Red Sox windbreaker, the billowing jacket covering a thickening middle. Ted Williams, the Splendid Splinter of twenty-five years earlier, was no longer splinterish but he was still loud. He was shouting instructions as the batting coach for his old team, training at Winter Haven, Florida. I had come here to ask baseball's last .400 hitter (.406 in 1941) a question: Why were there so few .300 hitters—only two in the American League in 1966—compared to twenty-five earlier, when there had been four .300 hitters on the 1941 Red Sox alone?

I walked to the cage and introduced myself. His deeply lined, leathery face crinkled into a friendly smile, which was a mild surprise to me since Teddy Ballgame, as he often referred to himself, did not always greet itinerant questioners with a smile. I told him why I had come and asked my question. He threw a question right back at me. "What," he asked in a voice that I later learned was heard a football field away, "do you think is the toughest job in sport?"

Before I give my answer—and *his* answer to his question—let me tell you what an ordinary conversation with Ted Williams could be like. It was more like a shouting match and Ted did all the shouting. His voice roared through a clubhouse when be bellowed a "good morning" to the attendants as he arrived. A few minutes after my conversation with Williams at the batting cage on the subject of the vanishing .300 hitter, a Red Sox player, who had been standing in the outfield during the conversation, came over to me and said, "Old Ted was real sore at you about something, wasn't he?" All he had heard was that booming Williams voice.

Actually this was the most pleasant conversation I ever had with Williams. I pondered his question for a few moments, deciding I would be perverse and not give him the answer I suspected he wanted: that the toughest job in sport was hitting a pitched baseball. I gave him two answers. "To me," I said, as he stared with a smile at a hitter in the cage, "the two toughest jobs in sport are one, the job of a golfer trying to hit his second shot onto the green next to the pin so he can get a par-4; and two, the job of a quarterback in trying to decide and execute a play in the closing minutes of a game when it's fourth down and five yards to go."

He kept on staring at the hitter, but I could see the amused gleam in his eyes, the look of a man about to blow away an opponent in a debate. "I say the toughest job is hitting a baseball," he thundered. "Your golfer is swinging at a stationary object. A baseball hitter has to swing at a ball coming at him at ninety miles an hour. There is silence when a golfer swings at a ball. A baseball player has fifty thousand people screaming at him to strike out or hit the ball out of the park."

He turned to face me, one elbow on a bar of the iron cage. "Then there's your quarterback. He has got ten other men and a coach on the sideline to help him get those yards for a first down. In baseball a batter is up there all alone and there is no one who can help him do it."

He turned to look at the next hitter stepping into the cage. The other players were silent, listening, or perhaps silent because any other conversation would have been buried under that avalanche of sound coming from Ted. "You're right, though, that averages have dropped from what they were twenty years ago. The slider's a big reason. There wasn't any slider when I first came up. If you figured the pitcher was throwing a curve, a fastball, or a changeup, you'd be right one-third of the time. Now you have to expect slider, changeup, fastball, or curve, so you could possible be right no better than one-quarter of the time."

He talked on for about twenty minutes about how new weapons in baseball—specialized relief pitchers, bigger gloves—had shrunk averages. He talked of the tendency among today's hitters to swing for home runs and, therefore, to strike out more often. He said too many hitters were unwilling to wait to get the possible pitch, jumping on bad pitches because they have one or two strikes on them and fear being called out on a third strike.

Later I recalled how often I had heard players say that Ted was a walking textbook on hitting. In 1959 I was talking to Red Sox catcher Sammy White at Yankee Stadium. "We were in Baltimore recently," the raw-boned six-foot-three White told me. "Ted had been watching Gus Triandos (a big Oriole slugger) and Ted suggested that Gus try a lighter bat. Gus did, and the next time he beat us with two homers."

He was just as generous, of course, with tips from the textbook to his teammates. In 1958 he and teammate Pete Runnels were running head to head for the batting championship. "We were a few points apart in late August," Runnels told me a few minutes after my conversation with Sammy White. "One day Ted told me I looked bushed. I was. He suggested I make certain changes in the way I was hitting. I did and went ten for twenty-one to move way ahead of him. You know how bad he wanted that title, but he was really glad to help me." Ted not only helped, he also nipped in ahead of Runnels to win the title with a .328 average, winning the title a month after his fortieth birthday.

"He's nearly always talking about hitting," another Red Sox star, Jackie Jensen, told me. "Mostly he stresses four fundamentals—hit a good pitch; get the fat part of the bat on the ball; don't swing if you're fooled by a pitch except if it's going to be a third strike; and choke up on the bat if you have two strikes on you. We all know these things, but often you forget. Ted, he's always concentrating, and he never forgets."

In 1969 Ted took over as manager of the Washington Senators. He was a manager by choice but a hitter by instinct. Just before the opening game of the season, the Senators' huge six-foot-five slugger Frank Howard once told me, Ted was pacing up and down the clubhouse. "Hey, Skip," one of the Senators shouted, "I bet you would like to be twenty years younger today."

"Ted grabbed a bat," Howard told me, "cocked it, his hands gripping it hard. He went into that batting stance of his, like he was looking out at a pitcher. 'Oh, geez,' he said, 'Would I? You bet I would.'"

Howard told me that as manager of the Senators, "Ted Williams taught me more about hitting in one season than I had learned in the previous ten." At spring training in 1969, Howard said, Williams took him aside.

"I think I can help you," Williams told Howard. "You know, you're the only guy in the history of baseball, the only one I've heard of, who ever hit forty-four home runs like you did last season and only got something like fifty walks. You should get one hundred walks every year."

Howard listened, but he was doubtful Williams should change him as a hitter. He was the kind of hitter who swung at anything close, figuring if he made contact once in three swipes, the ball would fly because of his strength. "You swing at everything like you had two strikes on you," Williams told him. "You're swinging at bad pitches or pitches that fooled you. You can afford to spot a pitcher a strike, if it's not the pitch you want. Spot him *two* strikes if you have to. Sooner or later he has got to give you a pitch that you can handle, in the good hitting zone. If you do it my way, I guarantee you'll make more contact, because you will be getting a better ball to hit ninety to ninety-five percent of the time."

"Skip," Howard said apologetically, "I don't feel I can afford to spot a pitcher two strikes to get a certain pitch. I might get the pitch and miss it. But I will spot him a strike, I'll go that far."

That year Howard, waiting more patiently for a good pitch, hit 48 homers, the most he ever hit. And he batted .296, matching his best average ever.

As friendly as he was to any ballplayer who needed help, Ted could be outspokenly nasty to people, like journalists, whom he thought didn't belong in a baseball club-house. The first time I met him, in 1956 in a clubhouse at Sarasota, Florida, where the Red Sox then trained, I showed him a photograph of himself fishing, which was his favorite sport away from baseball. An editor had asked me to show it to him and ask what kind of fishing gear he had used that day. Williams talked briefly about the photo. I made notes, thanked him, and left. The next day I came back, having forgotten to ask one more question about the photo. He saw me coming, stood and shouted so loudly his voice reverberated through the clubhouse, "What are you doing, writing a damn book about that picture?" He stomped right by me as I stood, red-eared, holding the picture and looking, I am sure, like a gaping-mouthed idiot.

Theodore Samuel Williams was born on August 30, 1918, in San Diego. His father left home early and he was raised by his mother, a Salvation Army worker. A tall and skinny teenager, he lived from early morning to late at night at a neighborhood recreation center where he swatted baseballs and imagined he was his idol, the Giants' Bill Terry, who hit .401 in 1930 when Ted was twelve. In 1936, only seventeen, he was signed by a local team, the Padres, then in the Pacific Coast League. The Red Sox bought him and in 1939, his first full season, the six-foot-three, one-hundred-ninety-pound Splinter hit .327 and 31 home runs in a ball park that did not favor a left-handed hitter like Williams (the right-field seats were over 350 feet from home). Some baseball historians have claimed that if Williams had played in a more favorable park, like Yankee Stadium with its relatively short right-field wall, he would have been the first to break Ruth's record of 714 homers; as it was, Williams hit 521 despite missing four seasons in the military.

In 1941 he was batting .3999555 on the last day of the season. In the official statistics that figure would have been rounded out to .400 and he would have become the first batter since his idol, Terry, to hit .400. On the last day of the season the Red Sox were playing Philadelphia a meaningless doubleheader. Friends advised Ted to sit out both games and "freeze" his average at .400. If he failed to get at least one hit in each game, his average would dip below .400. The Kid, as Williams was then called, refused. He whacked 6 hits in 8 at-bats to finish at .406, a level no batter has since come close to reaching.

Number 9 stood in left field at Fenway Park for eighteen seasons, missing the 1943 to 1945 seasons as a marine fighter pilot in the Pacific, and most of 1952 and 1953 as a fighter pilot over Korea. He was twice married and twice divorced. He feuded with Boston reporters, once spat at Boston fans, and would never tip his hat to Boston crowds who had booed and ridiculed him as a young ballplayer. Six times he led the league in batting, his second best year a .388 average in 1957 when he was thirty-nine. In his last season, 1960, now forty-two, he batted .316 and ended his career with his last hit—home run number 521. As he crossed home plate, the Fenway Park crowd roaring, he did not tip his cap. His career average was .344.

He retired to fish in the Florida Keys, where he had a home on Islamorada. In 1966 he was voted into baseball's Hall of Fame. He came out of the Keys only occasionally, usually to make an appearance for the Jimmy Fund, a charity he had long worked for to help sick children. Only years after it happened did a reporter reveal that Williams once chartered a plane to be at the bedside of a dying child he did not know but who had asked to see him.

In 1969 he was lured back to baseball as a manager by Bob Short, the millionaire owner of the Senators. The previous season the team had finish tenth. With much the same players, Williams brought the team home fourth and he was named the 1969 Manager of the Year. After the 1972 season, the team now the Texas Rangers and at the bottom of its division, Williams said another adieu to baseball and went back to Islamorada, where he still lives. In 1984, at a ceremony at Fenway Park, the Red Sox retired his famous number 9. Though he did not tip a cap—he was not wearing one. The Kid finally made his peace with those Boston fans he had warred with for so long. "Baseball is the greatest in Boston," he told them during the ceremony, "and the fans are the greatest—and I salute you."

Ted holds his old number 9 at a Boston ceremony in 1984.

Maury as a Dodger base stealer in 1962.

Maury Wills

MAURY WILLS AND I WERE SWEPT through the doorway of the subway car, part of a wave of rush-hour passengers. I stood chest to chest against a heavyset man in a pin-striped business suit. I twisted my neck to look for Maury. Sweat trickled down his brown face; his nose was snubbed against a taller man's shoulder. Perhaps being half-hidden by a shoulder was the reason he was not recognized on this January evening in 1966, this slim man who had been one of the heroes of the 1965 World Series only a few months earlier.

Maury was in Manhattan to sing and play the guitar at Basin Street East, then a popular East Side club. I had dogged his footsteps for much of a week. He was swaying on a subway train grinding its way to Queens because he had made a promise to the manager of the hotel where he was staying. The manager had a wife and daughter who were music buffs. He had asked Maury to come to their Queens home to play the guitar and sing with his wife and daughter. Maury had promised to come, forgotten, made another appointment, then forgotten that. Now, "running late as usual," as he told me, he had decided to board a subway car instead of taking a cab and being trapped in rush-hour traffic across the bridge to Queens. After we had wiggled out of the subway car in Queens, Wills bought flowers for the wife. "I think," he told me, "she might be miffed with me."

She wasn't. She and her daughter played the guitar and sang along with Maury through rousing rock 'n' roll versions of tunes like "Downtown." Their audience was one— me. I watched Maury with astonishment, one reason being I am always amazed when I see a musician look at black dots on white ruled paper, then somehow put fingers or mouth to an instrument and produce beautiful sounds. But, second, I knew that Maury, strumming away on the guitar like the professional that he was—a veteran of New York and Las Vegas clubs—had taught himself to play the guitar only three years before.

Several days earlier he and I had been sitting in Basin Street East a few hours before his show. He was lecturing me and Jim (Mudcat) Grant, a Minnesota pitcher who was also performing at the club, on how to play the guitar. As he showed us how to play a certain chord, I shook my head and said, "Too difficult for me."

He frowned and there was real anger in his vibrant voice. "No, no," he said firmly. "It's very easy. Anyone can learn to train his fingers. Don't even say it's difficult." He stared at me intently. "It is not difficult," he said, as if trying to brand that on my mind.

The son of a minister, Maury Morning Wills had an evangelical belief in the power of positive thinking. "Don't just think you are better than the other guy," he told me that afternoon at Basin Street, "you have got to believe it." His strong voice dropped in volume to a dramatic whisper. "John, if you are motivated enough, you can learn to do anything."

He pointed to himself as proof of what motivation can do. "For the first eight and a half years of my baseball career," the greatest base stealer of his time told me, "I was a baseball bum. But now I don't play baseball. I work baseball. There are a lot of blah ballplayers. They hit well, they field well, but they never do anything that grabs the fans. If you're a blah ballplayer, you'll always be a blah ballplayer. Some guys, they may hit .350, but when they get a hit they run to first base and they stop. You take someone like Lou Johnson (then a Dodger outfielder). When Lou hits a single, he dashes to first, rounds that bag, and tears halfway to second. He's got the crowd up on their feet yelling for him to get back. He's got them excited. One guy may hit .350 and Lou only .260, but Lou is bringing people into the park.

"Look, your primary job is to win games. But if you can entertain the fans too, this is great. If you bring people into the park, that's a salary factor in your favor that the owners have to consider when they talk contract with you. This is a business, pure and simple."

Making money had become important to Maury, who was born into a family that had little of it. One of eleven children, he was born in Washington, D.C., on October 2, 1932, close to the deepest valley of those Depression days. "Mostly," Maury told me, "we ate scrapple and chitlins and were glad to get it."

He grew up sinewy strong, the fastest-throwing pitcher in games played on sandlots within sight of the nation's Capitol. In 1952 the nineteen-year-old Wills happily accepted $1,000 to sign with the Dodgers. From 1952 to 1959 he played in minor leagues where he was often the team's only black. "We'd go into a town on a road trip," he told me, "and the bus would stop in front of an old hotel in the black section. I'd get out and then the rest of the guys would go to the good hotel."

He was fast—he stole 50 bases during one minor-league season. But at five-foot-nine and one hundred sixty-five pounds, he was thought too small to be a big-league hitter. In 1959 he was playing at Spokane. His manager, Bobby Bragan, suggested the righty-hitting Wills try to switch hit. The swift Wills, batting left-handed against righty pitching, suddenly was a .300 hitter. In mid-season of 1959, the Dodgers knew: 1) they had a chance to win the pennant; 2) they needed a shortstop other than the one they had to win it. They decided on Wills, now twenty-six. He hit .260 and the Dodgers won the pennant and the World Series. But during the next season, 1960, he was hitting so weakly that manager Walter Alston frequently embarrassed him by taking him out for a pinch hitter in the third or fourth inning. Wills sought help from coach Pete Reiser, who gave him technical tips on hitting. Reiser then added psychological advice that became a cornerstone of Wills's new personality. "Don't just think you're better than the other guy," the bald Reiser told Wills. "*Believe* it."

That season Wills hit .295 and stole 50 bases to lead the league. In 1962 the Dodgers moved from cramped Los Angeles Coliseum, a football field, to spacious Dodger Stadium. Alston did not have the people who could hit balls to those faraway seats. He built a team that scored runs with speed. Will was given a green light to steal whenever he could. For the next five years Maury was the base-stealing terror of the league.

Characteristically, he had prepared himself to be a base stealer. He had a book written by Ty Cobb, the Hall of Famer who had set a record in 1915 by stealing 96 bases. "I've read that book six or seven times," Wills told me in 1966. "Whenever I read it, I feel like Cobb is talking to me on every page, as if he is saying, 'Now Maury, you've got to put pressure on that pitcher, you've got to make him conscious of you out there . . .'"

In 1962 the pupil outdid the teacher by

breaking the teacher's record with 104 stolen bases. That season he was the league's Most Valuable Player. The Dodgers won the pennant in 1963 and again in 1965 and 1966, their popgun attack often consisting of Wills stroking a single to the opposite field, stealing second, and scooting home on another single. Then Sandy Koufax or Don Drysdale put a row of blanks on the scoreboard and the Dodgers had won another 3–2, 2–1, or 1–0 game. Wills led the league in stolen bases in 1963, 1964, and 1965, his best in those years, a total of 94 in 1965. In both 1963 and 1965 the Dodgers were world champions; in 1966 they lost to the Orioles.

"I've been very lucky," Maury told me early in 1966 shortly after our subway ride to Queens. "Lucky to be with the Dodgers, lucky to have teammates who helped me. That's the truth, but it isn't the entire truth. I've gotten the opportunities, what you call lucky breaks. But—and this is important—I've been prepared to take advantage of my opportunities. That's my definition of luck: opportunity meeting preparation."

Disputes with the Dodger front office led to his being traded to the Pirates in 1967. In 1969, after a short stint with Montreal, he was sent back to Los Angeles where he was again the team's regular shortstop and its unofficial captain. I talked to him in 1971 and he told me of his open eagerness to succeed Walter Alston when Alston retired, and to become the first black manager. "But they [the front office] worry about me," he told me. "They're afraid I might go off to play the banjo somewhere. But that nightclub stuff was two, three years ago. I've changed."

He retired in 1972, his career average .281. He still held the record for stolen bases in a season (it was later broken by Lou Brock and then by Rickey Henderson, who stole 130 in 1982). He joined NBC-TV as a commentator on "Game of the Week" broadcasts. Like most former athletes who are hugged by television when they retire, he found that the love affair lasted only until newly retired athletes, their exploits fresher, came along. Let go by television, he stayed close enough to baseball to be hired in 1980 as the manager of the Seattle Mariners, the second black (after Frank Robinson) to manage a big-league baseball team. By then his son Bump was a big-league baseball infielder with the Texas Rangers. When Seattle opposed Texas, Maury became the first big leaguer to manage against a team that had his son in the lineup. Early in the 1981 season, with the team stumbling and the players growling that Maury was too strict, he was fired.

The loss of the job he had wanted so badly knocked breath and confidence out of him. He went back to Los Angeles and became a recluse, watching television for hours, the door locked. He took to drugs. In 1983 he went into a clinic for 28 days.

"I feel strong, healthy," he told *New York Post* writer Maury Allen in the fall of 1984. "I'm confident again." Living now with his second wife in the Los Angeles suburb of Playa Del Ray, he appeared at Fantasy Baseball Camps in Arizona. At these camps a fan, after paying about $2,500 a week, gets a big-league uniform and the chance to play in games against former stars like Maury and Mickey Mantle. As I read about those camps, I could imagine Maury sitting next to a potbellied businessman and telling him that yes, the man could be better than Mickey Mantle—if he just believed it.

Maury as a manager in 1981, greeting son Bump at the plate.

Al as a Cincinnati Red in 1963.

Al Worthington

LATE IN HIS CAREER AL WORTHINGTON became what I once called "a sundown kind of pitcher." In movie westerns, a sheriff tells the gunslinger to leave town by sundown. The gunslinger grins a killer's grin. And at sundown, in the climax of those westerns, the gunsel and the sheriff walk toward each other, a time to kill or be killed. As a thirty-six-year-old pitcher for the Minnesota Twins, champions of the American League in 1965, Al came out of bullpens in the eighth or ninth innings, runners on base, the game so close a single run could win or lose it, knowing one wrong pitch could cost his team and a pitching buddy a victory. "It is," I once wrote, "a kill-or-be-killed kind of job."

Al was the perfect man for that kind of nervy job. Baseball had tested his courage twice and twice he had proved himself in conflicts that no athlete I know of ever had to endure, risking his career for a religious and moral belief. Baseball, I wrote, "had found an honest man and—as is its custom—it put a label on him: A Nut."

I talked with Al for much of a week during the closing portion of the 1965 pennant race as the Twins tried to lock up their first pennant. "You play a different game when you're in first place," he told me one afternoon as we sat in the lobby of the Kenmore Hotel in Boston, waiting to walk to Fenway Park for a game that evening. He sat in a large chair, but as big as the chair was, he seemed to dominate it. Six-foot-two and two hundred five pounds, he was built like a tight end, which he once was at the University of Alabama. The shoulders were blocky, the chest broad, the face square-chinned and large. His reddish crew cut got him the nickname "Red" early in his career with the New York Giants, but he disliked the nickname. He was dressed in a crisply pressed, conservative suit, a snow-white shirt with heavily starched collar, and neatly knotted tie. Most of the other Twins, lounging in the lobby, were dressed casually in open-necked sports shirts and slacks. The ruddy-faced, well-barbered Al looked like someone on his way to church to be a guest preacher—and, in fact, he did preach in Baptist churches during the off-seasons.

I asked him what he meant by playing a different game when you're in first place. "When you're on top," he said in his rolling Alabama drawl, "every out becomes a big out. Like last season, when we finished in sixth place, I'd pitch the seventh, eighth, and ninth innings. If I got them out, good. If I didn't, it didn't mean much on a losing club. This season, when we were in first place almost from the start, Sam [manager Sam Mele], he was saving me for one inning, maybe one out. Usually the last inning, the last out. Game after game, it was like that."

He had never been happy as a relief pitcher. "It is the hardest job in baseball," he said. "The only one that rates with it is pinch hitting. The big thing about pitching is consistency. Regular work, regular rest.

"But in the bullpen, pitching is everything but consistency. You pitch two or three days in a row, or you go six or seven days without

pitching at all. Then—*bang!*—they throw you in there and say, 'Get that man out.'"

I talked to starting pitcher Jim Kaat and asked him about Al's belief that relieving was tougher than starting. "No doubt in my mind that he's right," the gangling, raw-boned Kaat told me. "One day a reliever may have good stuff on the ball and they don't use him. The next day you may have nothing, but if they call down to the bullpen for you, you got to go in there."

"When you get up to throw," Johnny Klippstein, another reliever for the Twins told me, "you have to want to get into the game. That's part of being a good pitcher. On the other hand, you got to be hoping that the pitcher, who's your teammate, doesn't get knocked around. So one part of you wants to go, the other part of you wants to stay, and that's no attitude to have when you're trying to get ready."

I talked to twenty-one-year-old Jim Merritt, later a 20-game winner as a starter, shortly after he had pitched in relief for the Twins. "Sure, I was nervous out there," he told me, his fingers trembling as he lit a cigarette. "I'd never relieved up here before. In the bullpen my knees were knocking, my heart pounding, home plate wobbling like crazy. What kills you, you don't know when they'll call you to come in."

He drew on the cigarette. "You can make money in the big leagues starting or relieving," he said, "but I'd just as soon be a starter."

Worthington, dressing nearby, overheard. "Nineteen out of twenty pitchers say that," he said. "And the other one"—he tapped his head—"he's got something wrong with him."

In the specialty of relief pitcher, Al was one of the sub-specialists. "Modern baseball has become a battle of bullpens," Hal Naragon, the Twins' bullpen coach, told me at a time when the American League did not have a Designated Hitter rule. "If your starter gets knocked out early, you need someone—usually a hard-throwing young fellow like Merritt—who can hold off any more scoring until your hitters can close the gap.

"To get even, though, you may have to pinch hit for your pitcher in the sixth or seventh inning. Now you need a good short man who can hold them for an inning or two. But maybe he puts a man on base. He's a righty and a lefty hitter comes to bat. Now you need a lefty-against-lefty reliever—or a righty-against-righty reliever if the batter is right-handed. This kind of relief pitcher is in a groove against hitters who bat from his side.

"He may pitch to one batter, even two. If he does his job—and the game is still close—then you bring in a guy like Worthington."

"If you do your job," Klippstein told me, "they shake your hand. But you'd better be ready to pitch tomorrow and the day after tomorrow. The starter has four days off. But if you don't get them out tomorrow, they forget quick about that game you saved today."

Al Worthington had come to this kill-or-be-killed kind of job after an eleven-year roller-coaster ride through professional baseball. He was born on February 5, 1929, in Birmingham, Alabama. As a schoolboy, he once told me, he built up a strong right arm by throwing rocks at telephone poles. He played football at the University of Alabama, where he caught passes and punted, but left school to sign with a minor-league team. The Giants bought his contract in July 1953, and he made his big-league debut in sensational fashion by shutting out the Phils, 5–0. Five days later he shut out the Dodgers, 6–0. He was a rarity among pitchers: his fastball was a natural slider. Even when he threw a ball to first base, the ball hooked like a slider. At first puzzled, batters began to

time the hooks of that natural slider. He finished the 1953 season with a 4–8 record. He needed a second pitch to go with the natural slider and labored in the minors for much of 1954 and 1955. He came back to the Giants in 1956 as a relief pitcher who could get batters out before they got a second chance to time the natural slider. His best year was 1958 when he was 11–7.

In the summer of 1958, he told me in 1962, he had heard evangelist Billy Graham speak. "Suddenly I began to understand that good works would not get me into heaven," he said in his preacher's voice. "I had thought that if I was good to my family and neighbors, I'd go to heaven. But now I began to see that only through God's grace and faith in Jesus Christ could I receive salvation. I told God I was turning my whole heart over to Jesus Christ . . . I was making my break with the world. . . . Suddenly I became aware that I had been born again. And I knew that Jesus Christ had said, 'Except a man be born again, he cannot see the Kingdom of God.'"

Late in 1959 the Giants were racing head and head with the Dodgers for the pennant. Just before a win-or-lose series with the Dodgers, Al learned that the Giants had planted a spy in the grandstand who, with a telescope, could steal the signs the Dodger catcher flashed to his pitcher. By a relay system the signs were flashed to the dugout, then to the batter. Most batters, knowing what pitch is coming, will greet it with lusty enthusiasm.

Al told his manager Bill Rigney, he could not be a Christian and a cheater. Rigney later denied to me that the Giants had posted a spy. Al told me that Rigney promised there would be no spying. The Giants lost the series, and the Dodgers won the pennant. A year later Al was back in the minors. Late in 1960 he was picked up by the Chicago White Sox, also in the midst of a close race for a pennant. Al won the game and saved another. Then he heard talk that the White Sox also were stealing signs by posting a spy in the stands.

He went to manager Al Lopez, who later told me: "As a player it was none of his business what we were doing. But I did say, 'Show me in the rule books where it is wrong.'"

Al went to the front office. Hank Greenberg, then a Sox official and formerly the Detroit and Pirate slugger, told him: "Baseball is a game where you are trying to get away with anything you can. . . ."

Al packed his bags and went home to his wife Shirley and their three children in Birmingham. "I was scared," he told me in 1965. "Jumping a team is a serious business. I knew it could have washed me up in baseball."

The White Sox dropped him to a minor-league team at the start of the 1961 season. Despite his 15–4 record at Indianapolis, he seemed doomed to stay in the minors. Even the Mets, desperate as a new team, refused to draft him. "We have enough nuts on this club," said one executive. In 1963 the Reds finally took a chance on an honest man who refused to cheat. He started slowly, however, and the Reds sent him to San Diego. There, figuring he had little to lose, he toyed with a knuckleball. That was the second pitch he needed to go with the natural slider. The Twins bought him in 1964 and he posted a low 1.38 ERA for a sixth-place team. In 1965, with a pennant-winning team, he won 10 and lost 7, finishing with a 2.13 ERA. He led the league's relief pitchers with 18 saves. In the World Series he didn't allow a run in four innings of relief pitching but the Twins lost in 7 games to the Dodgers.

He stayed with the Twins through the 1969 season, when he retired. He appeared in 602 big-league games, won 79 and lost 85, mostly as a sundown kind of pitcher who

steps into trouble created by others and survives only if he doesn't make a mistake. As a reliever, he had 108 saves. Al was a coach with the Twins for several seasons. In 1975 he became the baseball coach at Liberty Baptist College in Lynchburg, Virginia. His teams have been among the best in the south, in 1983 winning 40 and losing 17 to win a district championship. He and his wife Shirley live in Lynchburg.

Al as a college baseball coach in 1984.

Tony puts Rocky Graziano onto the ropes in 1948
as the Man of Steel regains the middleweight
title.

Tony Zale

ON A SUMMER AFTERNOON IN 1969 I stood with Tony Zale at the bar in Gallagher's 33, a saloon near Madison Square Garden that has since become something else on a block where storefronts change as rapidly as traffic lights. The former middleweight champion of the world was working as a greeter at Gallagher's for $200 a week. At age fifty-five he still had the stony face and cast-iron build of his youth, his shoulders military erect, spine as straight as a flagpole. There was a pleased smile on his face because we were talking about something still very precious to him: the fighting skills of a man his contemporaries in the 1940s called the Man of Steel. I had just mentioned to him what one of his former antagonists, Rocky Graziano, had told me only a few days earlier: "When Zale hit you here [in the belly], geez, it made you bend over like he'd stuck something in there inside you, turned it around like it was a red-hot poker, and then left it there . . ."

When I repeated that quote to him, the Man of Steel stared at the floor for several moments, swirling ice cubes in a near-empty glass of ginger ale, the proud smile lingering. He was wearing a wide-lapeled, double-breasted brown suit and a flowered tie. He had worn that same kind of 1940s suit and tie thirty years earlier as a worker in the steel mills of Gary, Indiana, taking a date to the Saturday-night movies. His narrow eyes were set deep, his hair sparse and gray.

He turned to look at me, jamming his hands deep into the pockets of his pants. "I learned to be a body puncher in my first fight as an amateur." I could hear middle Europe as well as Indiana in his voice. "I had one of my mother's big Polish dinners and then I went to the gym to fight. In the first round I got hit in the solar plexus. I don't remember anything after that until I woke up, vomiting. Right then I decided I was going to be the one who hit other people in the body."

I had come to Gallagher's to talk to Zale about his three fights with Rocky Graziano some twenty years earlier. We had been talking only a few minutes about those fights, perhaps the bloodiest and most savage ever waged between the same two men in an American ring, when he laughed, the deep-set eyes twinkling, and said, "We gave them their money's worth, didn't we?"

Zale and Graziano battered each other from post to post, smashing the other's face until their gloves were stained crimson. Blood flew out of torn mouths and spattered their shoes. Each fight ended in a knockout. Yet, curiously, in two of those brawls, the one who was seemingly ready to be flattened at any moment rallied to knock out the other. In those two fights—the first two—the loser left the ring hardly marked while the winner left bruised and bloodied.

Tony ordered another ginger ale—he never drank alcohol or smoked—and then told me how he had come to those three fights. Tony Zaleski (he changed his name after becoming a boxer) was born in Gary on May 29, 1913. His father, a steel worker, died suddenly when Tony was two, killed by a car as he rode on a bike to a drug store to get medicine for Tony, ill with measles. His mother, eight months pregnant, was left with no insurance and a family of six soon to be seven. She walked home from burying her husband with five dollars in her purse.

"She and my father had come here from Poland," Zale told me, that pride in himself and his heritage making his voice rise. "Seven kids. She washed clothes, she took in washing, she worked when she could get work. She bought a cow that we kept in the backyard, so we could always have milk even if we didn't have money. She was some woman. She gave me my determination.

"I started boxing in gyms when I was twelve or so. My older brothers taught me. I had over two hundred amateur fights. After

I graduated from high school, I fought professional. That was in 1935. I fought a couple of years, then I got hurt. I was twenty-one then and I went to work cinder snapping around an open hearth for Illinois Steel."

It was hot, dirty, and noisy work, but it was also a living in that gray Depression year of 1937. A year later he went back to boxing. "I liked to work out in the gym," he said, jiggling ice cubes in another empty glass as he remembered, staring at the floor of Gallagher's. "My trainers had to stop me from overworking. People used to say, 'How can you enjoy fighting?' I couldn't explain it but I used to say that it was easier than working in the mills."

In 1941 he beat Georgie Abrams to win the world middleweight championship. His demeanor astonished people accustomed to the brutal, tough, and often-sleazy world of boxing. "If he's boxing and makes a mistake," his manager Art Winch once said, "he says, 'Please be patient, I'll do it right next time.' He is that kind of fighter—a real gentleman. Except he could kill you in a fight."

In 1942 he enlisted in the navy and served as a physical-training instructor at the Great Lakes Training Station near Chicago. A promoter offered him $25,000 to come to Chicago for a bout. Tony refused, saying it wouldn't look right for him to be fighting while his fellow sailors were dying on the burning decks of carriers in the Pacific. "We lost $25,000," his manager growled. "But we did the right thing," Tony said.

During the war years, Tony read about a flashy, squat brawler out of New York's tough East Side who was kayoing a string of middleweights. "I read a lot about Graziano while I was in the navy," Tony told me in Gallagher's. "I figured I'd have to fight him."

They met for the first time on September 24, 1946, in Yankee Stadium, Zale's middleweight title going to the winner. Graziano was twenty-four years old, Zale thirty-three, and Zale was six pounds heavier than the one-hundred-fifty-two-pound Graziano. Graziano was a 2–1 favorite, the gamblers figuring that almost four years in the navy had rusted the reflexes of the Man of Steel.

For six rounds they seemed to have figured correctly. Graziano's fists pounded Zale's eyes, nose, and mouth. Then, in the middle of that sixth, young Rocky decided to go for the middle. He leaned forward, aiming a body punch. He opened up his middle, perhaps the first but certainly his last mistake of the night. The blood-smeared Zale saw the opening and rammed his right like a sword into Graziano's belly. "Right there I put it to him," Tony said to me as he stood at the bar. He assumed a fighter's pose, fists clenched, and then he drove that rock of a right hand toward my midsection. I curved my back as that hand stopped inches away, and for a moment I thought I felt that sensation of a red-hot poker in the belly.

Rocky went down, sucking for air, eyes popping like a fish out of water. At the count of nine he was rising but referee Ruby Goldstein counted him out. As the two left the ring, the bloody Zale looked like the loser, the panting but unmarked Graziano the winner.

In his dressing room a drained Zale muttered, "Clean livin'. . . clean livin'. . ." Handlers had to carry him to the shower. In Gallagher's more than twenty years later he grinned, embarrassed, when I recalled for him how the Man of Steel had shown a weakness to the world. "I was exhausted," he said, the grin rueful. "You got to remember it was my first hard fight in four years."

They fought a second time in Chicago on the sultry night of July 16, 1947. Inside Chicago Stadium, an indoor arena, the temperature was a boiler-room 102 degrees at ringside. For the first three rounds Zale sliced Graziano's face into strips of bloody flesh. By the fourth Graziano's eyes looked like discolored eggs. But by the fifth the Man of Steel, now thirty-four years old, had begun to sag in the smoke-filled furnace. In the sixth he tried to swarm over Rocky, but the effort emptied his last bits of strength. Graziano hit him eleven straight times as Zale clung to the middle strand of the ropes, unwilling to go down, but unable to come up. The referee stopped the fight. Rocky was the new middleweight champion.

Again the winner, this time Graziano, wobbled from the ring dripping blood while the loser Zale, left unsteadily but without a wound. "The ref should never have stopped that fight," Zale told me. "The champion should only lose by being counted out."

Then the proud man's smile crossed his face. "I knew I would win back the title. I saw a look on Rocky's face in the third round when I cut his face good. He knew then that I was the boss."

They met for the third and last time in Ruppert Stadium in Newark, New Jersey, on June 10, 1948, and there Rocky indeed learned who was boss. The thirty-five-year-old Zale knocked down Rocky in the first, battered him through the second, dropped him on his back in the third. Rocky rose at the count of six. The Man of Steel stepped forward and threw the last punch, a left hook, he would ever throw in anger at Rocky Graziano. Rocky toppled backward, his head knocking against the canvas with the finality of a hanging-judge's gavel. A dazed Rocky was carried out of the ring. Tony had become the first middleweight champion to regain the title since Stanley Ketchel in 1908.

Later in 1948 he lost the title to Marcel Cerdan, a Frenchman with his own hands of steel. He retired, his war-curtailed record 70 victories, 46 by knockouts, and 16 losses, only 4 by knockouts. He had earned almost $300,000 from the three Graziano fights alone. During the 1950s the money vanished in a Chicago restaurant and then when his wife took their two daughters to California

and divorced him, Graziano, a close buddy now, tried to get him acting jobs in television, where Graziano had become a performer. Zale was supposed to play himself in the movie version of Graziano's life story, *Somebody Up There Likes Me*. During a rehearsal the Man of Steel threw a punch that breezed the chin of Paul Newman, who was playing Graziano. The producers gave Tony $1,500 and told him to take the next train back to Chicago. He still lives in Chicago, teaching boxing, telling people that "boxing makes you live better, cleaner, and righter." And by the erect, proud way he walks down a street, he shows people that there goes a man who once was the boss.

Tony points to the power of positive thinking during an interview in Chicago in 1984.